G000272712

Arabs of the Jewish Faith

Jewish Cultures of the World

Edited by Matti Bunzl, *University of Illinois, Urbana-Champaign*, and Jeffrey Shandler, *Rutgers University*

Published in association with the Allen and Joan Bildner Center for the Study of Jewish Life, *Rutgers University*

Advisory Board

Arabs of the Jewish Faith

The Civilizing Mission in Colonial Algeria

JOSHUA SCHREIER

RUTGERS UNIVERSITY PRESS

NEW BRUNSWICK, NEW JERSEY, AND LONDON

LIBRARY OF CONGRESS CATALOGING-IN-PUBLICATION DATA

Schreier, Joshua, 1969–
    Arabs of the Jewish faith : the civilizing mission in colonial Algeria / Joshua
Schreier.
        p. cm. — (Jewish cultures of the world)
    Includes bibliographical references and index.
    ISBN 978–0–8135–4794–7 (hardcover : alk. paper)
    1. Jews—Algeria—History—19th century. 2. Jews—Cultural assimilation—
Algeria. 3. Algeria—Colonization—History—19th century. 4. Algeria—Ethnic
relations. 5. France—Colonies—Algeria—Ethnic relations. I. Title.
    DS135.A3S357 2010
    305.892'406509034—dc22   2009043149

A British Cataloging-in-Publication record for this book is available from the
British Library.

Visit our Web site: http://rutgerspress.rutgers.edu

Manufactured in the United States of America

For Lise, Malka, and Noam

CONTENTS

MAPS, FIGURES, AND TABLES

Maps

Figures

Tables

ACKNOWLEDGMENTS

This book was a group effort, and I have many people to thank. Zachary Lockman provided advice, numerous careful readings, and unparalleled menschlichkeit. I am also a better thinker for having studied with Timothy Mitchell, Michael Gilsenan, Ariel Salzmann, Samira Haj, and Lila Abu-Lughod. Another brave cadre of scholars slogged through various incarnations of this work and survived to tell the tale: Edward Berenson, Julia Clancy-Smith, Alice Conklin, Susan Hiner, Patricia Lorcin, Aron Rodrigue, Jeffrey Schneider, Eliot Schreiber, David Shalk, Susan Slyomovics, and Paul Silverstein. During a memorable discussion in Poughkeepsie, New York, Henri Alleg provided invaluable inspiration to continue my work on colonialism. I extend a special thanks to Sarah Stein for the limitless help she afforded me by reading many versions of this manuscript and offering consistently excellent advice. Her confidence and support came at a difficult time and both were crucial to the success of this project. Nathaniel Deutsch has often expressed confidence in this project and I thank him sincerely for his encouragement. Michael Gasper has been a great friend, smart critic, and an invaluable support throughout graduate school and since. Beth Kressel, my original editor at Rutgers University Press, was helpful, efficient, and insightful, and Marlie Wasserman, also of Rutgers University Press, steered this project smoothly and capably through completion. I cannot thank these people enough for their suggestions, critiques, and insights.

I am also indebted to the host of brilliant friends, colleagues, readers, critics, panelists, mentors, and co-conspirators who have helped me through many long years of study, research, writing, and life in general. They continue to shape my thinking. This list of luminaries includes Sabri Ates, Laura Bier, Lia Brozgal, Koray Caliskan, John Chalcraft, Jessica Cooperman, David Deutsch, Marc Epstein, Rachel Friedman, Najib Hourani, Wilson Jacobs, Carey Kasten, Hartley Lachter, Max Leeming, Jared Manasek, Mitch Miller, Joe Nevins, Omnia el-Shakry, Michael Walsh, Owen White, Patricia Sloane-White, John Willis, and Eva Woods. My dear friends Heather Chaplin, Macabee Montandon, and Catherine Crawford provided consistent and necessary support; they know better than anyone that the final click is always in your heart.

My stellar colleagues at Vassar College's Department of History have provided greatly appreciated advice, support, inspiration, and constructive criticism: Nancy Bisaha, Bob Brigham, Mita Choudhury, Miriam Cohen, Rebecca Edwards, Michael Hanagan, Maria Höhn, James Merrell, Quincy Mills, Lydia Murdoch, Leslie Offut, Miki Pohl, Ismail Rashid, and Hiraku Shimoda. In addition to their roles in the creation of a fantastic work environment, they deserve additional thanks for their timely support of academic freedom. Marc Epstein, as a good friend and as chair of Vassar College's Jewish Studies Program, has also been phenomenally supportive. The helpful staffs of the Centre des Archives d'Outre Mer and the Maison Méditerranéenne des Science de l'Homme also deserve mention; Professor Robert Ilbert was particularly kind while helping me establish myself in Aix-en-Provence. Thanks also to the staffs of the archives of the Consistoire Central des Israélites de France, the Archives Nationales de France, the Service Historique de la Défense, the National Archives (United Kingdom), the Bibliothèque de l'Alliance Israélite Universelle, the Bibliothèque Nationale de France, the Library of the Jewish Theological Seminary, and the Royal Geographical Society.

The generosity of a number of institutions made this research possible. The Dolores Zorhab Liebmann Fellowship funded my major research in Paris and Aix-en-Provence. The Maison Méditerranéenne des Sciences de l'Homme contributed to my housing costs during my time in Aix. Vassar College's Committee on Research supported several crucial research trips through the Lucy Maynard Salmon Research Fund, the Gabrielle Snyder Beck Fund, and the Emily Floyd Fund.

Parts of Chapter 2 appeared originally as "'They Swore Upon the Tombs Never to Make Peace With Us': Algerian Jews and French Colonialism" in *Algeria and France: Identity, Memory, Nostalgia* (Syracuse, NY: Syracuse University Press, 2006). This material is preprinted by permission of Syracuse University Press. Elements of Chapters 3 and 5 first appeared in the article "Napoléon's Long Shadow: Morality, Civilization and Jews in France and Algeria, 1808–1870," *French Historical Studies* 30 (Winter 2007): 77–103. These sections are reprinted by permission of the publisher, Duke University Press. The postcard images of Oran's Jewish quarter and its main synagogue come from the private collection of Stephanie Comfort. The photo of Jews in Ghardaia is printed by permission of the Royal Geographical Society. Jamie Owen and the staff of the Foley Reading Room of the Royal Geographical Society were gracious, welcoming, and helpful. The cover image of Jewish children in Constantine's Jewish quarter is reprinted by permission of the Société Nationale de Géographie. Bill Nelson quickly and expertly created the map of Algeria included at the beginning of this volume. Portions of this work were shared and discussed at meetings of the Middle East Studies Association and the Society for French Historical Studies, as well as at Colby College, Swarthmore College, the University of Washington, Yale University, and UCLA. I thank my hosts and interlocutors at these events for their helpful thoughts and suggestions.

My family has been a great source of love and support. My dear mother, Arlene Richman, has listened to me, understood me, and put up with a great deal of my nonsense. She also spent many long and excruciating hours expertly editing this manuscript. I thank my father, Ethan Schreier, for his love and guidance, and for providing me with unwavering confidence that he would always be there. I am also blessed with the finest brother available to humanity, Benjamin Schreier. His humor, insight, and understanding of the Power of Negative Thinking were invaluable. Tremendous thanks are also due my brilliant, sensitive, and creative sister-in-law (and friend since college), Sarah Koenig, my fabulous niece, Ava, and my unstoppable nephew, Reuben. The influence of my grandparents, Sheva Schreier and Jacob Schreier (Z"L), is discernable in both my choice of topic and my approach. Sincere thanks also to Janet Levine, Geoff Taylor, and Norman and Rita Levine.

I thank my mother-in-law Monique Nathan for her acceptance, love, help, and wisdom. I could never have dreamed of such a spectacular *belle-famille*: Paul Merle, Martin Nathan, Vincent Nathan, Sandrine Billac, Lina Nathan, Colas Nathan, Alain and Denise Chapuis, and Vivette Weber. They have all been incredibly generous and welcoming.

My children, Malka and Noam, illuminate the finer side of reality and I am continually enriched by their full-spectrum brilliance. Finally, immeasurable thanks to Lise Schreier, my intercontinental wife: aishes hayil, super h., love of my life. She has sustained me with her insight, criticism, love, support, humor, and patience. I could not have written this book (or done much of anything else) without her.

Note on Transliteration of Names

In the French archives, the same name was often spelled numerous ways. I have elected to use the most common transliterations of Hebrew and Arabic names appearing in written materials of the time. That being said, some inconsistency within extended families is bound to remain.

Arabs of the Jewish Faith

Introduction

Arabs of the Jewish Faith explores how Algerian Jews responded to and appropriated the colonial campaign to assimilate them to France during the middle decades of the nineteenth century. It argues that France's policy of assimilation developed as a strategic response to the challenges of early colonial domination, including governing the demographically and economically important Jewish communities in Algeria's cities. As we shall see, members of the military administration drew on earlier French Revolutionary and Napoleonic debates about Jewish emancipation and citizenship to structure their policies toward the Jews of Algeria, but the colonial context dramatically transformed these ideas and policies. Thus, even when colonial lawmakers self-consciously borrowed from metropolitan legal precedents to understand and structure the prerequisites of French citizenship in Algeria, the colonial results were not analogous to what one might find in the metropole.

Local Algerian-Jewish individuals and institutions played vital roles in shaping the meaning and practice of civilizing. If French officials in Algeria found that Revolutionary ideals could be adapted to justify colonial domination, Algerian Jews forced changes in the application of those ideals into policies. Sometimes Jews in Algeria succeeded in thwarting objectionable colonial policies altogether. By the time of the Algerian Jews' collective naturalization as French citizens in 1870, many local Jewish institutions and practices that French reformers had originally decried as backward or uncivilized (and actively attempted to dismantle) were nevertheless still robust. (Certain Saharan Jewish communities were exempted from this measure.) As much as France exported the *mission civilisatrice* to Algeria, Algerians produced it in the colony.

Civilizing was a firmly rooted, meaningful colonial policy well before the latter decades of the Third Republic period (1870–1940), which historians often see as the apogee of the notion.[1] Consequently, this book departs from most treatments of colonial ideology by beginning the story earlier, during the 1830s and 1840s. While the cities were ostensibly friendly territories by the late 1830s, the colonial authorities questioned the loyalty of the various groups of Spanish, Italian, Maltese, and French settlers, not to mention local Arab and Berber communities that made up Algeria's urban population. Among them, native Jews attracted particular attention. They were not only demographically significant, but maintained a visible social role with extensive local, trans-Mediterranean, and trans-Saharan commercial contacts. Some conservative military officers feared their ability to keep local economic activity in native hands, and suggested expelling the Jews or sending them to France. More liberal voices hoped to "regenerate" them, which generally meant transforming them into a pillar of French colonial rule. The latter voices captured the Minister of War's imagination; within the first decade of the conquest, French authorities generally saw Algerian Jews as corrupt and immoral, but also as potentially useful allies in the conquest of Algeria.

Their solution was to establish Jewish "consistories," or officially recognized agencies charged with governing communal institutions and civilizing the local Jews. These agencies managed Jewish community finances and policed religious practice. They were staffed with French rabbis and officials who understood their mission to be a continuation of the French Revolutionary project of "regenerating" the supposedly oppressed and corrupt Jews of France.[2] True to the Revolutionary heritage of Jewish emancipation in France, French-Jewish reformers and their allies in the civil administration saw Algerian Jews as oppressed victims of despotism for whose enlightenment and emancipation they were responsible. In their effort to secure full citizenship for Algerian Jews, colonial officials helped develop a mythology holding Algerian Jews to be more intelligent, faithful, and redeemable than Muslims, their supposedly less-gifted former oppressors.[3] In other words, the culturally resonant teleology of Jewish emancipation was deployed in Algeria to justify and bolster French domination, reify preexisting differences and prejudices, and legislate new hierarchies.[4]

Faced with this policy, Algerian Jews were not passive, however, and their responses to efforts to assimilate them brought into relief the French colonial meaning of *civilization*. Frequently, the contests were over interior spaces, both literal and metaphoric; Jewish reformers and French civil administrators used the term *civilizing* in their efforts to secure access to homes, synagogues, and the family structure in order to monitor and control behavior, rituals, and hygiene. Reformers vainly tried to stop Algerian Jews from marrying solely according to the laws of their own religion, and condemned what they saw as immoral family practices, such as divorce and polygamy. They hoped instead that Algerian-Jewish families would conform to dictates of the French civil code. Colonial officials saw civilization as control over the interior of synagogues, in the structure of Jewish families, and in the status of Jewish women.[5]

On both intimate and institutional levels, however, Algerian Jews were often able to shape these policies. Many Jews avoided consistorial synagogues, preserving instead their own institutions and rabbis. Many parents sent their children to local schools, avoiding the official French-Jewish schools they regarded as either impious or substandard. French civil officials eventually found it necessary to bring local Algerian rabbis, previously condemned as "fanatic," into their official schools in order to attract students. Jewish couples contracted marriages beyond the gaze of French administrative authorities, frustrating local officials and forcing them to call upon their superiors in Paris or Algiers for clearer legislation. Elite Algerian Jews, meanwhile, joined the consistory and brought their own faith, interests, and networks of patronage to bear on the civilizing project. They supported certain rabbis, synagogues, and schools, while condemning those of their rivals. The civilizing project was thus interpreted, shaped, and sometimes even executed by the local Algerian actors it was originally intended to transform.

Despite the influence of local Algerians, emancipation maintained exclusionary qualities. Soon after the conquest, French military and academic interest in Muslim family structure brought polygamy and divorce—practices permitted by both Islamic and Jewish law in North Africa—into debates about citizenship. Many saw such obvious Jewish moral faults as products of Islamic oppression, and considered ways of emancipating Jews from their unfortunate milieu. By the 1860s, those interested in questions of indigenous naturalization—including politicians in Paris, judges in Oran, and Jewish reformers in Algiers—all turned for precedent to the earlier emancipation of French Jewry of 1791 and the Napoleonic policies of 1806 to 1808. They recalled that the Jews of France were finally naturalized only when Napoleon "corrected" their putatively immoral family code, harmonizing Jewish law and the French civil code by way of the Grand Sanhedrin, which he created in 1806. French lawmakers drew upon the Napoleonic precedent to formalize "personal status" laws in 1865. These laws barred Algerians from citizenship unless they agreed to formally reject the immoral Muslim or Jewish family codes permitting polygamy and divorce. In 1870, when Algerian Jews were granted citizenship, the Jewish personal status was legally eliminated. From that point onward, Algerian Jews enjoyed the same legal status as their colonizers, while Muslims were left to their own personal status laws, but without citizenship rights.[6] The logic of French-Jewish emancipation was paradoxically the same as that which justified Muslims' exclusion.

Colonial exclusion was so indebted to French logics of emancipation that French officials and legal scholars compared Muslim obedience to their "foreign" family code to French Jews before the Revolution and Grand Sanhedrin. One observer even took to describing the Qur'an as a "Muslim Talmud" that could theoretically be reformed to conform to French law. By banning polygamy and divorce, some argued, France could permit Muslims to be citizens, just as French Jews had been stripped of their personal status and emancipated. A second, more powerful, faction (also borrowing from earlier discussions of Jewish emancipation), however, compared Muslims not to Jews, but to the intolerant and oppressive Old Regime that had once persecuted them. While the Jews could be regenerated, the argument ran, Muslim rule was by nature corrupt and oppressive, so it had to be overthrown. Laws resulting from these conversations maintained a separate family code for Muslims that was ruled incompatible with citizenship. Most importantly, Muslims could not be French because they could practice divorce and polygamy (whether or not they actually did). Such laws distanced Muslims from Jews in Algeria: while benefiting Jews, the civilizing ideology functioned as a means of excluding the vast majority of Algeria's colonial subjects.

Conditions in Algeria, and notably the role of Jewish merchants, influenced how these precedents were transformed into colonial strategies. Jews in Algeria were a diverse lot, ranging from Haketia-speaking refugees from Morocco to local Arabic-speaking artisans to wealthy merchants from Livornese families.[7] The lives of many Jews were tightly interwoven with those of their Muslim neighbors. Correspondence of French generals reveals deep concern about the close relationships that certain rural Muslim tribes held with urban Jewish community leaders, the trading alliances that formed between Maltese fisherman and Jewish shopkeepers, and the ever-frustrating ability of Jewish currency traders in western Algeria to maintain the Spanish *duro's* preeminence over the *franc*. Such anxieties notwithstanding, the complexity of Jewish life on the ground was little reflected in colonial discourse. Indeed, by applying the template of Franco-Jewish emancipation to Algeria's Jews, military officers homogenized and reduced them to a representation of misery. In so doing, French officials structured the ideology of civilizing. There were two principle benefits to this strategy. The call to uplift the supposedly oppressed Jews living under the yoke of Islam justified a more intrusive colonial state structure that could better monitor Jewish economic activities. At the same time, colonial authorities hoped that the civilizing and assimilation of Algeria's Jews would produce a bloc of friendly urban subjects counterbalancing hostile Arabs or disloyal non-French settlers. For colonial officials and government ministers, civilizing the Jews was a strategic asset to securing the occupation of Algeria.

In this book, I draw on correspondence of the French army, archives of colonial prefectures, and archives of metropolitan and colonial consistories. I pay particular attention to petitions that Jews and Muslims submitted to French colonial officers in Algeria. British archives also provide insights into the economic role of notable Algerian Jews in the early colonial period. In addition, the chapters that follow make extensive use of numerous legal pamphlets, journals, newspapers, and court records that suggest how family customs served to rationalize exclusivist legislation. Woven into the study are the correspondences of colonial rabbis, educators, and military officials: these demonstrate how representations of colonized subjects' morality, hygiene, and gender roles became a vehicle by which civilizing came to demand an ever more present, intrusive, and disciplinary state structure. While such sources are undoubtedly colonial, they are also polyvalent in that they contain numerous narratives of mid-nineteenth-century Algerian Jews in their confrontation and cooperation with French colonial power. Such sources provide a rich tableau of the first decades of the occupation that open a vital window into Jews' experience of colonialism.

French archival records that relate these stories are written in an imperial prose that presents both challenges and opportunities; it masks, filters, and appropriates events it purports to record, but also unwittingly exposes the anxieties that haunted France's young and incomplete colonial administration.[8] Like earlier studies that deal with rural colonial subjects, this examination of urban Algeria requires us to "(read) records against the grain" to "uncover the subaltern's myths, cults, ideologies, and revolts that colonial . . . elites sought to appropriate."[9] Given French officers' consistent use of terms such as *fanatical* and *ignorant* to describe Jews, a good deal of reading between the lines is necessary if we are to endow them with a subjectivity beyond that granted by the colonial archives' "committed colonialist" perspective, to borrow Ranajit Guha's term.[10] Where officers saw "the spirit of intrigue," it is possible to read divergent interests, deep faith, and competing aspirations for local control.

Of course, these sources also make clear that the "colonialist" was not unitary, but actually a deeply fractured group that lacked consensus on some of the most basic questions of colonial policy. Furthermore, colonized subjects, out of necessity, conviction, or (most likely) a combination of the two, often spoke in the same "prose." Therefore, it is also in the local, Algerian responses that we may also explore the hegemonic but fluid ideology of colonial domination.[11] It is legible in the nervous belittling of Jewish feuds, requests, and complaints in military correspondence, and in the translated, transcribed, and highly formalized language in which Jews composed petitions to the cities' new administrators. French sources can thus shed light on relationships and disputes within their colonial milieu, and on the ways colonized Jews succeeded in being heard. They also suggest how Jews understood the new power's legitimizing ideology, as well as their own place in a rapidly changing North African landscape.

To emphasize the richness of the colonial archive is not to deny that we have more to learn from other kinds of sources, some of which have also informed this study. An examination of Algerian *she'elot u'tshuvot* (responsa) literature, for example, could provide another perspective on rabbinical responses to the transformations under discussion in this book.[12] Elite rabbis in Algeria were enmeshed in networks that connected them to other Jewish communities, notably in Palestine.[13] *Haskamot* (letters of approval or recommendation by other authorities that often preface religious volumes) in Algerian responsa literature attest to North Africa's integration into a wider Mediterranean Jewish world. Authorities based in Tunis, Jerusalem, Safed, and Paris had their Hebrew and Judeo-Arabic recommendations included in Algerian rabbis' volumes. Of course, the colonial archives examined here were not silent on religious issues, nor was Algeria a vital center for Jewish religious scholarship. Indeed, Algerian rabbis seeking recognition by the rabbinical elite often had their work published elsewhere, notably in Livorno.[14] But Algeria was not devoid of religious study either, and further investigation of Algerian rabbis' responsa on divisive issues such as ritual (kosher) slaughtering, briefly examined in the following pages, helps uncover other aspects of the fissures and transformations that accompanied colonialism in Algeria.[15]

Whether expressed in religious or administrative records, religious and communal alliances confound the resurfacing historiographic opposition between liberal French Jews and the colonized, supposedly traditional Algerian Jews.[16] North African Jews were simply too varied, divided, and influential in the structures and processes of colonial administration to be adequately described within this binary. Indeed, many consistory members categorized as French by the colonial administration were actually of Moroccan background. By the time the consistories were established in 1845, some of these French-Moroccan Jews were already active in the French military, while others were municipal councilors or members of chambers of commerce. Conversely, the Strasbourg-educated French grand rabbi of Oran occasionally took the side of local Algerian rabbis, while other Algerians accused him of backing "fanatics." This complicated reality forces us to revisit the oppositions established under the rubric of emancipation that helped format colonialism. In this respect, the study of Algeria's Jews can help us understand not only their own experience, but how the civilizing ideology was flexible and ultimately misleading, with implications for the surrounding (non-Jewish) population, as well.[17] Rather than scrutinizing French-Jewish snootiness toward Algerian Jews (which has been done), this book reveals the complicated processes by which emancipation was employed and appropriated in the consolidation of colonial rule.[18]

French-Jewish efforts to uplift Algerian Jews were both part of a wider colonial project and quite distinct from it. Historians' frequent use of the term "Jewish colonialism" to describe these efforts is quite understandable, but it can be misleading.[19] French-Jewish reformers concerned with the fate of Algerian Jews convinced Paris to establish colonial institutions (the consistories) to civilize and assimilate the Jews of France.[20] Certainly, French Jews hoped to remake North African Jews in their image, a stance that disparaged local Algerian beliefs, practices, and culture.[21] Twenty-five years after the process's initiation, Algerian Jews were naturalized, and to the great consternation of their many anti-Semitic Spanish, Italian, French, and Maltese neighbors, were actually voting.[22] It would seem that legally speaking, the expressed goal of many a colonial reformer worked, resulting in the social advancement of Algerian Jews.

But it is precisely this process that distinguished the Jewish experience from that of most colonized subjects in French North Africa. It would be naïve to reduce colonialism to a single set of processes, but it is fair to say that in the French case, it described France's use of a number of political, economic, and/or social policies to extend the state's authority and control over foreign lands and peoples. This process necessarily involved a great deal of violence. Most Algerians experienced colonialism as *cantonments* (land appropriations), diminished educational opportunities following the confiscation of charitable trusts, the establishment of a legal caste system, humiliating social hierarchies, impoverishment, wide-scale sexual abuse, and massacres.[23] As others have pointed out, this strategy was at odds with the French elite's view of itself: on several occasions, French observers themselves remarked on the contrast between their claims to be civilizing (or at least to being civilized) and the reality of French soldiers' actions and the society they were creating in Algeria.[24] Furthermore, many French administrators and educators championed a civilizing program for Muslim North Africans, yet few ended up educated or possessing full rights.[25] In other words, the encounter between French and Algerian Jews looked quite different from colonial practices directed at the far more numerous Muslim population of Algeria.

Despite these stark differences between various sides and strategies of French colonialism, their histories ought to be told together, and the (admittedly atypical) Algerian-Jewish experience does provide insight into the wider history of colonialism and its ideologies. Notably, the Jewish experience offers a perspective on the meaning of "colonial difference" in the North African arena—even if the Jews were eventually relieved of the legal 'difference' that divided them from their colonizers.[26] This is because the

French applied nominally similar standards of modernity and civilization to both Jewish and Muslim subjects. Questions of family morality, loyalty, industriousness, and linguistic affinity saturated debates about naturalization for both Jewish and Muslim colonial subjects. Moreover, at the time of their naturalization in 1870, Jews were arguably no more or less modern or French (by the varied, but generally bourgeois standards of most reformers or lawmakers) than other Algerians.

This fact was not lost on a number of French lawmakers. In fact, at the time of the 1870 Crémieux decree, which naturalized Algerian Jews en masse in October of 1870, some statesmen tried to repeal it. Their reasons were varied; some saw danger in permitting Jews, whom they saw as a natural commercial group, into the French military.[27] Others argued that Algerian Jews did not understand the principles of a republic, and would vote as a bloc following their leaders' instructions.[28] Still others repeated earlier arguments about citizenship's lack of compatibility with rabbinical jurisdiction over Jews' marriage and family laws.[29] Many saw the naturalization of Jews in Algeria as a dangerous provocation to Muslim subjects, and blamed it for the recent el-Mokrani insurrection.[30] In 1871, Charles du Bouzet, former prefect of Oran and special commissioner in Algeria, insisted that Algerian Jews' mother tongue was Arabic, and both their morals and their clothes were "oriental." Despite their recent naturalization, Du Bouzet argued, Algerian Jews were "strangers to the traditions of the French nationality," and "remain outside of Western civilization."[31] Du Bouzet claimed, "Indigenous Israelites are not Frenchmen, but Arabs of the Jewish faith."[32] According to the laws of the Third French Republic, Du Bouzet's claim was technically wrong, but it would have resonated among subscribers to an emergent right-wing, more racialist definition of Frenchness. Most importantly, Du Bouzet's exclusionary claim reflected the fact that French laws did not reflect observable cultural or behavioral differences between Muslims and Jews.

I borrow the title of this book from Du Bouzet's evocative statement to emphasize a certain contradiction in the civilizing mission toward Jews. Algerian Jews had actually spent the previous two and a half decades *resisting* French efforts to restructure their homes, schools, family relations, and synagogues. They had rejected France's emissaries of civilization, bringing their own leaders into institutions originally built to hasten local Jews' adoption of French culture. In the 1850s and 1860s, Algerian synagogues that French civilizers had decried as centers of fanatical resistance to the civilizing mission were still pillars of Algerian-Jewish institutional life. Even after emancipation was extended, many Algerian Jews were inclined to reject this ostensible reward. Du Bouzet, with his firsthand experience of Oran politics behind him, may not have been so far from a certain truth. Adolphe Crémieux, the longtime advocate of Algerian-Jewish citizenship who gave his name to the 1870 decree, might more aptly be accused of being out of touch with civilization's progress in Algeria.

The fact that Jews' legal inferiority was abolished in 1870 despite their enduring resistance to many French markers of assimilation illuminates an important aspect about the civilizing mission and the larger history of colonialism. Notably, the real referents for terms such as "civilized" and "Arab" existed in an abstract, political sphere, not in observable cultural forms. Similarly, the post-Enlightenment, French-Jewish historical narrative of emancipation could be deployed to change the destinies of people who would otherwise remain classified as "Arabs" and suffer the same political fate. By extension, colonizers, colonized, and others who existed in a state of tension between them (such as Moroccan Jews in the French administration) could draw upon the notion of civilization (or, conversely, Arab-ness or fanaticism), to serve varying ends. The use of the post-Enlightenment ideology of emancipation (itself contested in France) to define some people as "Jews" who ostensibly deserved equality, as opposed to simply "Arabs of the Jewish Faith" who did not, demonstrates how the ideology contributed to the construction of difference and an ever-evolving colonial hierarchy.[33]

This means that the metropolitan precursors to the civilizing policy were at once vitally important in Algeria, yet never imported completed and whole from France. Even when nineteenth-century reformers self-consciously sought to bring the French-Jewish "regeneration" movement to Algeria, what occurred in the colony was not a simple extension of the well-studied metropolitan efforts.[34] Instead, colonial administrators, reformers, and officers trawled for earlier precursors, principles, and concepts to help resolve the new problems facing them in the colony. For this reason, this narrative will occasionally shift its focus from Algeria to France, if only to illuminate how colonial reformers and administrators continued to find certain tropes from the Revolutionary and Napoleonic debates about Jews and citizenship helpful in their internecine struggles over the structuring of colonial difference.

Colonial lawmakers revived and interpreted earlier debates by putting domestic, familial, and even intimate practices at the center of their discussions about citizenship, especially of the Jews.[35] This emerges most vividly when one considers their focus on divorce and polygamy. These issues emerged in Napoleonic Jewish policy, which was formulated just as French women's legal gains were being reversed and a patriarchal and monogamous family was imagined as a central feature of civilization.[36] But while polygamy soon drifted from legal discussions of Jews in France, these discussions provided a powerful legal paradigm for colonial debates.

To a lesser extent, the "Jewish internationalism" that emerged in July Monarchy France (1830–1848) also demonstrates how metropolitan debates emerged with very different contours in the colony.[37] French-Jewish internationalism reflected a liberal, interventionist mentality, and its adherents aspired to weave emancipation into the colonial policy we explore in this volume. But this liberalism looked very different in the colony, where it was deeply shaped by local conditions—most notably by helping to justify a wider system of exclusion.[38] Metropolitan influences and models must be understood to be contested even within Europe, never taken at their word, and be examined in the light of colonial events and realities.[39]

Perhaps it is obvious that the place of Jews in the historiography of European empires is somewhat uncertain. Jews have been present in scholarship on modern imperialism, but for a number of reasons—some political and some historical—an overall theoretical approach to Jews and Empire has been elusive.[40] In some important ways, this work demonstrates why this is the case; within a single empire, Jews were at once colonizers and colonized, poor artisans whose livelihoods were destroyed by imperial conquest, and wealthy exporters of colonial products. While some Jews worked tirelessly to advance French rule in Algeria, others attacked colonial police or conducted trade with the chief of the resistance to French expansion, the Emir Abd al-Qader. Given this complicated reality, how is one to interpret the recent claim that "Jews were, as a group, objectively irrelevant to imperialism?"[41] As a group, the claim is fair—French imperial expansion would have happened without Jewish colonizers or the Jewish colonized. But Jews in France and Algeria both shaped and were shaped by imperialism, and their Jewishness was far from irrelevant in how colonial law was conceived and implemented. Moreover, the exigencies of French-Jewish political history provided a unique conceptual arsenal for actors in the colonial order. Notably, central (if bitterly contested) notions surrounding the Jewish experience in France, such as emancipation, liberty, freedom of conscience, and enlightenment all powerfully influenced French imperial policy. French colonial policy favored North African Jews without always benefiting them, while Muslims' putative intolerance (itself a notion rooted in Enlightenment claims) helped justify their dispossession. Whatever theoretical approach to Jews and Empire eventually emerges, it will walk a fine line: it must simultaneously question how and if the communal identity under examination actually preceded the analysis, while doing justice to the immense weight and breadth of meaning that Jewish emancipation and citizenship possessed in modern European empires.[42]

The Historical Context:
Jews in Early Nineteenth-Century Algeria

Given the pretensions of the civilizing ideology, it is important to separate emancipationist representations of Algerian Jews that emphasize their isolation and misery from their more complicated historical experience.[43]

This challenge is compounded by the fact that ultimate naturalization and integration in France has anachronistically obscured their ancestors' deep connections to North African society. The depth of this connection has prompted historian Benjamin Stora to call the emancipation of 1870 the Jews' "first exile" from Algeria—one that separated them from their Muslim neighbors.[44] To explore the meaning of the civilizing ideology, then, some light must be shed on the precolonial existence of Algeria's Jews in the late eighteenth and early nineteenth centuries. As we shall see, a great deal of evidence supports Stora's claim that the Jewish population in this context was not wholly separate, isolated, unitary, or miserable.

French descriptions of the Jews in precolonial Algeria painted a grim picture of preconquest life based in part on current understandings of Islamic legal categories, such as the *dhimmi*, a legal category of protected non-Muslim subjects that was frequently applied to Jews and Christians ("people of the book") in the Arab Middle East and North Africa. Dhimmi status protected non-Muslims but simultaneously gave them a subservient status.[45] This lower social rank was manifest in additional taxes, sumptuary laws, and restrictions on building or expanding non-Muslim places of worship. Doubtless, Jews in precolonial Algeria were not immune from humiliations, and at times, violence. In the best-known modern example, the great influence of Jewish notable Naftali Bujnah within the court of the *dey* (Ottoman leader of the Regency of Algiers) provoked anger among a number of rivals. The leadership of janissaries (Ottoman troops), apparently frustrated with the situation, assassinated Bujnah, and in so doing, unleashed a wave of violence against the local Jewish community in 1805.[46] Less dramatic than incidents of violence was the Jewish tendency to avoid ostentatious displays of power or pride, such as constructing synagogues out of scale with surrounding Muslim-occupied structures, or occupying ministerial posts in which their power over Muslims was obvious. Thus, if Jews served in any number of royal courts from Libya to Morocco, they were more likely to be invested with positions responsible for executing orders of the dey (such as treasurers or tax collectors) than with positions that carried decision-making authority.[47] While it has been suggested that Jews living in Ottoman North African regencies (such as those of Algiers and Tunis) possessed greater overall security than those in Morocco, Jewish life in (urban) Algeria was probably not characterized by perfect equality or security.[48]

This being said, a literal interpretation of dhimmi status should not stand in for social history; Jews and Christians living in Islamic societies experienced a wide variety of circumstances over different times and places.[49] While dhimmi status may not have been irrelevant, it is unclear what precise disabilities were attached to Jews *as Jews* in Algeria in the years leading up to the conquest.[50] The Jews' long history and presence in Mediterranean trade and culture, as well as the broad diversity of their social rankings, evident in the archives, suggest Jews were a relatively secure and integral component of late Ottoman and early colonial Algerian society. French descriptions of their universal isolation and abasement—in short, their lack of dignity or civilization—would then appear to be far more strategic than empirically based.

How did Algerian Jews live in the decades before colonization? One must start by considering that the Regency of Algiers lacked the unity and social integration associated with the modern state. The power of the Ottoman regency was centered in Algiers, but the 90 to 95 percent of the population who lived in rural areas probably felt its authority only irregularly.[51] As Julia Clancy-Smith has shown, the oases communities of the pre-Sahara simultaneously depended upon the urban center and tried to stay out of its reach.[52] The city was crucial to the rural economy, but the power emanating from it, generally manifesting itself in taxes, was to be avoided, if possible. This was a dynamic that colonialism colored but did not dismantle. Furthermore, the commercial and religious networks in which rural Algerians circulated did not necessarily conform to the future borders of Algeria, so one must not imagine that precolonial Algeria possessed a uniform political or social reality.[53]

In a world textured by considerable local autonomy and sharply different social realities, Jewish life was necessarily varied. Members of the mercantile elite in Algiers, for example, lived quite differently from Jewish traders in smaller Saharan towns such as Ghardaia. Quite different from both were the semi-nomadic Jews that escorted caravans between Morocco and Oran from the seventeenth century. As late as 1845, French observers reported the existence of "a considerable number of Israelites who live in equality with the Arabs, as cultivators and warriors. They are armed with the Kabyle rifle in order to fight in their ranks."[54] These were occasionally known as "Arab" or "Bedouin Jews." A report from a French consul in Tunisia noted the same phenomenon in caravans heading east from Algeria: "living exactly the same life as the Arabs, armed and dressed as them, mounted on horses and [in case of need] making war like them, these Jews are totally mixed with the rest of the population that it is impossible to distinguish [the Jews] from them."[55] Joseph Messas, a rabbi in the city of Tlemcen, cited a nineteenth-century responsum from Marrakesh (in Morocco) that outlined how to properly perform the ritual Torah reading after having spent successive Sabbaths in the desert.[56] As we shall see, itinerant Jewish traders were traveling great expanses between Morocco and Oran with their Kabyle partners well into the colonial period. Other reports from Libya offer further evidence that in rural North Africa, religion was often of secondary importance in defining social identities.[57]

As for Jews in the cities and towns of Algeria, they tended to live in semi-autonomous communities with no overarching national administration.

FIGURE 1.1. The majority of Algeria's Jews lived in larger cities such as Oran, but smaller communities inhabited towns that punctuated trans-Saharan trade routes. An English traveler took this photograph of the Jewish quarter of Ghardaia in the 1920s. Reproduced by permission of the Royal Geographical Society.

They were presided over by a Jewish notable often known as the *moqaddem*. The moqaddem often served as a community representative to the local Muslim leader and maintained an official position that provided an income. The moqaddem had the authority to enforce rabbinic judgments and local or imperial leaders' decrees, and also was granted powers of taxation over the community he administered.[58] It is unclear, however, how much political power the notable actually maintained over the community.

Furthermore, the existence of the moqaddem and official Jewish communal authorities does not mean that urban Jews' social identity was entirely defined by their religion. Instead, as in rural areas, many Jews had close commercial and social ties that extended beyond the borders of any given confessional community. In the cities, ties were forged between nomadic Muslim traders and Jewish shop owners. In the first years of the colonial period, even before the French dismantled the preexisting Jewish communal authority, Algerian Jews of differing social ranks would go into business with Maltese fisherman or British consuls. Furthermore, they were integrated into regional and extra-regional trading networks; one study estimates that Jews served as agents in two-thirds of all financial and commercial exchanges between Spain and Oran between 1792 and 1815, usually involving cereal crops, livestock, and wool.[59] Oran Jews worked with colleagues in British Gibraltar who in turn served as important intermediaries in commerce between Algeria, England, and Spain.[60] Like the desert caravans, these seaborne networks were far from purely Jewish in character.

Algerian-Jewish communal leadership in cities was itself often tied up with commerce. One of the privileges of the moqaddem of Algiers was to farm the 2 percent duty on (largely Jewish merchants') exports of ostrich feathers, tobacco, and wool.[61] The ostrich feather trade witnessed a particularly high involvement of Mediterranean Jewish merchants, suggesting that Jewish merchants in Algiers and other North African cities were sufficiently aware of global consumption patterns to profit from the trade.[62] David Duran, the moqaddem of the Oran Jewish community in the early years of the nineteenth century, held this post while serving both as consul general for the Republic of Ragusa (Sicily) and as an active merchant in the trade with Spain.[63] Similarly, the Jewish merchant Mordechai Darmon served as an advisor to several Ottoman deys and eventually used his enormous fortune to build what would later serve as the main consistorial synagogue. The ability of Jews to dominate the trans-Saharan and Mediterranean ostrich feather trade was tied to their international perspective, their connections in the Livornese and other extra-regional markets, and the role of the communal leadership within the governing structure of local regencies.[64]

Jewish life in precolonial Algeria was shaped by a "Livornese" elite and its trans-Mediterranean cultural orientation. This link dated back to Grand Duke Francis's 1593 proclamation known as the *Livornina*, which was intended to develop the city's commercial class. Hoping to profit from the same exodus of non-Christian talent from the Iberian kingdoms that had enriched southern France and the Ottoman Empire, Livorno invited persecuted people to settle in the city. By the eighteenth century, many Livornese Jewish merchants traveled back and forth between the cities of Algiers, Tetuan, and Livorno, while the Italian city's Hebrew press provided many of the Jewish books that would end up in collections in Oran and Algiers.[65] Hosts of Jews traveled back and forth across the Mediterranean throughout the seventeenth and eighteenth centuries leaving Algiers to settle in Livorno, acquire Tuscan nationality, and then return to Algiers as protégés of the Tuscan consulate.[66] Among these Livornese Jews were some of the greatest Algerian-Jewish mercantile families, including the Seror, Nahon, Levi, Valensi, Sforno, Tunes, Alvarengo, Lonsada, and Bongiorno families.[67] These families, and the firms associated with them, used their protected status, or formed partnerships with Christians, in order to facilitate trade or avoid taxes imposed on Jews in some Christian ports, such as Marseilles. Some of the elite Jews in Algeria who were well integrated into French institutions had Livornese protection.

By the time of the conquest, Algerian-Jewish merchants increasingly enjoyed direct commercial ties to France itself. In the eighteenth century, Algiers's trade with Marseilles had passed into the hands of important Algerian-Jewish trading houses. While this was originally conducted through intermediaries based in Livorno, by the end of the century Algerian-Jewish merchants had set up their own branches in Marseilles. Disruptions in trade caused by the French Revolution afforded some Algerian-Jewish families with Tuscan nationality—among them the Jakets, Boucharas, Busnachs, and the Bacris—the opportunity to seize a preeminent position in this trading route.[68] Jews' ability to control elements of urban commercial activity, or to profit from the trade in arms or grain with Spanish, Arab, and English merchants, also bespeaks an economically diverse community that was far from isolated or marginalized.[69]

The majority of Algeria's urban, Arabic-speaking Jews lived a modest existence in the late precolonial period, but probably did not resemble the isolated and persecuted wretches of many French colonial narratives. Most were artisans, peddlers, and shopkeepers at the time of the conquest, selling meat, fish, fruit, vegetables, and tobacco.[70] One traveler noted that Jews distilled brandy and kept taverns where members of Turkish garrisons were permitted to drink alcoholic beverages.[71] To the great annoyance of European officers and traders, they frequently served as valued (if not necessarily rich) intermediaries between parties in urban markets.[72] Local Jews also had influence in the trade of Ottoman, French, and Spanish currency in Algeria, a theme to which we shall return.[73] Among the artisans, there were many tailors, embroiderers, tinsmiths, coppersmiths, watchmakers, jewelers, goldsmiths, silversmiths, and shoemakers.[74] Such diversity suggests that local Muslim authorities did not severely restrict the trades or crafts open to Jews.

In addition to trade and social ties, the synagogue was another important aspect of precolonial urban Jewish life. Synagogues linked both the Jewish elite with the less wealthy mass of Jews, as well as Jewish commercial life with religious life. In the early colonial period, the French would derisively call Algerian places of worship "private synagogues."[75] Yet these synagogues had important social roles in precolonial Jewish life: they served as vehicles for wealthy Jews to invest in urban real estate while simultaneously increasing their social prestige. It is hard to know how much was earned by such investments, but they must have provided at least some revenue; in the 1840s, 17 private synagogues existed in Oran alone, and references to Jewish real estate holdings appear frequently in early colonial archives.[76] Synagogues were also centers of communal and religious life for different groups of Algerian Jews; when the colonial administration put pressure on communities through its centralizing measures, it opened up fissures between groups associated with different synagogues. While colonial policies changed and aggravated tensions, we must assume certain divisions predated the conquest. Synagogues owned by elite Jews shaped Jewish life in precolonial Algeria both by providing a source of income and by serving as centers for social and religious life.

Echoing commercial life, Jewish religious life was not isolated from its wider context. Instead, shrines to holy men, pilgrimages, and legends of miracle-working saints characterized North African Judaism as well as Islam. For example, Jews made (and continue to make) pilgrimages to the tomb of the legendary fourteenth-century Andalusian founder of the Jewish community of Tlemcen, Rabbi Ephraim ben Israel el-Naqawa (also spelled Ankawa, Enkaoua, or Elnkaoua).[77] Such visits are alluded to in archives of the early colonial period, and clearly predated the French conquest. Both geographically and culturally, these Jewish practices overlapped with local Muslim practices and there were many other Jewish and Muslim sites of pilgrimage in addition to the tomb of el-Naqawa in the outskirts of Tlemcen. Accompanying the rabbis' shrines were those of the patron saint of Tlemcen, Sidi Bou Médiène (Shu'ayb Abu al-Madayn), Sidi al-Halwi, and Abd Allah al-Shudi who, like Rabbi al-Naqawa, was of Andalusian background. Furthermore, Algerian Jews welcomed emissaries from Palestine who traveled across the Maghreb soliciting donations to support the pious communities of the Holy Land, while rabbis from Tunis, Jerusalem, and other Jewish communities of Muslim Mediterranean lands were called upon to give their blessing to religious volumes produced in Algeria. In addition to the commercial links discussed in previous paragraphs, it would appear that religious forms, the Islamic politico-cultural geography, and even a cultural memory of Andalusia connected Algerian Jews with their Muslim neighbors in the precolonial Maghreb.

Of course, different Algerian cities had different Jewish histories. Tlemcen (in western Algeria) and Algiers absorbed many refugees from the Spanish persecutions of 1390, while victims of the 1492 expulsion landed in Oran and the Moroccan cities of Fez and Tetuan (accompanied by many expelled Andulasian Muslims). In most of these cities, the new arrivals met Arabic- and Berber-speaking communities whose presence in North Africa has been dated as far back as the Roman destruction of Jerusalem in A.D. 70. In 1525, the Ottomans took Algiers, making it into an important military outpost in their wars against Spain, while also integrating it into the empire's far-flung Mediterranean trading network. Commercial and intellectual exchange tied Algiers to Istanbul, as well as to European ports, such as Livorno and Marseilles. By the years leading up to the French conquest of Algeria, many merchants in the western Mediterranean and North African worlds were Jews based in the ports and trading centers of Morocco, Gibraltar, Tunisia, and Algeria.[78]

MAP 1. Modern Algeria, as well as boundaries of the Province of Oran in the mid-nineteenth century.

This study focuses on the city and province of Oran for a variety of reasons, not the least of which being that its history presents such a stark contrast to the lachrymose French picture of Jews living under Islam in Algeria.[79] The city of Oran had spent much of the late medieval and early modern period under the rule of Spain, which had expelled Oran's Jews in 1668. Only in 1792, about forty years before the French conquest, did Muhammad al-Kabir conquer Oran and bring it under a more tolerant Ottoman rule. The leadership was eager to repopulate the ruined city and make it the regional capital for the province of the west (Mascara had formerly served as the capital), so the dey invited Jews from neighboring Mostaganem, Mascara, Nedroma, and Tlemcen to settle there.[80] After the initial founding of the community, immigrants from Algiers and Morocco augmented the settlement. By the middle of the nineteenth century, a considerable community of Haketia-speakers had joined the Arabophone local Jews of Oran, centered primarily in a Jewish neighborhood to the east of the old Casbah.[81] In addition to the fact that it left a rich archival record, nineteenth-century Oran presents an obvious focus of this study because even though it was small at the time of the conquest, overshadowed in western Algeria by Tlemcen, in subsequent decades it became the most Jewish (in both proportion and sheer numbers) of Algeria's cities. We must also remember that it was its earlier conquest by Islamic forces that actually ushered in Tlemcen and Oran's modern Jewish history.

MAP 2. The Jewish neighborhood in colonial Oran was located outside of the old city (casbah) and just south of the port. Rue d'Austerlitz, running north–south close to the center of this map, was the principal commercial street. From the author's personal collection.

FIGURE I.2. A postcard from the early twentieth century of Rue d'Austerlitz in the Jewish neighborhood of Oran. From the personal collection of Stephanie Comfort.

This tableau of a precolonial Jewish life tightly interlinked with the wider milieu helps frame this study. It is a base for understanding the changes that colonialism wrought, as well as the polemical quality of the reductionist French reports emphasizing the isolation and misery of Algerian Jews. Their perspectives were hardly understated: in 1836, for example, members of the central consistory in Paris described the French conquest as having "torn from slavery a [Jewish] population bent for centuries under the yoke of barbarism."[82] An 1839 letter from the minister of war to the minister of justice and cults reduced their complex and varied social standing to being "the object of the deepest contempt by the Muslims, cursed by the law of the prophet, [and] the victims of exactions and insults."[83] While other early reports noted the variety of Jewish industry and occupations in early colonial Algeria, they still insisted that the status of the Jews approached that of "slaves."[84] This puzzling contrast must be understood as stemming from both colonial exigencies and the legacy of Jewish emancipation in France. In the following chapters, we will explore how and why French colonialists imagined this economically integrated, diverse, and deeply rooted group to be a desperate community in need of dramatic transformation, and what role it played in the colonial effort.

Arabs of the Jewish Faith

I have chosen not to order the chapters that follow according to a strict chronology because a central claim of this book is that the historical exigencies of the colonial encounter distinguished it markedly from earlier French reform campaigns. Faced with the challenge of establishing a colonial order, military officers and Jewish reformers in Algeria cast around for previous models, which they often found in earlier French debates and legislation. Nonetheless, these precedents did not entirely predetermine the form colonialism would take. Instead, they helped colonizers imagine, justify, and build a colonial order in radical contrast to the republican order that was evolving in France by the middle years of the nineteenth century.[85] The organization that follows is dictated by the desire to understand colonial Algerian history both on its own terms and in dialogue with French metropolitan histories with which it conversed.

To this end, Chapter 1 begins in Algeria during the early days of the conquest. "Jews, Commerce, and Community in Early Colonial Algeria" examines both the historical context and the discussions and debates that led up to the founding of French *consistoires israélites* in Algeria. These consistories, presented as civilizing institutions, represented a French effort to better control the multiethnic, frequently non-French-speaking, and growing population in the cities. As we will see, for colonial administrators, the

Jews' profitable trans-Mediterranean commercial connections, combined with their potential utility as indigenous allies in the conquest of Algeria, made their close administration seem advantageous. Bolstering the case for civilizing, liberal French Jews, frequently connected to the metropolitan consistories, helped to develop a "Jewish mythology" through official reports and press articles. According to this vision, Jews were held to be more intelligent, faithful, and redeemable than the supposedly less-gifted Muslims among whom they lived.

Earlier scholarly treatments of this topic have identified the campaign led by liberal French Jews as uniquely responsible for the establishment of Algerian consistories. Here, I emphasize the military's role in the process. Doubtless, elite members of metropolitan Jewish consistories offered their services by bringing consistories to Algeria and by lobbying the appropriate ministries. But these institutions were only established once the Ministry of War was convinced that they accorded with France's colonial objectives. Drawing on military correspondence, my intention is to weave what might be mistakenly seen as a strictly inter-Jewish encounter between French and Algerians into the larger history of French colonialism. By extension, this chapter also reveals the complexity in what has often been reductively described as a stark ideological divide between liberal Jewish reformers and the anti-Jewish French generals in Algeria.[86] One need not deny the former's liberal convictions, nor the latter's antipathy toward Jews, to see that their shared commitment to military conquest was ultimately more historically important.

Though the goal of uplifting the Jews was imagined by its advocates as benevolent, the resulting campaign was not well received by its intended beneficiaries. Chapter 2, "Revolution, Republicanism, and Religion: Responses to Civilizing in Oran, 1848," explores instances of Jewish resistance to consistorial civilizing efforts in Algeria. In the eyes of these resistors, civilization as a concept was tightly interwoven with the experience of power, surveillance, and control. When Algerian Jews resisted civilizing institutions, they did not display the backward traditionalism of poor and oppressed people as contemporary observers described. Instead, the established community pushed back against a new and intrusive governmental effort to rescind previously enjoyed prerogatives. Indeed, both military and consistorial archives—upon which this chapter draws—reveal a range of pietistic, politically savvy, and thoroughly modern responses to Paris's efforts to intervene in local communities' affairs.

How was civilizing understood, used, and implemented as colonial policy? Chapter 3, "Synagogues, Surveillance, and Civilization," suggests that the effort to monitor and control interior spaces and domestic rituals was central to the French understanding of civilizing. To illustrate this, the chapter explores how the consistory of Oran tangled with the problem of private synagogues of the Algerian Jews and the practices that went on within them. Synagogues, as central institutions in both religious and commercial life, also provide a useful vehicle to explore many aspects of the colonial Algerian-Jewish social landscape.

Religious schools, too, became sites of resistance to colonial efforts to extend control and legislate morality, hygiene, and family behaviors. Chapter 4 shows that anxieties over cleanliness, health, control, and civilization were interwoven in the colony. "Teaching Civilization: French Schools and Algerian Midrashim 1852–1870" mines colonial surveys and inter-ministerial correspondence to illustrate how Jewish reformers in Algeria endeavored to close or remake the religious schools they saw as impeding Jews' progress on the path of civilization. Like reformers' efforts to control marital behaviors and synagogues, their success in transforming schools was limited. The power of local teachers, parents, and religious leaders forced the civil administration to alter and adapt its policies toward Jewish education. Struggles between these parties illustrate how authoritative discourses and the intertwined notion of civilization were wielded to justify control over would-be citizens.[87]

If demands of hygiene legitimized increased French control and surveillance of favored colonial groups, various family laws and customs were consistently evoked as the ultimate bar to citizenship. Chapter 5, "From Napoleon's Sanhedrin to the Crémieux Decree: Sex, Marriage, and the Boundaries of Civilization," uses court transcripts, official correspondence, and legal brochures to show that colonial debates about the naturalization of Algerian subjects frequently referred back to Napoleon's 1806–1807 Sanhedrin and, particularly, how it linked French citizenship with family law. I show that in 1850s Algeria, as in France at the opening of the century, Jewish laws about polygamy and divorce became a focal point of discussions about the meaning of citizenship. And while the newborn Third Republic saw naturalizing Algerian Jews as part of the emancipatory legacy of 1789, it explicitly excluded Muslims from citizenship rights. Colonial policy in Algeria echoed Napoleonic doctrine by maintaining the family as an index of a given group's capability to be naturalized. The level of civilization, it seems, could be read in family practices.

The Conclusion casts glances both backward and forward. It briefly considers two legal cases, one before and one after the period studied here, suggesting how family life has maintained a prominent position in French notions of citizenship. It then resumes this book's exploration into how understandings of civilization were frequently linked to the ability of the state to monitor and control previously intimate, religious, or familial arenas. It argues that civilization was consistently tied to the concept of emancipation, a concept that had become an authoritative trope in late eighteenth-century discussions of Jews in France. This term, "civilization," was then evoked in the colonies not only to mobilize concern for the Jewish minority, but also to support legislation that maintained the inferior status of the colonized majority.[88] The colonial encounter thus helped transform the revolutionary call for emancipation into an imperialist ideology.

Insofar as Jews gained citizenship, French lawmakers—and no small faction of scholars—considered them to have been successfully civilized. And yet to the historian, their story can be considered the exception that proves the rule. That is, the same logic that structured debates about whether Algerian Jews could become French citizens (and if so, how), also rationalized the exclusion of the vast majority of Algerians from the French body politic. The experience of the relatively small and ultimately emancipated Algerian-Jewish community is thus valuable, paradoxically, in so far as it sheds light on the exclusionary power of the French civilizing mission. Civilization has always been, first and foremost, an ideology whose promise of emancipation played host to the rationale for exclusion.

1

Jews, Commerce, and Community in Early Colonial Algeria

In March 1832, General Pierre Boyer sent a report to the governor general of Algeria describing the commercial life of Oran. The French had occupied this formerly Spanish city the year before, and the officer, nicknamed Pedro the Cruel for his public use of corporal punishment, including group beheadings, was the local French commander.[1] As Boyer put it, Oran's "commerce was composed of at most forty Jews" who managed to "pool their money together and buy the cargo of a ship of between seventy and one hundred barrels (*tonneaux*)."[2] They would then take the merchandise, which was generally shipped from Gibraltar, and "as quickly as possible, transport it to their boutiques and stores in the upper part of the city and display it for sale." This was their method of avoiding the fees of the customs warehouse, and simultaneously keeping potential competitors at bay. The result, according to Boyer, was that "there is not a single French businessman installed in Oran."[3]

Thirteen years later, on November 9, 1845, King Louis-Philippe signed a law that "organized" the Jewish communities of Algeria. The "Ordonnance portant sur l'organisation du culte israélite en Algérie," as it was called, was modeled in part on Napoleon's 1808 decree that had created a network of Jewish consistories in France. Consistories were official, state-supervised communal organizations generally staffed by wealthy and assimilated Jewish notables whose responsibility was to represent, police, and regenerate the Jewish communities of their circumscription. The 1845 decree called for a new central consistory in Algiers that would oversee two provincial consistories, in Oran and Constantine. Like the consistories Napoleon had established in France in 1808, the new consistories were staffed by government-approved (French) chief rabbis and lay members charged with the regeneration of their communities. To this end, the new Algerian consistories were granted full

23

control over the local Jewish community's budget, including the right to tax kosher meat and wine and to distribute alms to the needy. In addition, they were responsible for maintaining order in synagogues, suppressing unauthorized religious assemblies, and, if necessary, preventing local religious leaders from exercising their functions. And while Boyer's frustrated letter to the governor general suggested that a significant group of Jews was already integrated into Oran's trans-Mediterranean commercial life and doing well for themselves, the consistories were intended to encourage Jews to learn "useful professions."[4] Carrying the official motto *civilisation et patrie*, consistories were also chartered to help the Jews learn French, to swear fidelity to France, and to uplift a population whose very commercial prowess had provoked complaints by French officers less than a decade and a half before.[5]

During the intervening thirteen years, French colonial references to Jews in Algeria traced an uneven arc. For most of the 1830s, officers such as Boyer either discussed rifts and rivalries in Jewish communal leadership that boiled over into the realm of colonial administration, or complained about the Jews' undo commercial influence. By the early 1840s, however, many French observers and writers were calling on Paris to "emancipate" men whose status approached that of "slaves." What explains these radically different encounters with Algeria's colonized Jews? Did they arise from the appearance of more "liberal" spirits on the colonial scene? Did they reflect the changing ways French officers, possessed of their own colonial ideologies, responded to the evolving exigencies of the conquest? Answering these questions requires us to turn to the decade and a half between the installation of French commands in Algerian cities and the 1845 ordinance, to examine the role of Jews in cities under French rule, and to consider how influential men in the French service integrated the Jewish populations of Algeria into their nascent colonial ideology.

The exigencies of conquest, rather than real cultural differences between the colonized, led the Ministry of War to pursue the establishment of Jewish consistories in colonial Algeria. Jews were a significant component of the social and economic fabric of Algeria's cities, and were intimately interwoven into regional and trans-regional trading networks. These factors attracted the attention of French authorities as much as they sparked a vocal campaign by metropolitan Jews to uplift those they came to regard as their Oriental cousins. The significance of the Algerian-Jewish community led seemingly internal problems of communal leadership to ripple through the urban social landscape, affecting other European and indigenous Arab or Berber groups, and ultimately caused French generals to worry about the state of the occupation. Establishing consistories represented an effort to better control Jews and the growing and multiethnic urban population of which they formed an important component.

Previous work has usefully underscored the important role of French-Jewish liberals in the subsequent history of Algeria's Jews. Prominent Jewish reformers influenced by July Monarchy liberalism were the first to suggest that consistories should be extended to Algeria's Jews, and that such institutions would help uplift a fallen race. Here, I emphasize the crucial role of the French military—both the army and the Ministry of War in Paris—in shaping the future of this Mediterranean Jewish population.[6] Anti-Jewish comments of leading military officers have made it all too easy to overlook the confluence of interests between them and the metropolitan liberal Jewish reformers who were so crucial in shaping colonial Jewish policy.[7] Yet, by the time the Jewish reformers convinced the Ministry of War that establishing colonial consistories made sense, at the end of the 1830s, military officers already had nearly a decade of experience governing urban Algeria's unwieldy Jewish population. By emphasizing the military's perspective, the story of Algerian Jews is more properly integrated into the larger history of early French colonialism in Algeria.

The Military, Commerce, and Jews in Algerian Cities

What, then, were the considerations that eventually led the Ministry of War to install institutions whose very motto suggested a French desire to civilize Algerian Jews and attach them to France? As we saw in the introduction, different groups of Jews constituted an important element in a diverse urban demography. In the decades following 1830, non-French Europeans quickly outnumbered French settlers in Algeria, with most coming from Spain, Italy, and Malta, along with smaller numbers from Switzerland and the German states. In 1840, for example, Algiers counted 14,434 Europeans, but only 6,861 of them were French.[8] There were also 18,387 local Algerians called by the French *indigènes* (indigenous), most of which (12,322) were Muslims and the remainder (6,065) Jews. As for Oran at the time of the conquest, the soon-to-be named capital of Algeria's western province counted about 17,000 residents, of whom about 3,700 were Jewish.[9] There were also 4,837 Europeans, including 2,333 Spaniards, and about 1,342 Frenchmen.[10] From the very beginning of the conquest, contemporary reports and memos offer glimpses of a colorful, religiously diverse, and truly international population in Algeria's coastal cities. Neapolitan coral-fishers dominated the trade in Bône, for example, while Maltese fishermen helped set prices in Oran.[11] Accompanying them were Haketia-speaking Moroccan Jews, Judeo-Arabic-speaking local Jews, a Livornese Jewish elite, Turks, liberated slaves of sub-Saharan origins, and transient bands of Italians, French, and Spanish.[12] Former Christian captives may also have augmented the poor European population of Algerian port cities, as was the case in Tunis.[13] In Oran, a community of fifty-seven

M'zabi merchant households had lived under written contract with the Otto-man administrator for years before the conquest, facilitating trans-Saharan caravan trade, while in Algiers, M'zabis also ran urban mills and furnished slaves to wealthy households.[14]

A series of incidents that occurred in the early years of the occupation provide a window into Jews' place in this multiethnic fabric and hints at their relationships with other groups that predated the French conquest. Such incidents also provide fascinating illustrations of French frustration with Jew-ish commercial influence in the Algerian cities during the first days of the occupation. As Boyer's angry report suggested, Jews emerged as significant if not always appreciated commercial players on France's new colonial frontier. Importantly, an element of their troublesomeness stemmed from the partner-ships and interactions they maintained with the local urban milieu. In an 1832 report to the governor general, for example, the local French commander noted that an increasing number of fishing boats were returning to service in the harbor of Algiers. The commander estimated that the number of boats had jumped from about seven or eight in March 1831 to about fifty-six in Feb-ruary 1832. The city's new leadership would normally applaud Algiers's return to commercial life, as the French hoped to keep Algeria's cities commercially viable. Yet, in this case, the partnerships that were sprouting up amid the non-French population were cause for concern. "Around June," noted the local commander, "complaints were made against a company of Maltese fish-ermen and Jews who take all the fish and sell them at very high prices." At the time, the French general Pierre Berthezène ordered the local administration to "end these abuses" and even ordered the creation of a local sheik (leader or deputy of a higher authority) whose purpose would be "to monitor the exchange of fish." While the initial efforts appeared to be successful, "since the end of last December the same abuse began again."[15]

The archives are silent on how the case of the Algiers fishmongers might have been resolved, but the incident sheds light on Jews' local visibility, as well as on the alliances of convenience they brokered with other local groups. Taken in combination with Boyer's complaints that Jews could cor-ner trade in Oran, a pattern of frustration with Jewish economic prominence emerges. This frustration continued into the 1840s, when General Thomas-Robert Bugeaud described Jews as "the greatest obstacle to the rapproche-ment between Arabs and Frenchmen." The reason for this, according to Bugeaud, was that "Jews insert themselves between the two parties, in order to cheat both. Since they speak the language and they know the customs of the country, they pose as the arbiters of commerce, and they only rarely allow an Arab to deal directly with a Frenchman."[16]

In a November 1843 visit to Oran, Bugeaud echoed earlier comments by Boyer, noting that it had become "a pretty little city, cool and picturesque," but also lamenting, "unfortunately, the major part of its population is made up of rapacious Jews" who "have become insolent because we have emancipated them too early."[17] A week and half later, he complained that Jews "controlled the better part of commerce, which French nationals could conduct very well."[18] These were not isolated vexations. Military correspondence about Jews during the first 15 years of the conquest prominently featured complaints about their commercial dominance.

Popular accounts added additional dimensions to the French understanding that Jews dominated the economy of Algeria. A number of popular French writers painted a picture of Algerian Jews as indispensable to local commerce, but also as greedy and dangerous to the French occupation. Louis de Baudicur, a prolific writer of the early colonial period, wrote a book on the "indigenous [peoples] of Algeria" in 1852, in which he observed that "trade [was the Jews'] principle occupation," so if a Jew felt any affinity for another people, "it will be for the one with whom he can trade most gainfully." He went on to warn his countrymen, "Let us not fool ourselves, the English are worth more to the Jews than we are."[19] Journalistic accounts that appeared in such regional publications as *Le Journal de Rouen* also described Jews' commercial significance in Algeria. A. de Genvray and A. Lapointe, for example, described the Jews as "obligatory intermediaries for our relations with the natives."[20] Baron Baude, a *conseiller d'état* who had formerly served as the king's commissioner in Algeria, wrote that "the Israelite population is called to play an important role in Africa," and that "the Jews [have] an ease of access to the Muslims which we will lack for some time."[21] Military observations about Jewish commercial prominence were hence reinforced and possibly even fueled by such popular accounts.

Anxieties about Jews' commercial dominance led French officials to monitor Jewish merchants' relationships with the interior. To understand the issues at stake, it is important to have a sense of the regional economic situation at the time. The occupation of Algiers and Oran had disrupted trans-Saharan trade networks on which the French had hoped to capitalize, since the destruction of the central authority unleashed chaos in the interior. Different tribes and clans quickly split over whether to do business with French-held towns or not. Different groups inhabiting the periphery of French control had to weigh the benefits and risks of trading with those whom many native Algerians regarded as the enemy.[22] Some pastoralists found their previous means of existence threatened or eliminated by the interruption of trade routes and the impossibility of obtaining grain, and many had to subsist on products available from desert oases, such as dates.[23] Well into the 1840s, the French administration was scrambling to encourage caravans to cross through the Sahara and into the northern cities and towns in order to reestablish a disrupted economy and ensure the provisioning of the littoral's population. General Bugeaud bragged in 1842 that he had finally convinced bedouin to come back to French markets, while General Eugène Daumas was still eagerly predicting the caravans' return from Tunis to Algiers as late as 1845.[24] In a context in which the French ardently hoped to bring trade back to their new conquests, city-based Jewish traders were an important resource.

Archival documents suggest that when strains in relationships between Jewish urban merchants and the tribal interior emerged, French officials became anxious about their ability to control the local economy. From one 1839 case, we get a sense of how certain Jewish commercial groups made arrangements with representatives of Muslim tribes to secure a favorable trading environment. In the late spring of that year, a member of the Hashim tribe who had recently purchased a piece of calico in Mostaganem, a town about forty-five miles east of Oran, encountered a *wakil* (pl. *wuka'la*), or tribal representative, of Emir Abd al-Qader of Mascara (and leader of the Hashim). It is uncertain what the Hashim tribesman planned, but he probably hoped to make a profit in the active caravan route that brought European-made cottons through such Saharan trading towns as Ghedamis and Ghardaia (where Jewish merchants also operated) to Kano, in contemporary Nigeria.[25] The men with the wakil insulted the Hashim merchant, took the recently purchased fabric, and insisted that upon orders of the emir, he buy nothing more from French-held cities. While the fabric was later returned to the purchaser, according to the lieutenant general of the Province of Oran, the wakil's actions were part of a larger racket involving certain tribes and influential Jewish merchants. The French official guessed that Abd al-Qader was probably hoping to stop all commerce with French-held cities. This would make sense given strains in the treaty of Tafna (negotiated in 1837 to cease direct hostilities between French forces and the emir) and the imminence of war in 1839.[26] However, the French officer suspected that the wakil was acting on more local concerns, notably trying to "favor certain privileged Israelites": "I have remarked that a number of them, for example Mr. Israel Serfati, make considerable shipments of merchandise into the interior with the agreement and protection of the wakil, at the exclusion of the others. The Jews have always had good relations with the wakil, who, naturally benefiting from this favor, prefers (dealing with the Jews) over the others."[27]

There is not enough evidence here to draw definitive conclusions, but the anecdote does raise potentially fascinating questions about the relations of Algerian-Jewish merchants with the anticolonial forces under Abd al-Qader.[28] As we shall see, on at least one occasion an Oran Jew explicitly condemned a communal leader for having close ties to the emir. The letter also fleshes out Jews' place in the early colonial economy and provides some indication of French responses to it. Whether or not the lieutenant's memo accurately captured the wakil's motives, it would appear that urban Jewish merchants possessed important contacts in the interior, including tribal representatives with whom they negotiated favorable working relationships.

Men such as Israel Serfati had probably established agreements with the Hashim's wakil before the occupation as part of an effort to secure favorable trading conditions and trustworthy partners in a decentralized political environment. As Francesca Trivellatto has explained, establishing trustworthy partnerships was a difficult but essential task incumbent upon early modern Mediterranean and Maghrebi merchants (Jewish and gentile). Even in the relatively proximate world of the Italian Sephardic trading communities upon which her work has focused, legal action was rarely a desirable means to ensure upright behavior. In addition, confessional alliances were insufficient as guarantees of either honesty or competence.[29] French military concerns with Jews' trading with Muslim tribes in the interior continued to surface after the establishment of the consistory. In 1853, for example, a Moroccan Jewish immigrant to Algeria was arrested along with several Kabyle Muslim associates for a series of thefts near the town of Sidi-Bel-Abbes. According to military correspondence, he had previously been "living among the Kabyles of Morocco."[30] In 1855, the *bureau arabe* (an arm of the French military charged with dispensing justice in rural areas inhabited entirely or almost entirely by Muslims) in the province of Oran requested a list of all itinerant Jewish merchants (*colporteurs*) operating among the Arab tribes in the interior, as well as their authorizations to do so.[31] The new French administration in Oran thus had to manage a populace that was at once indebted to the occupier for security but still enmeshed in far more expansive ties of business and loyalty.

An important consequence of Jewish prominence in both the urban milieu and in surrounding networks was that disputes seemingly internal to the Jewish community found their way into the domain of French colonial politics. Reports from the early colonial period suggest that a series of crises of communal leadership during the 1830s entangled the French administration, and by 1839 officials at the Ministry of War were seriously considering alternative proposals by which they might more effectively govern the Jewish component of the civil population in Algeria. As we shall see, metropolitan Jewish reformers were to participate in reform that would establish the consistories and totally reorganize Jewish communal governance.[32] Before this reform and after its adoption as well, the French administration fielded complaints by urban Jews about their leaders. These crises of communal administration affected other non-Jewish groups on the Algerian littoral. In other words, Jews in Algeria quickly made themselves a matter of imperial administration. These problems inspired the development of a colonial ideology of regeneration that would later justify the establishment of consistories.

We now turn to several such episodes, considering what they tell us about Algerian colonial history.

In February 1832, an Oran Jewish merchant by the name of Amar, who had made considerable money shipping cattle to Gibraltar, stepped down from his French-approved position as head of the Jewish Nation (*chef de la nation juive* in French).[33] Amar was from a powerful family with ties in both Livorno and North Africa that had a presence in Algiers at least since 1723.[34] The precise circumstances surrounding Amar's resignation remain elusive, but he may have fallen sick, for he later succumbed to the cholera epidemic that swept the Mediterranean basin at the beginning of the 1830s.[35] Amar had worked closely with the French leadership to provision Oran with food and had served as an intermediary between the French garrison and the local Jewish community; he had also regulated and policed interactions among the town's Jewish merchants and members of the (Muslim) Doua'ir and Smela who brought goods to the Oran market.[36] General Boyer apparently chose him for the position after Amar was elected by his co-religionists, but a subsection of Jews had vocally manifested their desire that the French authorities reverse that decision.[37] Many were partisans of Joseph Cohen-Scalli, another local notable, and hoped to install their man in Amar's place. The most recent election for moqaddem, however, brought only 80 votes to Cohen-Scalli, while Amar won by what one French official called an "imposing majority."[38] When Amar left his post, the French did not appoint a replacement, but Cohen-Scalli retained his position as adjunct to the French authority. Amar's departure had a significant effect on France's ability to effectively administer the city.

In the absence of the respected moqaddem, the Cohen-Scalli subsection of Oran's Jews apparently began to take advantage of the lack of oversight. In February, Muhammad al-Qadi, the brother of Mustapha Agha, who led the Doua'ir tribe, wrote to the French command in Oran. The Doua'ir had usufruct over state lands mostly to the west and south of the city and had previously enjoyed a privileged relationship with the *bey* (leader, governor) in the west.[39] Dating from the times when the Spanish held Oran, before 1792, the Doua'ir also owned property and stored grain harvests in the western city of Mascara, and had a historic role provisioning the city with goods from the interior.[40] By 1832, the Doua'ir were making overtures to the French, though many of their members also served as officers for Abd al-Qader.[41] Muhammad al-Qadi complained that Jews were taking advantage of their position, insulting Arab traders, cheating them, and even stealing the goods they had brought to sell.[42] He pleaded with General Boyer to do something about the leadership of the Jewish community in Oran. "We only ask for peace and tranquility," he assured the general, which would return once Boyer "restored the safety that we enjoyed under Amar." He then begged

Boyer to put Amar "back at the head of the Jewish nation," for "he is the only one who understands the interests of Arabs and Jews, and knows how to restore order."[43]

Boyer could ill-afford to ignore the complaints. On February 13, a captain at the military post in Mers al-Kabir in Oran wrote to Boyer to announce that "twenty or twenty-two" Arab leaders of the same tribe had presented him a petition that they had not managed to deliver to Boyer themselves.[44] Their complaint had to do with "Jews and several foreigners" who abused the tribe members when they came to do business in Oran. The captain confirmed the allegations against the Jews, and noted that the insulted traders refused to bring their wares to market for fear of further abuse by foreigners or Jews. Wasting no time, Boyer wrote Muhammad al-Qadi the same day, assuring him that "I, like you, have the highest regard for Amar" who would subsequently "remain the representative of your rights to my person."[45] He then assured the Arab leader that his people could "come with your goods," and "if you find yourself in need of a [trustworthy] Jew, address yourself to me. You will promptly receive justice."[46] Two weeks later, Boyer was still dealing with the fallout of the power vacuum. He wrote to the minister of war in Paris to complain that Jews continued to taunt Arabs who came into the city, and that after fifteen days the markets were still suspended.[47]

What does the crisis that surrounded Amar's departure from a leadership position teach us about the place of Jewish communal structures in Algeria's urban economy in the early days of French colonial rule? While our window remains narrow, it appears that Jews' demographic and commercial prominence, as well as their integration into surrounding regional and extra-regional trading networks, made their behavior a real concern for French leadership as early as the 1830s. In some sense, Jews' historic economic success in Algeria pointed to contemporary French failures. After all, the disappearance of Amar, or at least of the authority he was seen to possess, led to a series of problems that wracked the commercial life of Oran. Not only were petitions signed and complaints filed but the French also had problems provisioning the city in his absence—or more specifically, when Ottoman institutions of communal governance (such as the moqaddem) were allowed to disintegrate. Whether the divisions expressed by the struggle between Joseph Cohen-Scalli and Amar neatly traced ethnolinguistic divisions (Judeo-Arabic, Haketia, Italian), economic boundaries, or other ideological, social, geographic, or religious groupings, they clearly had strong repercussions for the commercial life of early colonial Oran. Jews maintained enough influence on local markets that a failure to enforce discipline upon local clans could send ripples out into the countryside or up the chain of colonial command. The story of Amar suggests that by the early 1830s, the leadership and administration of Algerian-Jewish communities had proven itself to be a consequential element in the larger project of colonial domination.

There was an important ideological dimension to the early encounter between Algerian Jews and their French occupiers. Part of what made it so hard for French officers to deal with the Jewish population of cities such as Oran was their assumption that Jews were natural allies of French colonialism. Early reports and correspondence make it clear that despite the frustration over trading monopolies and inside deals with local wuka'la, the French assumed Algeria's urban population was dependent on the security they provided, and believed these cities harbored populations more interested in commerce than holy war; therefore they also believed that urban Jews shared common interests with their French occupiers. This assumption is reflected in early descriptions of these cities as housing "Jews and Turks" who are "favorable to our interests" and willing on occasion to go out on "sorties to push back Arabs."[48] A similar sentiment led French officers to defend the Jewish moqaddem as someone charged with "missions of [a great] importance."[49] Nor was this perceived bond with the French occupiers limited to Jews in official roles. The French law of 1834 legally abolished Jews' juridical autonomy (aside from personal status issues), making the Algerian Jews governable as "Europeans." The disconnect between this ideology and the reality of Jewish interconnectedness with the tribal interior, as well as with British Gibraltar, Livorno, and Morocco, demanded official attention. This gulf would inform the decision to establish Algerian consistories that aimed to teach, among other things, fidelity to France.

The distance between an official French ideology that envisioned a friendly civil population of Europeans and Algerian Jews and the actual practices Jews maintained was perhaps most visible when the actions of Jewish notables emerged as security risks for the French. For example, in March 1832, Boyer complained to his overseers in Paris about Oran's relationship to the surrounding tribes. "I had obtained agreements with the tribes to renounce hostilities . . . and protect [traders bringing] our provisions. For three months we have enjoyed this, but now it has changed," complained Boyer. In addition to Jews insulting and stealing from Arabs, a meddlesome Jew by the name of Sabah had returned to Algeria, and "the words exchanged and correspondences with these same Jews with [hostile] Arab chiefs, has all conspired to put us in the same state of hostility [with the tribes] we were in last October."[50] Earlier, Boyer had also complained of an unnamed Moroccan Jewish merchant (perhaps Jacob Lasry, discussed below), based in Oran and involved in cattle exporting, whose tendency toward "intrigue" managed to "harm [French] relations with the Arabs." The same Jew was also suspected of conspiring with the vice consul of England to raise cattle prices in Oran and "harm the interests of the French occupation of Oran."[51] The events suggest that Jewish mercantile activities, whether or not they posed actual threats to France, were seen as threatening by the nascent French colonial authority in North Africa.

It is hard to know exactly who Mr. Sabah was, or what was the nature of these "conspiracies." Indeed, it is difficult to determine whether Boyer's note reveals a real conspiracy among Jewish merchants and various tribal chiefs to weaken the French position, or simply an eagerness to assign blame for faltering supplies in Oran during a time of war. However, given the historical context in which deals between Jewish merchants and British or Arab traders were standard, Boyer's anxieties in and of themselves illuminate a complicated relationship between the would-be French masters of the country, Jews, and various tribal groups in the interior. In this instance, as in so many others, the complicated colonial reality clashed with the French ideology that held Jews to be natural allies, as essential components of their colonial cities. The fact that the emergent French authority was forced to rely upon the Jews made it all the more crucial for officers to address issues of Jewish communal leadership and Jewish-brokered trading arrangements. By the close of the 1830s, the minister of war would be eager to establish institutions geared toward Jews that would address these questions.

The story of Haim Israel Raphael Jacob Lasry (Arabic: al-'Asry) provides another example of how Jewish merchants in Algeria presented challenges to the French conquerors, occasionally bringing them into diplomatic scuffles with their European rivals. At the same time Jewish intermediaries like Lasry maintained an uneasy relationship with French authority in Algeria, they were forced to negotiate with new colonial authorities while not necessarily benefiting from the conquest. Given Lasry's stature in western Mediterranean commerce, tracing his relationship with local, French, and foreign powers in Algeria requires the puzzling together of British and French imperial archives. Lasry was emblematic of how a certain wealthy Algerian-Jewish elite maneuvered with French power at the dawn of colonial rule in North Africa.

Lasry was a British-protected subject based in Gibraltar and Oran. His exports of Algerian cattle (both sheep and cows), wheat, and barley were high-value affairs in which British merchant companies and foreign consuls were involved. In 1831, the French General Bertrand Clauzel, faced with inadequate numbers of troops to maintain control of the Algerian littoral, experimented with indirect rule by asking Bey Ahmed of Tunis to appoint beys for Constantine and Oran as proxies for the French. Subsequently, the Tunisian bey Kheir al-Din Agha took over the administration in Oran. Shortly afterward, Jacob Lasry and James Welsford, Lasry's business partner and British vice consul in Oran, made a deal with Kheir al-Din, who was in need of money. Kheir al-Din offered Lasry a substantial discount off the standard price for rights to export grain and cattle from Oran in exchange for a loan.[52]

Soon after Lasry paid for the rights of export, however, the new French governor general, Pierre Berthezène, replaced the Tunisian with General Pierre Boyer. Meanwhile, the French government refused to ratify the agreement that Clauzel had originally made with Bey Ahmed that had led to Kheir al-Din's installation, casting doubts on the validity of privileges he had sold to Jacob Lasry and other merchants like him.[53] Lasry and Welsford found that under the rule of Boyer, "some impediment was thrown in the way of the exportation" of grain and cattle, so they called upon the new French ruler to verify that the French would respect existing export agreements.[54] In August 1831, the French General Behaghel, the military sub-intendant in Oran, met with Jacob Lasry, Joseph Zermaty, a Jewish merchant based in Algiers, as well as several other merchants (both Christian and Muslim) in the palace of the bey to discuss the matter.[55] The meeting's minutes would later provide "proof" that all local authorities (French, Tunisian, and British) agreed that the permits were valid. According to the British vice consul's notes, the French civil intendant sent subsequent assurance to his British counterpart that the rights would be honored as soon as Boyer issued his formal permission.[56]

Lasry and the British consul were soon disappointed; they continued to face obstacles trying to export grain from French-held Oran. In an October letter to London, the consul reported that he had "an interview with General Berthezène yesterday, and [I] showed him this document signed by every authority at Oran, and I ventured to add that British merchants residing there would be ruined, if no dependence could be placed on the official acts of the head of the Government at that place."[57] Both Boyer and Berthezène, according to the consul, agreed that Lasry's claim was just, but insisted that it should be taken up against the bey of Tunis, not the French.

The French leadership's change of heart and subsequent rejection of Lasry's agreement with the former bey of Oran suggests one way the onset of colonialism may have disadvantaged North African Jewish merchants—a tendency that scholars have only recently begun to explore.[58] According to Welsford, he and Lasry had managed to export some goods, but "it was not in the power of the said Her Edin (Kheir al-Din) to pacify nor to induce the inhabitants to become friendly,"[59] so they could not take full advantage of the permits they had purchased. Furthermore, they claimed that they "experienced a great hindrance in our commerce from the circumstance of the troops of the said Her Edin being frequently supplied with grain from our magazine."[60] In other words, Welsford and Lasry claimed to have lost money due to the dislocations caused by the French war of occupation and from subsequent resistance to it, as well as suffered exactions on goods by French proxies' troops.

The case also sheds light on why the French leadership might have feared Algerian-Jewish merchants' close partnerships with France's rivals in the Mediterranean basin. Lasry's claim, after all, attracted the attention not only of British consuls in Algeria and Tunisia, but of officials in London as well (ineffectively, it would prove). In response to the British consul's interest in Lasry's case, General Boyer wrote to Her Majesty's consul in Algiers in October, informing him that "the Tunisian agent had no right to dispose of the future, which did not belong to him."[61] The fact that the French conquerors had both installed and removed Kheir al-Din was insignificant in the French general's estimation. Boyer added that another agreement made by Clauzel, with Mustapha Bey of Titteri, to export 15,000 *fanegas* of wheat to Europe was similarly annulled.[62] If Lasry sought to recover the cost of his rights of exportation, he would have to take up the question with the Tunisian government, which Kheir al-Din had rejoined. It would appear that the French were not overly eager to honor trading agreements they thought benefited Britain more than themselves. Of course, the French also faced British complaints when they prevented Jewish merchants from exporting goods.

When Welsford and Lasry realized the futility (or imprudence) of pressing the case with the French in Algeria, they turned to Tunis. In early 1832, they went to Tunis and set up meetings with Mathieu de Lessups, the French consul, as well as with Hussein Basha Bey.[63] While the bey told Lasry and the British and French consuls that he understood the justice of their claims against Kheir al-Din, he also insisted that Tunis had claims against the French, without whose resolution he could not demand restitution of Lasry's money. Within several days, both French and Tunisian leaders had promised Lasry and the British that the matter would be satisfactorily resolved, but with little result, in fact. Unappeased, Lasry and Welsford then turned to the British consul in Tunis, Sir Thomas Reade. Despite British (and to a lesser extent Sicilian) efforts, both French and Tunisian authorities appear to have denied Lasry and Welsford's requests.[64] By May, the bey wrote to Reade, insisting that Lasry and Welsford had actually taken advantage of the rights of export, and so Tunis owed them nothing. The French appear to have backed the claim. The ultimate resolution appears to have been against Lasry and Welsford.

Lasry's story suggests that the beginning of French colonial rule in Algeria disrupted established trading networks in which certain Jews were tightly enmeshed. At the same time, attempting to assert control over commercial exchanges presented France with challenges from both the restive interior and its chief European rival. Lasry himself was not commercially ruined by the French invasion, his claims against Kheir al-Din notwithstanding.

Indeed, as we shall see in the following chapter, Jacob Lasry remained a considerable social and commercial presence in early colonial Oran. Although British documents occasionally describe him as a "Jew of Gibraltar," Lasry maintained an important presence in Oran and by the early 1840s he not only had family there but also had made significant real estate investments in the city. As Lasry's commercial prominence grew so did the French reckoning with him. Thus, Lasry will reappear in our story in the 1840s, when he made a notable real estate investment in the form of a private synagogue, and again when we reach the early 1850s, at which point he was featured at the head of consistorial lists of Oran's Jewish notables.[65]

The tension between the desire of the French for a supportive civil population and the vagaries of commercial and communal life in Algeria's cities also helps explain why civilizing would emerge as colonial policy in Algeria. This is most evident in the ongoing push and pull in colonial policy over Jewish communal leadership. In 1835, for example, a number of Jews of Oran, cognizant of an imminent visit to Oran by the head of the French Army of Africa, known as the governor general, composed a letter to request that "a man represent the Hebrew nation of Oran" and that this man be empowered to "judge the crimes . . . of the above named nation."[66] At first glance, this might appear a transparent request for French interference. Given the fractiousness of the urban Jewish population, it may very well have been. However, we could also read this document as an effort on the part of Algerian Jews to perpetuate a tradition of local control. The Jews noted that a representative would be as useful in Oran as it was in Algiers, and that the governor general would be well advised to "assemble us" and "name our choice before you depart."[67] (By this time, the merchant and community leader Amar had passed away, and the de facto representative of the Jews to the French was Joseph Cohen-Scalli, a member of the municipal council and the favored candidate of a portion, if not the entirety, of local Jews.)

French response to the request sheds light on why the French soon opted to reform Jewish community structures. The local civil governor took a dim view of the request, seeing it as a bid to reestablish Jewish religious-communal structures that should have been superseded by French authorities. This interpretation was technically apt; in August 1834, a new law subsumed Jews in cities to French law. Since the death of Amar, who had served as head of the nation, it was now "superfluous" to maintain such a position charged with enforcing communal (religious) rulings. Reflecting on the historic role of Amar, the administrator who rejected the request mused that Amar's "principal functions," after all, "consisted of assuring the execution of sentences of the Rabbinic tribunal" which no longer possessed official competence. With the establishment of French municipal structures in Oran, "three notables of this nation have been named municipal councilors." As for the management of communal finances, there were "a certain number of rabbis, treasurers, and commissioners" who offered "all sorts of guarantees." Furthermore, no complaints had ever been filed against them. The response explained further that honoring the petition to install someone who did not already belong to the municipal counsel appeared to invite "difficulties" and was motivated by a "spirit of opposition" more than anything else. As a result of French policy, the Jewish population must be regarded as having already been "dissolved into the European population."[68]

The problem for the French, of course, was that Jews were not dissolved into the European population. Not that European was itself a necessarily reliable or stable category in North African cities early in the colonial encounter.[69] But even assuming the officer was merely referring to Jews' legal status, as opposed to commenting on their loyalty, events suggest that Jews were far more enmeshed in the wider Muslim society. Social realities in Algeria's cities also bespoke a contradiction in French efforts to neatly categorize the populations over which they ruled and formulated policy. Despite the August 1834 ordinance that assumed Jewish juridical assimilation with the European population, and the help French officers acknowledged receiving from urban Jewish notables in provisioning towns and building civil defense, Jews were far too fractious, diverse, and implicated in local networks to be reliable pillars of support. According to the French vision, the civil population of the cities, where most Algerian Jews and European settlers were housed, needed to be civilized.

Subsequent struggles during the mid- to late 1830s over communal leadership would further accentuate the need to effectively administer and assimilate the Jewish population to the French colonial project. For example, in Mostaganem, Jews also asked the French to install a community leader, locally known (along with his counterpart at the head of the city's Muslim community) as the *hakem*. The petitioners demanded that he be chosen based on their votes, and indicated that the hakem they chose would have a responsibility to the surrounding non-Jewish community. Indeed, following the election among the Jews, the local civil administrator testified,"the hakem announced his pleasure [with the result of the vote], and promised to expend all efforts to maintain the harmony between the Muslim and Israelite populations."[70] Interestingly, several years later, a group of Jews rose up against the chosen hakem. Apparently, by 1839, Israel Serfati, the merchant accused of enjoying a "privileged" relationship with the Hashim's wakil whom we encountered earlier, also hoped to install a leadership more to his liking:

"Israel Serfati . . . is a very troublesome character. He has recently left Oran to establish himself in Mostaganem, and he seems to be one of the leaders of the uprising against the hakem. It is he who in 1836 was imprisoned on

the island Rachgoun [off the western coast of Algeria, near Beni Saf] for having insulted Mustapha ben Ismail."[71] As this fragment suggests, Jews such as
Serfati were "suspect" friends to the French authorities—as urbanites, they
were beholden to French protection, but they remained resolutely enmeshed
in larger and unpredictable (for the French, at least) socio-commercial networks. Given the ongoing contradiction between French wishes that the
urban population be firmly planted in the colonists' camp on the one hand,
and the reality of how this process was evolving on the other, the Ministry
of War would turn to institutions meant to "attach" the "Israelites" to France
through a process increasingly described by the term "civilization" by the
early 1840s.

These vignettes reveal how issues of communal governance encouraged
the French to consider more effective institutions for managing the urban
civil population. They provide few details, however, about local religious
belief or how it affected French responses to local Jews. One final example
of a communal dispute from the 1830s, in contrast, provides a fascinating
perspective on the tense intersection of Jews in French colonial ideology,
their commercial networks and communal squabbles, and the ways in which
Jews' religious beliefs interacted with colonial policies. In this instance, the
complaints of a Jew of far more modest means drew official French attention.
David ben Shimon was a poor Algiers Jew who had sent his daughters to work
as domestic servants in the home of an affluent French officer or merchant
to supplement the family income.[72] On the fifteenth of Tishrei, 5596, corre-
sponding to October 8, 1835, ben Shimon entered one of the principal synagogues of the city to complete the requisite prayers for the festival of Succot.
Here he was accosted and (perhaps) beaten by Mr. ben Duran and his men.[73]
A scion of one of the established Spanish-Jewish rabbinic and mercantile
families in Algeria, related (like Amar) to the Bujnah clan, ben Duran was currently one of the leading Jewish merchants of cattle and grain in the city, and
he served as head of the Jewish Nation, an adjunct to the civil authority, and
a favored local advisor to the French military.[74] Ben Duran was also to serve
as an emissary between the French general Desmichels and Abd al-Qader.[75]
By his own admission, ben Duran did not owe his official title to popular
election as did the Oran-based Amar, but, rather it was his social position,
service to the French occupying forces, and position of "Israelite adjunct" to
the city administration in Algiers that brought him his office.[76] Despite his
rank, a significant number of Jews in Algeria challenged the French decision
to install ben Duran—they not only convened and voted for a local by the
name of Lévi Bram in his stead, but also demanded that the French honor
their decision.[77]

Despite ben Duran's imposing wealth and authority, ben Shimon dared
complain that the wealthy merchant prevented him from completing his

prayers and subjected him to a beating "upon the balls of my feet (*baston-nade*) . . . in the presence of all assembled," and then expelled him from the synagogue. All this, according to ben Shimon, because "I have sent my daughters to work in the home of someone who does not belong to our religion, a French lady." Ben Shimon recounted that he had been ordered to stop sending his daughters to work with the French before Succot, but protested that "scruples of religion do not concern me," so he continued to allow his daughters to work among the gentiles. He argued in a letter to the governor general that this "intolerance" and "prohibition to work among Christians" appeared "very strange" coming from Mr. ben Duran. "Since the conquest of Algiers, [ben Duran] has engaged almost without interruption in commerce with Europeans, and . . . receives his appointments from the French nation for functions that he must carry out in the interest of this nation."[78] At the same time, ben Shimon wished to point out that ben Duran was not dealing with only the French. The "hostility" of his tormentor, ben Shimon insisted, "explains the well-known relations he and his family have with Abd al-Qader, the emir of Mascara, the enemy of France." Clearly, he went on, "the goal of the measures he took toward me was to avoid relations that could lead to a rapprochement of the indigenous [Algerians] and the French, and to meld their interests."[79] Ben Shimon accused ben Duran of working against the French by doing business with the leader of Muslim resistance and by discouraging local Jews from working with Algiers's small French elite.

These accusations hint at the tensions and contradictions that characterized relationships between the French colonial authority and the urban Jews upon whom it relied but whom it simultaneously mistrusted. Ben Shimon's comments, in fact, are in close dialogue with those of the French civil officer who rejected the pleas of the Jews of Oran for a new moqaddem. Both responded to, and helped to create, an official discourse that held Algerian Jews to be "dissolved into" the European population, a discourse that fused Jews' interests with those of the French occupiers. The implicit arguments contained in these transcripts take as a point of departure the goal of welding the Jews of Algeria to the French. Yet they also reveal the contradictions and half-truths of this same ideology. The letters suggest that many Algerian Jews felt the continuing pull of communal identification more strongly than any attachment to the civil authority or to the French nation it represented. They show that the lingering strength of commercial and perhaps social networks compromised French hegemony. The French would eventually attempt to bridge the gap between colonial myths and realities with a more concerted effort to attach these Jews to France.

The efficacy of ben Shimon's petition itself is unknown; we do know, however, that doubts about Duran's efforts to bring Jews and the French authority into a tighter relationship became a central concern in French correspondence. Indeed, by the end of November 1835, Duran no longer served as head of the Jewish Nation in Algiers, and he was complaining of having been "disgraced in the eyes of the French government." The condemnations aimed at the Jewish leader elicited the concern of the governor general himself, and was the subject of nervous exchanges between French officials and with Duran himself. Worried by ben Shimon's accusations, the governor general insisted that the details of the case against Duran were irrelevant, but that "the principal issue . . . is Duran's prohibiting his co-religionists from having relations with the French." He then asked the local civil authorities whether it could be true that "the Head of the Jewish Nation would have used against us the authority and influence he owes to us . . . [as opposed to] facilitating a fusion that it is his duty to obtain."[80] He ordered that the civil administrator "investigate the details of this affair" and prepare a detailed report.[81] The civil intendant complied, effectuating a preliminary investigation that discredited the accusations. Ben Shimon and his colleagues issue from the "lowest class" of Algerian Jews, assured the intendant, and their hope is merely to bring down a man of power and influence.[82] While archival clues about the affair trail off at this point, it is safe to say that Duran did not lose his important stature in the western Mediterranean commercial world; one source mentions him as a principal partner in the sale and export of 350 head of cattle in 1839.[83] What remains evident is that the size and significance of the Jewish community rendered communal fractiousness in early colonial Oran a French political issue, and that the same officials expected their chosen Jewish leaders to abide by a colonial ideology of "fusion" despite harboring lingering doubts about Jews' loyalty.

How did the Algerian Jews' "myths, cults, ideologies, or revolts" during the first years of conquest express themselves in such dramas?[84] We have seen that the divisions within the Jewish community were understood as intrigue and clannishness in colonial narratives. Nevertheless, the disputes also present fissures in the colonial ideology that hint at how Jews perceived and responded to the realities of early colonial Oran. In the wake of accusations against him, for example, Duran denied having beaten ben Shimon, and asserted being nothing but dedicated heart and soul to the victory of French forces throughout Algeria. At the same time, he did justify in strong terms expelling ben Shimon from the synagogue. This action had nothing to do with the fact that ben Shimon's daughters worked with the French (which, Duran asserted, was permissible), but rather the fact that ben Shimon permitted his wife to have a "scandalous" sexual relationship with "a Moroccan," an affair also attested to in French correspondence.[85] "Adultery, according to our principles," Duran explained, "is a religious infraction, punished under the Regency by expulsion from the synagogue and the bastonnade." This practice changed, according to ben Duran, at the time he was called upon to be head of the Jewish Nation. At that point, "I convened rabbis and notables, and in agreement with them, I modified this punishment and softened the most ignoble disposition, now incompatible with the civilization of the nation that dominates us—the bastonnade was thus suppressed."[86] At the same time, insisted Duran, the arrival of cholera in Algiers had made family laws particularly relevant to communal governance: "Cholera having invaded this city and exercised ravages particularly among the Israelites, public prayers were ordered. In the sermons of rabbis it was recommended, above all among heads of family, to watch over the purity of morals and forbid adultery, the sin that most greatly offends the Divine Majesty."[87] Duran accused ben Shimon of deliberately confusing the issue of his daughters' employment at a French home with the fact that he was encouraging the "debauchery" of his own wife. The wording presents the possibility that David ben Shimon was accused of *hillul ha-shem*, or the public disgrace of God's name through flagrant sinning.[88] Since the expulsion of the Jews from Spain, North Africa (especially Morocco) had emerged as a center for Jewish mysticism in the early modern period.[89] Spanish kabbala-rooted beliefs often held that human actions reverberated in the divine realm, so Duran (or the rabbis) might have seen a sin such as adultery (according to Jewish law, punishable by death) as inviting dire heavenly retribution.[90] Duran insisted that sexual misconduct was both unacceptable and potentially calamitous: "David [ben Shimon] was denounced to the rabbis as encouraging the debauchery of his wife with a Moroccan. The rabbis called David to them, providing paternal recommendations that he distance from his family any suspicion of misconduct.[91] But David, deaf to the rabbis' voices, only continued his lamentable line of conduct, and he was convicted of having strongly favored the pollution of the marital bed with the same individual who had passed a night with his wife."[92] Given the poverty of ben Shimon and evidence of the presence of prostitution in the Jewish quarter, it is not inconceivable that ben Duran's account was sound and ben Shimon was prostituting members of his own family.[93] Whether or not prostitution, or any other form of sexual misconduct, had actually taken place, however, Duran's account sheds light on the moral universe of early colonial Jewish Algeria.

Duran's note reveals a tension over the responsibilities incumbent on the communal leadership. The job's mandate appears to have extended beyond the oversight of trading relationships with merchants in Gibraltar and the Doua'ir, and encompassed the spiritual and physical health of Jewish community members. Exceeding the responsibilities given to them by the French, the moqaddem and rabbis invoked their duty to prevent the real or apparent sexual misbehavior of their communities from causing or contributing to outbreaks of disease. Corporal punishment may have been putatively incompatible with the ideology of the land's new masters (the French actually continued to use the same form of punishment), and the law of August 1834 may have legally placed Jews on a par with other Euro-peans.[94] But local Jewish leaders saw their responsibilities to the Jewish community as touching on spheres beyond that envisioned by the French. Notably, the moqaddem's functions included looking after Jews' moral con-duct and attempting to avoid divine punishment. The French would seek to intervene in the private realm of religious behavior once civilizing had become an official policy. However, the clash between Duran and Shimon suggests that private, sexual behaviors already represented a charged loca-tion for contests invoking communal, colonial, and divine authority in the early colonial period.

The tension between French policies of legal assimilation and the main-tenance of communal autonomy provoked a final legal/religious dispute that warrants our attention. In this case, the soon-to-be installed grand rabbi of Algiers, the Metz-educated Michel Aron Weill, provoked a storm of protest among local rabbis by suggesting in 1845 that local Jews were bound by Jew-ish law to oaths demanded by or made in French courts. This justification was in all likelihood made in the wake of the 1841 and 1842 decrees that officially disbanded the rabbinical courts in all matters aside from personal status. A number of local rabbis were outraged by Weill's announcement, accusing him of directing "damaging words" and "grave insults" against Algerian Judaism. The local rabbis also accused Weill of implying that Alge-rian rabbis have a different (and presumably less accurate) understanding of the law than French rabbis. While it is unclear exactly what form the local Algerian-Jewish outcry took, Rabbi Weill felt compelled to publish a substan-tial argument entitled "To the Rabbis of Algiers" in the French newspaper *Courrier d'Afrique*. In it, he noted that local rabbis were wrong to extrapolate the Talmudic rules concerning *shevu'at ha-dayanim* (oath of judges) to cover all religiously binding oaths. The shevu'at ha-dayanim is an oath invoked at times when it is impossible to determine the truthfulness of contradictory claims, and requires the presence of the *sefer torah*, an actual scroll of the law. In response to this assumption, Weill cited a section of the Talmudic tractate *shevu'ot* (oaths) that put the emphasis on the biblical commandment to not take God's name in vain, regardless of the juridical circumstances. In other words, "any oath, private or public, ordinary or judicial, is valid, legal, and carries for those who take it falsely all the penalties of perjury."[95] The dispute evoked earlier dramas in French-Jewish history regarding a Jew's religious obligation to obey the prevailing law of the country in which he or she dwells. For example, representatives serving in Napoleon's Assembly of Jewish Notables in 1806 evoked the Talmudic dictum *dina d'malkhuta dina*, or "the law of the kingdom is law" as part of a larger effort of demonstrating Jewish and French law to be compatible.[96] In a very different manner from the dispute between ben Duran and ben Shimon, the influence of native rabbis and their religious views proved an obstacle to the imposition of French law in Algerian cities. As we shall see in the pages following, this dynamic would prove increasingly frustrating for colonial authorities.

Thus far we have considered how Jewish commercial prominence, leadership of fractious communities, and even religious beliefs created tensions for the French occupiers. But let us now consider how the more modest stratum of Jewish commercial intermediaries also caused problems for the French authorities. This class brokered smaller deals between European and Arab traders, and also participated in the exchange of currencies. This was an important feature of the colonial economy, as the arrival of the French did not spell the demise of locally used currencies, such as the Spanish *duro* or the Ottoman *boudjou*. The influence of Jewish merchants and their business orientation westward toward Spain and Gibraltar produced a steady flow of doros into Algeria, notably through Oran, where more than 2,000 Spanish nationals lived by 1838.[97] Military and other correspondences are rich in allusions to the use of foreign currency in French Algeria well into the 1840s. While some of these references are neutral observations, generals such as Bugeaud bitterly complained about the dependence of the local economy on Jewish money traders and intermediaries.[98] Wresting control of the early colonial economy represented another challenge to the French administration, and Jews' real or perceived threat to this process represented another motivation to reorganize the community by the end of the 1840s.

The use of Spanish or Ottoman monies may have been business as usual for urban merchants in early colonial Algeria, but it constituted a thorn in the side of French military administrators. Archives of Ministry of War correspondence from the late 1830s reveal, for example, that Bugeaud felt compelled to intervene in local economies to curb confusion over the values of various currencies in use. Thus, in 1839, the French declared that a coin known as the *mabul*, which was used in markets in and around Constantine, could no longer be accepted as currency, as "the weight and gold content (*titre*) of this coin is essentially variable, [so] it will no longer be accepted by official agencies and shall now be considered as merchandise."[99] Two years later, the German travel writer Morritz Wagner noted that French currency still had "no general circulation among the natives, the Spanish dollar being the principle currency."[100] Corroborating Morritz's account, the correspondence of Captain Eugène Daumas, who in 1838 was the French consul stationed in the eastern coastal city of Mascara (still under the nominal administration of Abd al-Qader), mentioned the theft of Spanish and local Ottoman money in routine correspondence.[101] As late as 1848, a French guide for travelers and new colonists advised, "even though French money is in use throughout Algeria, there are still tribes that will only accept local currency (*la monnaie du pays*), or sometimes Spanish duros."[102]

It was General Bugeaud, however, that most clearly defined the role of native Jews in the colony's currency market as posing a problem for the French. According to Bugeaud, the Jews had enough commercial power to "veto" all trade that was not in their preferred Spanish currency.[103] Furthermore, he accused the Jews of exploiting their role as commercial middleman, since colonists and the French authorities had to purchase Spanish money at high rates from Jews in Oran in order to do business in Algeria.[104] Jews "made a double profit," according to Bugeaud, since they "gained both on the merchandise sold [to the Muslims] and on the money which paid for it." Only forcibly substituting the French franc for Spanish currency, the officer believed, would terminate Jewish economic hegemony. To that effect, in May 1842, Bugeaud requested permission from Paris to prohibit Jews, on pain of expulsion from the towns they inhabited, from dealing in other than French currency.[105] Bugeaud's aggressive stance fit with his wider antipathy toward Algerian Jews, but even if he were exaggerating the specifically Jewish role in controlling the exchange of currency in Algeria, his comments are revealing. In the early 1840s, the French military leadership clearly aspired to exert a more direct control over the economy, and the continuing use of doros compromised this mission. Once again, the French found the Jewish place in the urban economy important but frustratingly difficult to manage.

The preceding pages have illustrated that governing Algerian Jews presented a number of challenges to the nascent French colonial administration. They represented an entrenched religio-commercial community that had strong and, to the French at least, dangerous links to other Mediterranean ports, as well as to the tribal interior of North Africa. Their dependence on the French for protection did not guarantee their loyalty, and French officers occasionally fretted about Jews such as Sabah, whose own business created (or were imagined to create) problems between French garrisons in the cities and local tribes. Even communal governance often led to headaches for French officials, as clashes within the Jewish community sent ripples through local markets even as certain factions cried for French support. These circumstances gradually led the Ministry of War to take seriously the proposition of metropolitan Jewish reformers that the system of consistoires israélites be extended to Algeria. In the pages that follow, we see how the adoption of this system constituted a pragmatic response to the challenges of colonizing Algeria's cities.

Toward the Consistory System:
"Tolerance" in the Service of Domination

In 1833, a member of the central consistory in Paris, Adolph Crémieux, wrote to the minister of the interior regarding France's new conquest in North

Africa. At the time, Crémieux was a young, left-leaning activist who would go on to serve as a deputy during the short-lived Second Republic. As noted earlier, he would live to see his name attached to the 1870 law granting Algerian Jews full citizenship rights. In his 1833 letter, Crémieux directly addressed some of the problems the military had been facing while governing Algerian cities in the preceding year or two. He argued that the installation of Jewish consistories in the cities of Algeria would be advantageous, given France's "political goals," as it would advance "religious and moral" interests.[106] Several years later, on December 12, 1836, the consistory launched another appeal, this time to the minister of justice and religions. The second appeal expanded the points made in the first, arguing that Jewish consistories in Algeria would advance colonial interests. "The numerical significance of our Algerian co-religionists," argued Crémieux, "as well the manifold relations enjoyed between this new possession and the mother country, lead us to believe . . . that some advantage for the government could result from a Jewish consistory at Algiers, placed like all the departmental consistories under the direction of the central consistory."[107] On September 4, 1839, the central consistory in Paris asked the minister of war to "legally organize" the Jewish religion in Algeria. The consistory again requested permission to prepare a draft for a law establishing Jewish consistories in Algeria, and reminded the ministry that unlike the Jews, the Protestants and Catholics in Algeria were already organized. The consistory underlined "the significance of the Jewish population in these countries," as well as the positive "results that have already come of the schools that have been established for it." The members of the consistory argued that a religious organization for the Jews would be just as beneficial for colonial authorities as for "our co-religionists."[108]

Crémieux's hope for the establishment of Jewish consistories in Algeria under the direction of Paris's central consistory would not come to pass. Instead, when consistories were eventually established in Algeria, they were answerable to the Ministry of War. The fact that consistories were established at all, however, attests to the influence the letters of the central consistory had upon the Ministry of War. Furthermore, the Jewish interlocutors in Paris directly addressed the problem of the Algerian Jews' demographic and economic importance, as well as their dubious loyalty, thereby assuaging the suspicions of the French colonial authorities. "It seems that [the consistory] could attach to France a major component of the African population," they wrote, "and thus hasten, [through] administrative and religious relations, the progress of civilization and moral regeneration of our new co-citizens."[109] In their letters, the consistories of France presented themselves as potentially useful servants of the colonial venture. In so doing, they helped tint the solutions they proposed for advancing France's colonial conquest with a liberal, emancipatory hue.

The central consistory proposed to resolve nearly a decade of difficulties France had experienced while managing Algeria's Jewish urban population. Of course, by 1839, the situation in the colony presented new challenges. The treaty of Tafna was soon to unravel, the cities hosted an expanding European (non-French) population, and the opinion at the Ministry of War had shifted from "limited occupation" toward "total conquest" of Algeria.[110] In 1838, the administration had begun publishing annual statistical reports regarding French establishments in Algeria emphasizing, among an array of other observations, the relatively low mortality rates of Algerian Jews and their demographic importance in Algerian cities.[111] On April 3, 1839, the Ministry of War (under the brief command of Lieutenant General Despans-Cubières) wrote to the governor general of Algeria, who at the time was Comte Sylvan-Charles Vallée, in order to lament the fact that "the Jewish *culte* has not, since the ordinance on justice of 19 August 1834, been the object of any disposition on the part of the French administration."[112] Vallée was referring to the aforementioned law that had legally "dissolved [the Jews] into the European population" by dismantling the legal foundation of Jewish autonomy; native rabbis, from that moment, possessed *legal* authority only over marriage and infractions of religious law.[113] This reform notwithstanding, as we have seen, Jews' commercial and social prominence continued to plague the French colonial authorities, and the Ministry of War hoped to establish civil institutions that would more tightly weave the urban Jews into the fabric of colonial domination.

The Ministry of War expressed a similar vision of the Jews' place in the imperial order as did the local authorities. Notably, both parties associated Algerian Jews with the European population (as opposed to other native Algerians) and aspired to exert more effective control over them. The ministry compared the local Jews of Algeria to European religious communities, such as Catholics, who had a diocese, and to the Protestants, who were on their way to having their own consistory. In contrast to Muslims, who "respected the effects of our protection" and were thus to have "their laws . . . maintained and respected," Algerian Jews were directly comparable to their French-Jewish counterparts and should not have any particularistic legal autonomy. "It seems odd (*difficile*) that our domination should not bring . . . modifications to [the Jewish religion's] practice, and harmonize it with the new institutions and rules of the religions in the metropole."[114] In other words, the religious and social institutions of urban Algeria should begin to resemble those of France. The minister concluded by requesting that the governor general appoint a commission to examine the current "problem" and propose a solution. The commission should include "the most respected (*considérables*) Jews, and those most apt to be consulted on religious matters," as well as non-Jews "whose participation would be recognized as useful."[115] In 1839, the Ministry of War itself ordered the creation of a commission charged with investigating the possibility of establishing a religious organization for the Jews in Algeria; it is unclear if anything arose from this initial effort.[116]

By the late 1830s and early 1840s significant liberal voices were reverberating through the July Monarchy's Ministry of War, paving the way for reform of Jewish institutions in Algeria. Figures such as Alexis de Tocqueville and his friend and collaborator Gustave de Beaumont had turned their attention to Algeria, actively supporting colonization and the establishment of civic institutions. Through them, they hoped, Europeans would naturally be drawn to settle in France's colony. For example, in a circular he wrote for members of parliament in the early 1840s, Beaumont urged his countrymen not to give up on the colonization of Algeria, or to "attempt nothing grand after having followed this enterprise for so long," which would be to "admit impotence and abandon it; after having striven to extend so far, to fold in upon ourselves and condemn ourselves to a sad inertia, haunted by the memory of past . . . glory."[117] Beaumont and Tocqueville's commitment to centralization, liberal institutions, and colonialism would make their mark at the Ministry of War in the years leading up to the establishment of the consistories.

In the early 1840s, both men served on the Ministry of War's Commission de colonisation de l'Algérie, with Beaumont eventually becoming the group's reporter to the ministry. He argued that "in order to attract colonists to Algeria" a number of measures must be taken, but "without question, the establishment of good civil institutions must rank as our first priority."[118] For both Tocqueville and Beaumont, France's imperial grandeur was important, and both denied the possibility that France could abandon Algeria. Both wished Algeria to follow in the republican steps of the United States rather than allow Bugeaud to create a military-colonial society. "No one ever leaves one's country of birth . . . to seek out a far away land where he will live under the capricious rule of a soldier," warned Beaumont. "If there exists a common sentiment in Europe . . . it is repugnance for the rule of force. Look at the immense current of European emigration—where is it going? To the United States, to Canada, to Australia, to New Zealand, everywhere where there is liberty."[119] Liberal institutions, thought Beaumont, would encourage European settler colonialism.

According to the commission, liberal institutions would also facilitate French domination of the cities. While Beaumont supported war to pacify the countryside, he saw liberal institutions themselves as rendering the cities more European. The report of the commission assured the minister of war that "we have no need to chase [the Moors] violently [from the cities], as they are leaving on their own accord," indeed, "it is an ongoing phenomenon today; the Moors are gradually disappearing from Algeria." This was because "Our graceful and refined way of being (*nos moeurs faciles et livrés*), our character, our religion—or rather our irreligion—our developed and effective policing which penetrates everything, even domestic space, the superiority of Europeans in commerce and industrial professions; it all distances the Moors from us. Such is the very nature of our civilization before which the Muslim populations of the cities retreat, due to their sentiment of impotence to either adopt or struggle against it."[120] Civilization itself, here defined by liberal commercial practices, policing of domestic space, and religious nonchalance, was putatively ridding the cities of presumably undesirable Muslims. According to the commission, good civil institutions were in themselves bulwarks for French domination of the cities. By the early 1840s, the Ministry of War's commission on colonization provided a vehicle by which prominent July Monarchy liberals influenced how colonization, and colonial Jewish policy, would proceed.

The commission's report provides some idea of why a rift formed between the generals in Algeria and their superiors in Paris. The latter leaned toward civil institutions such as consistories. The generals, while understanding the urgency of dealing with a religio-commercial community that represented an obstacle to French economic and social power, were concerned about reinforcing institutions of civil rule in Algeria. Bugeaud, notably, was vocal in his disregard for civil authority and for the civilian population it governed.[121] General Nicholas Valée, Bugeaud's predecessor as governor general, had a different perspective, but was also frustrated with the reforms Paris was putting in place to extend and rationalize the civil administration. The ordinances of October 31, 1838, and August 21, 1839, did not satisfy Valée, who hoped to maintain a strong and clear division between civil and military spheres of competence. Valée's idea was to divide Algeria into three zones. The first would be a civil administration governing the cities where a significant European population had settled; the second would be a militarily governed area stretching to the desert, where the foundations of future colonization would be laid; and the third would be an area run by indigenous chiefs answerable to the military.[122] It is difficult to be certain, but Valée's silence in the face of numerous requests for information about civil institutions for Algerian Jews may have reflected his general frustration with how his superiors in Paris were administering the conquest.

Regardless of the reason, the Ministry of War seems to have agreed with the commission on colonization that civil institutions should be established to resolve France's Jewish problem in Algeria. With Paris's ministries leaning in this direction, it is not surprising that July Monarchy liberalism flavored the discourse about consolidating control over Algeria's cities. "*Maréchal*," wrote Minister Soult to General Valée on November 6, "In a message dated

3 April (#33), my predecessor invited you to submit, as soon as possible, your propositions regarding the definitive organization of the Jewish religion in Algeria." Unfortunately, he chided, the invitation had remained unanswered. Conflating the population of Algerian Jews with Europeans once again, the minister pointed out that "it has now been quite a long time since we addressed the spiritual needs of the Catholic religion, as well as members of the Reform Church. . . . The government must not delay in taking care of the Jewish religion." Echoing the liberal reform discourse espoused by consistorial reformers such as Crémieux, the minister of war argued, "the spirit of tolerance which animates it [the government], as well as the current requests of the central consistory of France, impresses upon (us) a sense of duty."[123] The project of devising more effective institutions to govern the colonized population had become one with the project of spreading "tolerance."

The minister's sharply toned letter to Valée resonated with the larger struggle over zones of military and civil control. He noted, "discussions are already underway between my department and that of religions regarding the means of satisfying the needs of the Jewish population of Algeria." Given this state of affairs, the minister threatened, "You can easily understand . . . just how urgent it is that I receive a response to my request included in the letter of last April 3." Furthermore, he warned that "if this communication is delayed, I will regrettably be obligated to approve a plan which the local administration will have had no involvement [in designing]. You yourself [above all can] appreciate just how harmful such a measure would be."[124] The lack of any archival trace of a response, combined with the failure of the measure to advance for another several years, suggests that Valée did not respond to the minister's request. The situation on the ground in Algeria, as well as the suggestions of metropolitan liberals, had convinced the Ministry of War to add to the civil institutions already serving Europeans in Algeria's cities. Yet the generals, whose correspondence had originally signaled that they perceived the Jews of Algeria to be a problem, were unconvinced that a civil bureau was an effective way to deal with this group.

The clearest indication of how the generals hoped to solve the problem of Jewish power in Algeria emerges in Bugeaud's correspondence. Notably, in 1838, when discussing the idea of peopling his military-agrarian colonies with fallen women and orphans, Bugeaud suggested that the cities of the littoral would benefit from *removing* the troublesome Jews and "sending orphans to our cities [in Algeria], for those [colonists] who ask for them." This would have the advantage of dealing with a social problem at home while "add[ing] to the French population, the augmentation of which we have a great interest in order to solidify our occupation. Oh that we could replace through this means, or by another, the Jewish population!"[125] Such

comments have helped construct an image of Bugeaud as at odds with efforts
to civilize the Jews. More important for our purposes is the point that both
liberal civilian and military figures sought to remove obstacles to effective
colonial domination. Later, Bugeaud more fully articulated his desire to
expel the Jews from Algeria, but insisted that his plan, like that of the consistory, was an attempt to facilitate the conquest while helping to regenerate
the Algerian Jews. Strikingly, Bugeaud recognized that his plan might be seen
as cruel, but nonetheless saw it as advancing a greater goal:

> [W]e could even permit them [Algerian Jews] to establish themselves
> wherever they like in France. I know that they will tell me: "What? You
> want to act with even more cruelty to the Jews than the Turks and
> Arabs!" I answer that our position is quite different from that of these
> peoples. As a power, the Jews were nothing more than an atom to
> them, for us they are almost as numerous as Europeans in our coastal
> cities. . . . By permitting the Jews of Algeria to establish themselves
> in France, their moral transformation will be accomplished earlier
> than by the measures of which you have informed me, which will only
> achieve their goals in Algeria quite slowly.[126]

Despite the consensus of historians that Bugeaud fell well outside the
liberal camp, it is worth noting that, by 1843, he was echoing aspects of the
civilizing liberal language emanating from the July Monarchy's ministries. At
the same time, he proposed his own solution to the Jewish problem. Rather
than reinforce civilian rule, Bugeaud hoped to simply remove the population
he viewed as obstructing French control.

Given his negative opinion of civilians, Bugeaud's objection to the consistories was well founded. The organization of Jews in the cities of the Algerian littoral was bound up with Paris's effort to develop the colony's civic and
governmental institutions. This was made quite clear in another war ministry letter of November 1839. This one, addressed to the Ministry of Justice,
again referred to Protestant establishments in Algeria as a model, insisting
"the organization of the Jewish religion, practiced by a very considerable
portion of the civil population, remains to be achieved." Demands have
multiplied, the ministry noted, and the "King's government [must] concern
itself with religious issues." Citing numbers demonstrating that Jews made
up about a quarter of the population of Algerian cities and were numerically
only slightly less numerous than Muslims, the minister of war insisted that
"we cannot delay in concerning ourselves with a religious community [that
was] left in state of total abandon by the former rulers, [an abandonment]
that the conquest has yet to end." The minister argued for a consistory-type
structure by noting that new Jewish communal organizations could be made
financially self-sufficient, and that while the August 1834 ordinance had

removed all but marriage from rabbinical competence, "It seems that the moment may have come to remove this [last] exceptional area of competence, which has been rarely used well."[127] The Ministry of War was proposing reforms that would have mimicked the sorts of administrative transformations in Algeria that French Jews had experienced since they acquired citizenship in 1791. Algeria's Jews, from the perspective of this office, had to be made French in order to advance the cause of colonialism.

In 1842, the Ministry of War appointed two prominent French-Jewish reformers to carry out a detailed study of the Algerian Jews and to propose a solution. Joseph Cohen, an attorney based in Aix-en-Provence, traveled to Algeria several times and wrote frequent articles in support of establishing Jewish consistories in the reformist Jewish journal *Archives Israélites*. When the report was commissioned, he also became an official advisor to the war ministry in Algiers.[128] Several years later, when the July Monarchy established Algerian consistories, he became president of the consistory in Algiers. He would later return to France and take up journalism. Perhaps more influential was his partner Jacques-Isaac Altaras, a wealthy Marseilles-based ship-builder. Born in Aleppo to a prominent rabbinic family, he had come to France as a boy, made a considerable fortune, and by the 1840s had become the president of both the Tribunal of Commerce of Marseilles and the Jewish consistory of the city. Altaras's dwelling in Marseilles (the primary French port for ships bound for, or coming from, Algeria), his prominence, and his knowledge of Arabic led Paris reformers to encourage him to take an active role influencing the fate of Algerian Jews. With Cohen, Altaras produced a much-celebrated report for the minister of war, "Report on the Moral and Political State of the Israelites of Algeria, and the Means of Ameliorating It."[129] Native Jews, the report stated, "need us to initiate [them] to the principles of civilization . . . and that we develop, in a word, their intelligence for the journey toward political and moral progress."[130] Given their loyalty to the nation that delivered them from Turkish despotism, wrote the authors, a proper "initiation" would only increase their attachment to France—and consistories could achieve it. It would be necessary to abolish the position of moqaddem and the vestiges of civil autonomy, the report argued, but Algerian Jews could eventually be transformed into a "pillar" of French domination.

Following the distribution of the report in 1843 and its partial publication as a series of articles in *Archives Israélites*, the Ministry of War named a commission charged with preparing a law to organize the Jews of Algeria. This body included Adolphe Crémieux, several members of the chamber of deputies, and representatives from the Ministry of War and the Ministry of Justice and Religions.[131] Theirs were not the only voices in favor of such reforms. Several years later, Albert Cohen, an Orientalist and close associate

of the powerful Rothschild family (which had advanced loans to the July
Monarchy régime) also began advocating for a consistorial organization.[132]
By August, drafts of a new law that would bring consistories to Algeria were
being circulated between the war and justice ministries.[133] Clearly, a consensus had emerged in higher military and civil circles that the consistories
would provide more effective governance of Algeria's Jews than would the
continued enfranchising of the head of the nation or the Israelite adjunct
positions. This new institution, advocates argued, would better aid the colonial mission of transforming Jews into a more reliable component of the
colony's European population. The task remained for reformers to convince
the generals that this strategy would serve their interests as well.

Bugeaud remained unconvinced that strengthening civil institutions for
Algerian Jews would aid French control of Algeria. He expressed a particular
concern about the consequences of what he called the emancipation of the
Jews. The minister of war assured him that he was "exaggerating" potential
negative effects, and that "this ordinance will not, in effect, result in the
complete emancipation of the Jews of Algeria," and "will be conceived in
such restrictive terms that I do not doubt that it will satisfy you." At the same
time, the minister reminded Bugeaud that "the effects of legislative dispositions" were "destined to . . . affect a moral reform amidst such a significant
portion of the Algerian population, which should be the goal of our common
efforts." Bugeaud, who himself had proposed relocating the Jews as a means
to regenerate them and secure France's hold on its colony, was nonetheless
losing ground to the liberals. Underlying the inevitability of the reformers'
consistorial project and implicitly advising Bugeaud that his interests lay in
cooperating with the ministry, the minister announced, "I hope to be able
to . . . [soon inform you] of a royal ordinance . . . with precise instructions
regarding its execution."[134] Whether or not Bugeaud was convinced of the
strategy, the decision had been made to help resolve the problem of urban
governance with civil institutions.

Despite French-Jewish reformers' hopes to be made responsible for
governing Algeria's consistories, the new civil institutions would remain
under the Ministry of War's power. Altaras, Crémieux, and other consistorial reformers, all of whom had hoped to see Algerian consistories under the
wing of the central consistory in Paris, were disappointed in this respect.
Indeed, soon after the decree was issued on November 9, 1845, discussions
of it in the Jewish press were mixed. They noted in particular the inability of
the central consistory to name the rabbis and lay members of the new Algerian consistories.[135] On November 8, 1845, one day before the project became
law, the minister of war ordered his staff to quickly rewrite it to ensure that
it conform to principles outlined by members of King Louis-Philippe's cabi-
net. The orders make clear that the consistories would serve the military

and the conquest rather than the members of the consistories. For example, while reformers such as Altaras had wanted to suppress the remaining forms of Jewish civil particularity, the minister of war insisted that the new decree offer "no modifications . . . to the civil condition of the Israelites of Algeria. No portion of administrative authority should devolve to the consistories."[136] Furthermore, the new consistories would be forbidden to "intervene in questions of [religious] dogma." The king would "prescribe no belief, no formula, no sort of religious practice (*culte*). It forbids no conversion and no change." Finally, all taxes imposed by the new consistories would be "voluntary."[137] In other words, as influential as the French consistory's liberal reformers may have been in proposing the idea of Algerian consistories, the Ministry of War had no intention of abnegating any control of civil institutions to metropolitan agencies. The consistories would remain a military tool of conquest.

On November 9, 1845, King Louis-Philippe signed the draft into law, bringing a new institution to work in support of the military's campaign to advance and consolidate French colonial domination. In keeping with the assurance Minister Soult made to Bugeaud several years before, the law was not to be confused with Jewish emancipation. The minister of war assured the king, for instance, that the "new redaction of the ordinance relative to the Israelites" had "removed all elements that tended to allow the central consistory in Paris to involve itself (*immiscer*) more or less directly in the affairs of Algeria." In other words, the "proposed institution will have a purely Algerian character."[138] By subsuming the Algerian consistories to the Ministry of War and preventing the metropolitan reformers from directly influencing policy, the intention was for the French administration to maintain control of the conquest. As the minister explained to the king within a day of the law's proclamation: "the Algerian Israelites will be able to become useful and safe auxiliaries to French domination in North Africa, and I dare to hope that your majesty, sharing these views, shall deign to grace this proposed ordinance with his signature."[139] Metropolitan reformers were welcome to participate in this venture, but they were denied control over it.

The minister of war's approach to governing Algerian Jews was conceived in the liberal tradition. Though reformist in hue, the 1845 law that brought consistories to Algeria did not attempt to break the hold of Jewish merchants over commerce, nor did it subsume Algerian Jews to new restrictions, as had efforts to change Jewish commercial behavior in France.[140] Rather, the decree aimed to fuse the Jewish community's institutional structures to the French administration. Article 3, for example, held that both rabbis and lay members would be appointed by the minister of war; Article 4 stated that Algerian rabbis' salaries would henceforth be paid by France. Perhaps most revealing of the intention of the new institution was the oath to be signed by all members of the ministry's new religious arm: "before

God all the all-powerful, creator of heaven and earth, who forbids taking his name in vain and who punishes perjury, I swear allegiance to the King of the French, and obedience to the laws, ordinances, and regulations published or to be published by his government."[141] The new law also instructed rabbis to teach obedience to France, to instruct parents to send their children to French schools, and to teach Jews to learn agricultural work. At the same time, Articles 16 through 21 regulated how the Jewish communal treasury would come under the wing of the consistory and thus be ultimately overseen by the war ministry.

The ministers in Paris understood these tasks as spreading French civilization. The members of the new consistories were to be both European Jews and indigenous Jews; the latter should have their origins among the Algerians, speak the same language, and be able to "exercise a great influence" on their co-religionists.[142] The ministers specifically asked for Algerian members that "have adopted French mores and customs, and can become in the assembly [of Algerian Jews] . . . a representative of our civilization."[143] The indigenous members included Amran Sénanès, who was "an honest, mild-mannered man who is closest to us (regarding) our ideas and our civilization."[144] In 1847, when the Metz-educated Rabbi Lazare Cahen was applying to the Ministry of War for a job as rabbi in Algeria (he would end up in Oran), he boasted that he was uniquely qualified to "help raise the holy edifice of civilization on the immutable and ancient foundation of the Israelite religion, to dissipate the shadows of ignorance and prejudice." He was also eager to "teach them to appreciate the benefits of liberty which they now enjoy."[145] Civilization, and the accompanying principles of enlightenment and emancipation, had become not only justifications, but also actual principles to be employed in the service of colonizing Algeria. Both liberal and interventionist, the consistories would strive to attach the Jews of Algeria to France during the 25 years leading up to Jewish collective naturalization in 1870. If they expressed a French-Jewish liberal ideal, they were also a significant component of French colonial strategy.

Conclusion

The civilizing mission in Algeria was born out of the needs of French colonial rule. The Jews of Algeria were a demographically significant and commercially prominent force in Algeria, and French generals quickly experienced (or perceived) trouble governing them. Generals blamed Jews for French settlers' inability to break into local markets, while Jewish internal disputes occasionally jeopardized ongoing French efforts to reestablish trade in cities. A liberal discourse of regeneration, rooted in Enlightenment and Revolutionary debates over Jewish citizenship influenced the language in which the 1845 "Ordonnance" was discussed and written, but exigencies of the conquest convinced the Ministry of War that the Jewish population of Algeria needed a more effective governing institution.

Previous scholarship has correctly highlighted the influence of the campaign by metropolitan liberals, such as Altaras and Cohen, on the reorganization of Algerian Jews. But it must be remembered that only in late 1830, after the French presence in Oran and Algiers was nearly a decade old, did the Ministry of War begin to seriously consider the central consistory's proposal. The central consistory in Paris had sent its first letter advocating Jewish consistories considerably earlier, in 1833; yet, it was only at the end of the decade that France's colonial experience inspired the Ministry of War to consider the consistory's proposal for governing Algeria's Jews. At this point, not coincidentally, the government was definitely close to adopting the strategy of "total conquest," manifest in Bugeaud's 1841 appointment as Governor-General of Algeria. By then, it was far more obvious to officials in the Ministry of War that maintaining the moqaddem or transforming the position into the Israelite adjunct did not adequately address problems such as Jewish commercial independence or their questionable loyalty to France. Forming Algerian consistories represented a significant move toward establishing civil institutions for the growing urban population, and by extension, laying groundwork for a permanent French establishment in Algeria. The debate about how to administer Algeria's Jews, and the decree that was eventually produced to resolve this problem, both furthered the politics of imperialism in North Africa and infused them with a civilizing tone.

2

Revolution, Republicanism, and Religion

Responses to Civilizing in Oran, 1848

Amran Sénanès was disappointed. During a meeting at the beginning of September 1847, three months after the consistory's founding, the representative shared his belief that it was "regrettable" that the powers of the consistory were so "restrained." The consistory, with its current competencies, he thought, was perfectly geared to France, "where the Jewish population is civilized," but not to a country "as backward as this one."[1] A particular problem, he felt, was that the local population had been under the impression that the "new administration," meaning the consistories, would be considerably more powerful than the moqaddem and his council had been before. Since Jews' discovery that the consistory had no more power to enforce their will than had the earlier communal representative, the organization's mandate became extremely difficult, if not impossible, to achieve. In one of the first uses of the emblematic phrase justifying France's colonial expansion, Sénanès described his and his colleagues' goal as their "*mission civilisatrice*, the most noble hope that the consistory possesses, and to whose realization it devotes all its efforts."[2]

It is telling that in one of earliest colonial appearances of the term *civilizing mission*, it was employed to highlight its apparent failure. Sénanès's frustration and anger over the hopelessness of the civilizing ideal exemplifies the contradictions of the consistorial project. The French officers who created the consistory were imbued with liberal ideals and imperialist fervor, and wished to attach the urban population to France. At the same time, the centralizing ideal these officers defended prevented the consistory's functioning as anything like a semi-autonomous, confession-based police force. Consistory members were, quite simply, powerless to force major changes in the educational, occupational, or moral lives of their charges. Notes from the initial meetings of the consistory reveal a fledgling bureau attempting to exert influence over a community in dramatic flux and suffering the effects of the recent war with Abd al-Qader. As noted in the previous chapter, the war that recommenced in 1839 interrupted trade routes and threatened pre-existing economic activities in Oran and other cities. Although wealthy Jews, often owners of urban real estate, managed to get by, disruptions brought on by the colonial conquest had had a disastrous effect on Jews of modest means. Early notes of the consistory bespeak a great need for communal charity, while civil authorities noted that many Jews, often with massacred or missing family members, had recently come to Oran and Mostaganem from towns, such as Mascara, that were devastated by Abd al-Qader.[3] Given his relative powerlessness, Sénanès found it difficult to quickly transform the community with whose moral regeneration he was charged.

In the first years of the consistory's existence, its civilizing policy did not show signs of success on its own terms, even as elements of the local Jewish elite adopted a political and moral language based on the civilizing ideal. Jewish responses to the consistory's installation reveal an established, secure community both resisting and adapting to the intrusion of new French institutions. In their efforts to maintain elite prerogatives or pre-serve local religious custom, Algeria's Jews often rejected French reformers and rabbis who were charged with overseeing their communities, refused the option of being governed by French personal status laws (*statut personnel*), and attempted to maintain newly outlawed schools and synagogues. Their discontent was articulated in various lexicons; they stressed piety and fidelity to their traditions, but they also used the political language of French colonial ideology—vocabularies that stressed patriotism, civiliza-tion, and at times even republicanism. At the same time, Jews in Oran were particularly hostile to colonial-administrative intervention in financial and religious spheres, governed until 1847 by local Jewish communal authorities. As we shall see, the Jews of Oran made use of the enlarged space for politi-cal expression that accompanied the revolution of 1848. At the same time, Jews' petitions and complaints resonate with expectations and perspectives forged in the period of the Regency, illuminating the continuities as well as the disjunctures between the precolonial past and the colonial order.

Scholarship on the French-Jewish intervention into the lives of their colonized co-religionists is generally conducted along the axes of French liberalism and Jewish emancipation in France.[4] Doubtless, exploring how French authorities and Jewish reformers understood the Algerian Jews and attempted to civilize them has proved fruitful as a way to draw out patterns and contradictions in the Franco-Jewish experience. Altaras and Cohen's liberal and pro-naturalization "Report on the Moral and Political State of the Israelites of Algeria," discussed in the previous chapter, has rightfully been identified as one of the "key texts in the history of Jewish emancipation."[5]

Older treatments that held to this axis were less cognizant of the contradictions between liberalism and emancipation à la française, and viewed resistance to the process of emancipation as fanatic or traditionalist rejection of
salutary reforms.[6]

Here, the focus has less to do with the limits of liberalism or the incom-
pleteness of French-Jewish emancipation than the meaning of civilizing—
both to the consistorial officials appointed by the minister of war and to the
local Algerian Jews experiencing it. In his study of the Egyptian 'Afandiya
in the late nineteenth century, Michael Gasper observed that 'civilization'
functioned as a claim to political authority.[7] For consistorial officers, civilization functioned similarly. It also meant securing control, extending surveillance of hitherto personal spheres of life, and centralizing administration,
liberal currents also present in other July Monarchy reforms. These efforts
threatened local power structures and moral sensibilities, but our understanding of civilizing must also take into account that such policies did not
immediately succeed or effect a significant moral, ideological, or educational
transformation. Jewish responses to the civilizing project, on the other hand,
point to a leadership reasonably secure, self-confident, and occasionally able
to use colonial ideologies of civilization and progress toward its own ends.
Brought together, these stories offer a nuanced definition of civilization and
the civilizing mission that does not assume a monolithic colonial modernity
born of an incontestable post-Enlightenment rationality, nor write off the
civilizing mission as "window dressing."[8] Simultaneously, they present a
picture of colonized Jews entirely at odds with the slavish and disoriented
victims that inhabited any number of colonial narratives.

Once again, the 1845 "Ordonnance portant sur l'organisation du culte
israélite en Algérie," provides a useful starting point as an example of how
metropolitan institutions and ideologies were adapted and transformed in
the colonial context. As noted in the previous chapter, the decree was a
response to colonial realities and strategic considerations, but its form and
language were shaped by July Monarchy liberalism; it also echoed a centralizing decree issued a year and half earlier, in May 1844, that had "reorga-
nized" the Jewish religion in France. The May 1844 decree gave the central
consistory in Paris considerably more rights to censure or even dismiss local
consistorial rabbis—even grand rabbis—than Napoleon granted when he
originally founded consistories in 1808. Furthermore, the 1844 law called
upon consistories to approve kosher slaughterers, mohelim (who perform
Jewish ritual circumcision), and the ministres officiants (leaders of religious
services). By extension, the consistories were also expressly given the right
to dismiss these officials.[9] Following in this centralizing vein, the Algerian
decree also gave substantial powers to the consistorial officers. No one had
the right, for example, to "exercise religious functions, whether as a rabbi or

[other] officiating minister" without the official authorization of a central or provincial consistory. Much like their metropolitan corollaries, these bodies were imbued with the authority to name "agents of the religion, and notably *shochets* [sic] kosher slaughterers)."[10]

Together, the 1844 and 1845 decrees represented a further centralization of the institutions overseeing Jewish practice in France. Of course, the 1808 decree that established consistories was itself a great step toward centralization; it demanded that consistories monitor rabbis, prevent them from teaching anything contrary to the rulings of the assembly of notables and Grand Sanhedrin, prevent any unauthorized prayer assembly from meeting, and encourage Jews to "exercise useful professions and to inform the authorities of those who do not have a recognized means of existence."[11] The 1844 decree, however, concentrated more power in the hands of the central consistory, and by extension, the agency that oversaw it, the Ministry of Justice and Religions. This new centralization was striking enough to inspire critiques by both Jewish and non-Jewish circles, as would the Algerian decree of 1845.[12] Both the ordinances of 1844 and 1845 reflected the liberalism of the July Monarchy by increasing the power of state-sanctioned (and often secular) consistorial officials in making doctrinal and communal decisions.

While both decrees had liberal elements, they did not necessarily grant or respect rights. The 1844 decree in France was a centralizing effort that never threatened Jewish citizenship, while its Algerian counterpart placed consistories under the supervision of the minister of war as part of a larger effort of colonial domination. The 1844 decree was part of a campaign aimed at Jewish integration with their non-Jewish neighbors, but the 1845 ordinance for the Jews of Algeria was an effort to sever the Jewish population from the local majority that would never be granted citizenship rights.[13] In keeping with its colonial nature, the minister of war had the authority to approve the selection of both lay consistorial members and the grand rabbi of the central consistory in Algiers. Indeed, all decisions taken by the consistory in Algiers had to be approved by the "administrative authority," which at this point was also under the authority of the war minister; even local community rabbis were ultimately to be approved by him. While the 1844 decree in France subsumed French Jews under the Ministry of Justice and Religions, the decree of November 9, 1845, technically made Minister of War Nicholas Soult the ultimate arbiter of the Algerian rabbinate.[14] As France expanded the civil administration in Algeria, the Ministry of War maintained ultimate control. How, then, did the Parisian ministers try to remake the governing structures of Algerian Judaism to aid the consolidation of colonial power in the city of Oran?

On June 22, 1847, the provincial prefecture presided over the ceremony officially opening the consistory of Oran. Three lay officers and a French rabbi publicly swore to uphold the duties incumbent upon them and to be faithful to the French crown.[15] In keeping with the 1845 decree organizing the Jewish religion in Algeria, members were selected from among indigenous and French Jews, with the position of grand rabbi reserved for a Frenchman. The term "indigenous" (*indigène*), less a reflection of the realities of Algerian-Jewish culture than a colonial convenience, was a commonly used, imprecise phrase that reappears frequently in official correspondence and published materials. It was used to describe a diverse population of Jews who did not possess French citizenship in Algeria.

The term "indigenous," used as both an adjective and a noun, was a colonial term that simultaneously misrepresented its subject and helped create new colonial identities. The word represented and symbolized a larger French misunderstanding of Algerian Jewries. It applied to both Livornese and local Judeo-Arabic-speaking Jews, as well as to Moroccan immigrants coming from Tetuan or one of the Spanish enclaves. Indeed, by 1850, it was estimated that between 600 and 800 Jews in Oran were recent immigrants from Morocco. As we shall see, the deliberate but flawed French notion of a unitary indigenous Jewish identity proved problematic when rabbis of one rite or background were chosen by the consistory to represent Jews with differing sensibilities. Just as importantly, however, the colonial regime made indigenous into a socially and legally salient term that inevitably affected Algerian-Jewish self-perceptions and behaviors.

The consistorial use of the term "French" as a social category also masked a more complicated reality. The first officially designated "French" officer of the Oran consistory was Emmanuel Menahem Nahon, a Jew of Moroccan background. Nahon had acquired French nationality and had been working as an interpreter for the military at the time of his selection. While his outlook was very much in line with the French grand rabbi's, he had not necessarily spent much (or perhaps any) of his life in France.[16] The administrative vagaries of the designations French and indigenous were not isolated miscues. From the beginning, the consistory reflected both its colonial inception and a lack of concern for the local Jewish cultural landscape.

The Ministry of War's choice of grand rabbi also indicated a certain disconnect with the reality of Jewish life in colonial Oran. Metz-educated Lazare Cahen was chosen perhaps because of his experience in education; he had founded Jewish schools in both Phalebourg and Nîmes (in France). Officers of the Ministry of War were particularly impressed by Cahen's background as a prison chaplain in Nîmes. His prison experience, he assured his future employers at the Ministry of War, had given him the opportunity "to observe the customs and habits of the indigènes and to study their mores and characters a bit."[17] Indeed, it was his experience working with Jewish inmates, more than his educational background that received explicit notice in ministerial correspondence concerning his candidacy for grand rabbi.[18] The ministry was probably aware of the fact that local Jews represented a not-negligible proportion of the inmates in Oran's civil prison. In 1847, for example, Algerian Jews accounted for 27 of the 115 convicted inmates, or nearly a quarter of the incarcerated population.[19] Imbued with liberal ideals and a romanticist appreciation of work's inherent value, Cahen was convinced that the Jews of Algeria did not naturally understand the importance of work. He assured the minister that he was capable of inspiring "in my *barbaresque* co-religionists the love of work" which, according to Cahen, "was extinguished under the malignant influence of Oriental lassitude and sloth." Furthermore, he assured the liberal July Monarchy–era ministry that he could "teach them [local Jews] to appreciate the benefits of liberty" of which they were not aware, and "to love and cherish France to which they owe this celestial gift."[20] Cahen's Alsatian religious training, elite liberal outlook, and preconceived ideas about his "Barbary co-religionists" well suited his superiors, but did not prepare him for dealing with Oran's diverse and deeply rooted Jewish population.

The two Jews chosen to fill the allotted role of "indigenous" lay members of the consistory of Oran exhibited qualities respected by the Ministry of War but they, too, were poorly prepared for the actual duties they were to undertake. Both were wealthy merchants. The first, Amran Sénanès, was actually the brother-in-law of Emmanuel Nahon, almost certainly of a Moroccan family, and was chosen for his status as *éclairé*, or enlightened.[21] The ministry probably arrived at this description because of Sénanès's social prominence and the fact that in 1847 he was already sending his children to French schools. Sénanès also served prominently in the civil and governmental life of Oran, on both the municipal council and the chamber of commerce. When he died prematurely several years after joining the consistory, prominent French officers, such as the prefect, attended his funeral, suggesting a close association with the French administration.[22] Abraham El Kanoui was the second consistorial member considered indigenous. He was also a local merchant with roots in Oran who was regarded as "highly respected" locally by officers in the Ministry of War.[23] Although he reportedly entrusted his children's education to French instructors, he was also the only member of the group incapable of speaking French, and needed an Arabic translation of the required consistorial oath.[24] While wealth and prominence were clearly vital to the ministry's selection of consistorial members, they would prove to be inadequate guarantors of the loyalty of all the factions of Oran's Jewish population.

The consistory's first priorities consisted of securing control of community finances and public religious practice, both of which proved flashpoints for the local populations. The first meetings were devoted to naming (and securing the tax revenue from) a limited number of ritual slaughterers and merchants of kosher alcohol.[25] The consistory also took control over the properties that had belonged to the former communal organization and which had guaranteed a certain income used to subsidize the charitable and educational institutions it maintained. This included a community mill, an oven, and several stores.[26] The officers directed revenues into the (now consistory-managed) community charity fund and burial society. The consistory also began choosing those rabbis who were to be designated as official ministers at various synagogues in Oran and smaller towns in the province, such as Mostaganem and Tlemcen. This process did not necessarily involve the introduction of new personnel, but since western Algeria had witnessed significant Moroccan Jewish immigration, in some cases it did involve privileging one community's rabbi (and therefore its customs) over another's. The officers required owners of all independent synagogues of Oran to register with the consistory and obtain its permission to remain in operation. The owners were local notables, only some of whom were represented in the consistory by El Kanoui. The consistory thus set out to apply the July Monarchy's policy of centralizing institutions and limiting the power of non-state religious institutions to the colonial context.

Among the officers of the consistory, the larger French goal of colonial consolidation was articulated through the immediate project of moralizing local Jews.[27] For example, within several months of their installation, Rabbi Cahen and Emmanuel Nahon vocally (if briefly) turned the consistory's attention from charity and the regulation of ritual services to Jewish prostitution. According to them, Oran's entire population of *filles de joie* was "housed in the quarter of the Jews," a terrible thing for the reputation of the neighborhood. "It is with justified indignation," they noted in the consistorial meeting, "that honest people refuse to frequent this quarter, due to the odious interchanges they must face at each instant."[28] Altaras, in his report submitted to the Ministry of War five years earlier, had also decried the existence of prostitution among Jewish women. Now, insisted the consistorial rabbi and president, "inhabitants (of the quarter) cannot even step outside without rubbing shoulders with women of ill repute (*mauvaise vie*)." The outraged French consistorial officers quickly resolved to confront the Jewish property owners who allowed the trade to go on in their homes. Subsequent reports by the (French) Rabbi Cahen suggest that these attempts were less than perfectly successful. Perhaps out of their powerlessness to eliminate it, consistorial discussions of prostitution following the first several months of its existence were rare.

This brief crisis over prostitution suggests that the urban Jewish community's new administrators were dealing with problems aggravated by the same historical processes that brought them to power. The existence of prostitution in the Jewish quarter was probably not a new phenomenon, but the discussion surrounding its elimination suggests that it had grown more prominent with the occupation of the city by French soldiers and with the subsequent growth in the European population. From 1838, as the government started keeping statistical track of French establishments in Algeria, it also began keeping track of the number of prostitutes in Algerian cities and charts became available of *filles publiques* divided by nationality and race. Without demonstrating an overrepresentation of Jewish prostitutes, they did suggest significant involvement.[29] Combined with the plague of the early 1830s and the disruptions of war, it must be concluded that poverty was a prominent feature of early colonial urban life.

In addition to shedding light on the social conditions that shaped Oran's Jewish population, the consistory's concern for the social problem of prostitution points to the ambitions of the organization's officers. These men hoped to burnish the reputation of Algeria' still-non-emancipated Jews in the imaginations of their superiors both at the Prefect of Oran and the Parisian ministries. Ridding this community of prostitution would prove it well prepared for the reforms consistory members advocated. Though this theme will be addressed more fully later, it is worth pointing out that the consistorial concern with prostitution represents an early example of how women's morality became a key measure and marker of colonial difference.[30] For consistorial reformers committed to the now official colonial policy of distancing Algerian Jews from what they saw as an Oriental cultural milieu, representations of their moral status (occupations, sexual behaviors, use of time) were vital to control.[31] The visibility of prostitution in the Jewish quarter undermined the consistorial mission of recasting Jews as Europeans ripe for legal recognition. Colonialism both aggravated the problem and introduced the mission to solve it.

Other apparently short-lived consistorial efforts at moralizing the Jews of Oran were aimed at children, youth, and public gambling. Like prostitution, gambling and the putatively raucous behavior of Jewish children were visible challenges to the claim that Algerian Jews maintained disciplined households that would conform to an ordered, bourgeois ideal. Once again spearheaded by Cahen and Sénanès, the consistory took up the question of young Jews spending hours at cafés that had become "veritable dens of perdition for the [Jewish] youth," and where, to "satisfy their passion for gambling," they come and end up "reducing their families to misery." Every day, insisted the consistorial officers, "one sees young people of good families passing the entire day at the café," while the reproaches of their parents fell on deaf ears.[32] It was the noisy side effects of the purported neglect of parents that caught the attention of the consistory. On the Sabbath, consistory members insisted, the streets of the Jewish quarter filled with noisy children who were allowed to play on their own when their fathers "abandon[ed] them" to either go to the synagogue or rest at home.[33] The commotion was such that the Sabbath was indistinguishable from the festivities that accompany annual holidays. The consistory resolved in the two cases to write to the sub-director of the interior in Oran. To resolve the problem of gambling in cafés, the consistory demanded "the closure of these establishments." As for the problem of the noisy and disruptive children, the consistory decided to ask the sub-director to inform the police and request a special detail that would watch the Jewish quarter for three or four consecutive Saturdays. The consistory hoped the police officer would then arrest the offensive children, put them in jail, and upon the parent's arrival to retrieve them, "severely reprimand the parents for according them so little surveillance."[34] The fate of the cafés remains unclear, as the police were decidedly uninterested in the matter. "The police do not take care of children who run about in the streets of the city," they informed the consistory several days after the inquiry, "as long as these children do not commit any blamable action."[35]

The way the consistory attempted to intervene in the perceived problems of prostitution, gambling, and public rowdiness illustrates several disconnects in the early colonial Jewish quarter of Oran. It is clear that the rhythm of life of the largely poor artisan families inhabiting the Jewish quarter of this Mediterranean port city struck consistory officers as chaotic, decadent, and immoral. Dedicated to teaching his co-religionists the love of work, Cahen saw Arab-Jewish café culture as improvident, a menace to class boundaries, and even a danger to family integrity. Cahen described local understandings of parenting as deeply flawed, for parents should be far more active monitoring and disciplining their children. Furthermore, there was a question of the use of space; public streets, in his view, were not to serve as playgrounds for unsupervised and noisy children. Despite, or perhaps because of, these men's distance from Oran's Jews, the Ministry of War assigned Cahen and Sénanès a role in the colonizing effort that they took to be a moralizing one—a process of "attaching to France" a group that was both a component of the wider North African, Arab-Islamic cultural context, as well as one negatively affected by recent economic and social disruptions.

Yet, a certain powerlessness represented a second disconnect separating Cahen and Sénanès's civilizing mission from that of the ministerial and colonial authorities. The Ministry of War empowered the consistory to take over the Jewish community's finances, to grant monopolies and tax the sale of kosher wine and anisette, and to control the production and sale of kosher meat. Such ritual-related activities were also the official reserve of the Jewish consistories of France. In their colonial incarnation, they represented a strengthening of French civil institutions in the shaping of (Jewish) life in Algeria's cities. Nevertheless, the civil authorities themselves were not invested in the micro-management of Jews' religious habits, recreational activities, or child-rearing practices. Unless given orders from higher authorities, institutions such as the Prefecture of Oran or the Commissariat of Police were not willing to arrest children for playing in the streets, or eliminate the widely accepted practice of prostitution. In the eyes of the early consistory, the civilizing mission was a noble but frustratingly toothless policing campaign.

Perhaps for related reasons, the consistory's first months received decidedly mixed reviews from local Jews. As we shall further discuss, some wealthy Jews quickly learned to navigate the new communal landscape. Others, however, bristled at the consistorial effort to secure control over the community's institutions. For example, in October 1847, Joseph Levy, a Jew living in the inland town of Tiarat, wrote to the consistorial officers in Oran. He had been appointed representative of the consistory in his town, and was running into problems. According to his letter, he could not convince the local Jews to accept as shochet Abraham Kalfoun, the man chosen by the consistory to be the official kosher butcher of the town. Instead, they insisted on maintaining the former shochetim in their functions.[36] In response to Levy's request for instructions, the Oran consistory insisted that Kalfoun had been nominated locally and that the town's Jews had to accept him. The response of the town to the appointment of Kalfoun represented a small, early example of how communal divides and loyalties would profoundly complicate the consistory's centralizing program. These communal seams would dramatically unravel in subsequent months.

The prevalence of private synagogues was another early concern of the consistory that sheds light on both the social landscape of Oran Jewry and on how this population tangled with new colonial authorities. The seventeen private synagogues of Oran were a form of property in which well-off Algerian Jews invested, and they catered to the religious needs of a considerable portion of the Jewish population in the city.[37] Out of 7,000 or so Jews in Oran, the official synagogue that the consistory directed could hold only about 60 people.[38] With the establishment of the consistory and the eventual opening of official houses of worship in the various cities and towns of the Province of Oran, officials operated on the assumption that the social function of private synagogues had expired. According to the consistory's officers, "The existence of . . . synagogues outside of any administrative control or religious discipline" constituted a real problem that had to be investigated and solved. "They are essentially private companies (*exploitations privées*), a sort of commercial industry, and they profoundly compromise the dignity of the religion."[39] Yet even the designation of "private" reflected official misunderstandings of the local cultural terrain. With no consistory or ministry of religion paying the clergy's salary, public Jewish religious spaces were nonexistent prior to the introduction of colonial authority in Algeria and, what is more, commercial and religious interests were often intertwined in this and many other Jewish contexts. Regardless, in the eyes of the authorities, so-called private synagogues represented a tacit (and later on, explicit) challenge to the French grand rabbi's monopoly on moral oversight and *hallachic* (Jewish legal) guidance. By late summer of 1847, the owners of private synagogues in Oran had been informed that they would need official permission to remain open, and by the beginning of September, they had all formally requested authorization.[40] In late December, the director of civil affairs in Oran announced that upon recommendation of the consistory, one month would be given for private synagogues either to be officially approved or to be shut down.[41]

Actually shutting private synagogues, however, was a complicated affair, and was to preoccupy consistorial officials for many decades to come. They were, after all, private property, and their owners, as mentioned earlier, were often wealthy and well-connected merchants. With contacts extending internationally and occasionally high in the French administration, these merchants often had the ability to overstep the limited competence of consistorial leaders. Furthermore, because private synagogues fulfilled a variety of charitable and ritualistic needs, shuttering them was not necessarily advisable. Vividly illustrating this point is the affair of the synagogue of Jacob Lasry, whom we encountered in the previous chapter. Briefly returning to this merchant's story provides some indication that "private synagogues" were both commercial ventures and centers of community in nineteenth-century Algeria, and as such became targets for consistorial struggles to regulate Jewish life.

As we recall, Haim Israel Jacob Lasry was a wealthy exporter of grain and cattle from Algeria. His primary bases of operation appear to have been Gibraltar and Oran, and given the earlier solicitousness of the British consul, he probably possessed a British passport.[42] According to a charter translated by Emmanuel Nahon from Spanish (probably Haketia) into French, Lasry founded the "European Bait ha-Knesset Lasry" in the city of Oran on the fifth of Sh'vat, 5603, or January 5, 1843. According to the charter, the purpose of Lasry's "European synagogue" was to officiate according to the rite of "European Sephardim."[43] This could have indicated Livornese, but it was more likely a Spanish Moroccan rite. Lasry's synagogue was to function (according to what was certainly the norm) as both a revenue-generating enterprise and a charitable foundation. The revenues were to pay the employees of the synagogue, any necessary reparations, and to subsidize the continual study of Torah by a *yeshiva* (school or group of scholars of Torah) of ten rabbis. At the beginning of every month of Nisan (in which Passover falls) and Elul (the final month of the Jewish calendar), the synagogue would pay for the *tefillin* (phylacteries), leather boxes containing portions of scripture, worn by men during certain weekday prayers, of two (male) orphans or two impoverished men.[44] Every three years, if the funds existed, the synagogue would pay for the marriage of an orphaned girl who would otherwise not have the necessary funds. A *junta*, or governing council, would make decisions about the rabbis chosen for the yeshiva and about charitable disbursements, but the owner of the synagogue would retain power to approve their decisions. Jacob Lasry also reserved certain ritual honors to himself— notably, the reading of the *haftara* (ancillary passages of scripture associated with a given day's regular Torah reading) during *minha* (afternoon prayers) on Yom Kippur (the holiest day of the Jewish year). He also reserved the right to recite the first blessings made in synagogue following those made in favor of the king of France. As this suggests, private synagogues such as Lasry's served as avenues to produce or reproduce social prestige, perpetuate Jewish learning, help needy members of the Jewish community, and even, at least in this case, to offset their owners' costs of maintaining investments in urban real estate.

Lasry appears to have been aware that these dynamics would threaten the new authorities. Shortly after the decree of November 9, 1845, Lasry became nervous that his recent religio-financial investment might be closed by the incoming consistories. Having had a significant role in the pre- and early-colonial export economy, he already had long experience working with European consuls, but France's imperial presence in Algeria required a new approach. In a letter written directly to the minister of war in Paris, Lasry attempted to explain that ritual differences existed among Jews in Algeria, a fact that the law creating the consistory effectively denied. European Jews and Algerian Jews observe different rites, he explained, and his synagogue administered to what he called the population of European Sephardim in Algeria.[45] In addition to addressing their religious needs, the synagogue would also dedicate itself to "lightening the suffering of the poor class of Israelites."[46] Lasry's appeal, expressed in the third person, reveals the interweaving of profit and charity that underlay the private synagogues that the consistory reductively characterized as commercial ventures: "the petitioner sincerely desires, Mr. Minister, and even dares to hope, that this relief to suffering will quickly be renewed, and to do this he is entirely ready to continue undertaking the numerous sacrifices that he has taken upon himself out of love of charity (*le bien*). [The synagogue's] ornamentation cost him forty-five thousand francs."[47] If the consistory to be established in Oran would not grant him permission to stay open, Lasry hoped, the minister of war would rectify the situation. As if to ensure this possibility, Lasry assured the minister that he himself was quite influential among his co-religionists, that "industry and agriculture" are his constant occupations, and, lifting directly from the text of the 1845 decree, that he had "never ceased to encourage the exercise of useful professions." Of course, he also assured the minister that "in all circumstances," he teaches his fellow Jews "obedience to laws, the loyalty they owe France Their Benefactor, and their duty to defend her."[48] Lasry presented his synagogue and investment as a potential ally to French colonial domination and the mission to assimilate Algeria's Jews.

Lasry's synagogue remained open. The minister of war forwarded the letter to Governor General Bugeaud, who appears to have ignored it. It is because the consistory's efforts to intervene in Lasry's affairs failed that this story is so illuminating. The interchange between Lasry and officials in the colonial apparatus reveals how an elite representative of Algerian Jewry adopted elements of the civilizing discourse (such as loyalty to France and social utility) that justified the consistories, even as he preemptively maneuvered to avoid their censure. Within the correspondence, we see Enlightenment-inflected colonial ideology becoming a shared and pliable moral register, a language by which one advanced one's own authority. Lasry was one of a number of wealthy Jewish notables who recast themselves as eager soldiers in France's colonial effort. This effort, as Lasry's letter to the minister conveys vividly, required local Jewish elites to know and effectively use the language of the civilizing ideology. Lasry's case is particularly representative of this evolution, and of its importance to the remapping of power relations in Algeria: in 1855, a decade after he wrote to the minister of war, this quintessentially Jewish Mediterranean merchant who had navigated between Oran, Gibraltar, and Italy became the president of Oran's consistory.

1848: Jews and the Second Republic in Algeria

Before Lasry became a representative of France's civilizing mission in Algeria, the upheavals of the 1848 revolution disrupted the life of Algerian cities. The advent of the Second Republic occurred only months after the installation of the consistory in Oran in June 1847, and by this time Algerian Jews were coming into increasing contact with European settlers. The population of Oran had grown from about 17,000 in 1830 to almost 23,000 in 1847, the year of the consistory's establishment.[49] In addition to a native population of 4,763 Jews and 2,504 Muslims in 1847, the city counted 15,591 European immigrants. This fact became particularly important in 1848, when the overthrow of the July Monarchy inspired the political aspirations of the largely working-class, left-leaning European colonists of Oran.[50] If Paris was the epicenter of the 1848 events, the civic activism and widespread proletarian participation in political clubs that characterized the early Second Republic echoed powerfully in colonial Algeria.[51] While Oran's immigrants included far more Spaniards then Frenchmen (the official figures for Europeans include 8,520 Spaniards, 4,954 Frenchmen, and 1,056 Italians), the population was deeply moved by political events in France.[52]

As in France, the revolution in Algeria was marked by the formation of a profusion of political associations. Masonic lodges became centers of political discussion, occasionally leading to public demonstrations, while larger cities hosted a number of republican clubs. On several occasions, demonstrations by European colonists led to violent confrontations with the police. In Bône, for example, the disorders eventually led to the dismissal of the director of civil affairs for the province, while disorders in Oran brought about the mayor's downfall.[53] Colonial republican activists printed brochures and petitions, planned meetings, and attended public gatherings throughout the colony.[54] The press, though regularly harassed by the military authorities, benefited from a judiciary that often sympathized with the journalists.[55] This civic activism was not confined to the European settler population; the urban Jewish population participated as well, using a democratic lexicon to understand and respond to challenges to local structures or religious authority.

What this suggests is that not only elite Jews like Lasry, but also many less privileged Algerian Jews drew on French political language, in this case republicanism, during the explosion of political debate in France and Algeria in early 1848. The political atmosphere of the early Second Republic created a fissure in the edifice of authority, allowing Jews in Oran to act against the new consistorial leadership. Just as many European colonists hoped the Second Republic would bring an end to the military regime, Jews in Oran were hopeful that the rise of democracy in France might augur the fall of the consistories. Jewish complaints about the consistory were rooted in their perception that the governance of their communities had been transferred from local leadership to a group of corrupt outsiders. Furthermore, many local Jews sensed that the new structure had installed a religious order that was insouciant of local custom. The points of religious-communal fissure were between the European grand rabbi and his new community, on the one hand; on the other, it was between the Moroccan rabbis whom the consistory granted official titles in other cities and towns of the province. In the city of Oran itself, the rebellion succeeded in changing the face of the local consistorial structure. Exploring the form and language of the unrest, we gain insight into how the concept of civilization was both deployed and challenged by an established Jewish community—one that evidently did not see itself in need of regeneration.

In 1848, Jews in cities throughout the province of Oran began vocally rejecting the religious and temporal authority of the consistory. As early as January, deputies from the consistory of Oran encountered problems fulfilling their duties in provincial towns such as Mascara and Mostaganem. For example, local Jews had forced the consistory-appointed rabbi out of the major communal synagogue in Mostaganem, obliging him to conduct services elsewhere; on February 18, 1848, forty-four Jewish heads-of-household in this town petitioned the director of civil affairs with the intention of ridding themselves of the consistorial representatives who had been sent to lead them. They complained of abuse of authority, religious transgressions, disrespect to revered local rabbis, and even physical mistreatment. So strong were these objections that the civil commissioners reported a "complete insurrection" of local Jews against the authorities and the eruption of "disorders."[56] The prefecture of the province was not long in responding with orders to "severely repress" the uprising.[57]

Notwithstanding the resultant repression (the exact nature of which remains unclear), the disturbances spread to other towns. Rabbi Moshe Abou of Oran drew up a subsequent petition and addressed the Governor General Henri d'Orléans, duc d'Aumale, who had taken over from Thomas-Robert Bugeaud in September 1847. The petition leveled further complaints against the consistorial delegate to Mostaganem, a Jew of Moroccan descent by the name of Salomon Sarfati.[58] Sarfati had been a favorite of the consistorial administration; a note from the grand rabbi several years later noted that he was dedicated to the "progress" of his co-religionists. By 1850, he had founded a "pious society," founded a synagogue, and opened two schools in the province.[59] Nevertheless, he quickly made enemies, and, in early February 1848, the consistory of Oran was actively soliciting the colonial administration's help in repressing the disturbance at Mostaganem. Consistory President Nahon urged the civil commissioner of Mostaganem to solve the problem with a strong hand: "This task would be rendered easier . . . , if the instigators of harm (mal) were removed (écartés), if their poorly wielded influence were eliminated, in a word, if in punishing them [we provided] a severe example warn[ing] all others that obedience is due to our laws and that the administration has a strong will to have them respected."[60] Meanwhile, the affair had become troublesome enough to concern the governor general, who demanded an explanation of the recent disturbances among the Jews.[61] By mid-February, he commanded the director of civil affairs of the prefecture of Oran to investigate the complaints.[62] On April 6, he ordered announcements to be placed in Oran's synagogues alerting Jews that the consistory's president remained in power. He also ordered "severe" treatment of the agitators, to be "an example demonstrating that consistorial authority must be respected."[63] In the same note, he chastised the director of civil affairs for his "reprehensible weakness" in not having acted more severely. The Orléanist governor general, however, would not reign over the subsequent events. The leaders of the Second Republic soon sent the officer into exile and appointed the brutal, if politically republican, Louis-Eugène Cavaignac as governor general of Algeria.[64]

In March 1848, the Jewish movement against the consistorial leadership increased in intensity. Fully 100 Jewish heads of households in Oran petitioned the new governor general asking for the complete overhaul of their consistory. Citing corruption, religious ignorance, threats, insensitivity to local custom, and the inappropriate Moroccan origins of its leaders, the Jews of Oran implored the highest-ranking officer of French Algeria to remove both Cahen and Nahon and to reform the structure of the consistory into an elected body.[65] These petitions accompanied a level of civil unrest in Oran that continued to worry the authorities. The director of civil affairs wrote a letter to the consistory noting that he viewed with "extreme discontent the conduct of the Jewish population."[66] The consistory agreed that the recent actions of elements of the Jewish population were disturbing and added that the rebellion had spread to other parts of Algeria. In April, a newspaper article in *l'Echo d'Oran*, reproduced in the metropolitan Jewish press, reported that Jews in Oran were rioting and that troops had intervened to suppress the disturbances, resulting in numerous arrests. Similar problems were reported at Mostaganem, where the local community was understood to have rejected the consistorial system. According to the report, local Jews had "manifested a systematic opposition to the measures required by the organization of the Israelite religion that the government has carried out."[67] Astonishingly, in the city of Medea, southwest of Algiers, the army was even called in to back the appointed heads of the Jewish community.[68] Soon thereafter, the director of civil affairs ordered posters placed on the walls of Oran synagogues assuring local Jews that the authority of the consistory would remain intact and that France would not allow its laws or functionaries to be insulted by men who "did not understand" the meaning of liberty.[69] On the following day, Jews rioted again, tearing down the posters and stoning the police. Around the same time, many small-scale merchants, especially Jews and Muslims, who had contracted loans in order to purchase real estate or other investments, saw the change of regime as an opportunity to cease payment. Officials, such as the British consul in Algiers, fretted about the fate of the comfortable classes, speculating that the rebellious parties were taking advantage of new French laws eliminating imprisonment as a punishment for debt.[70] While it is unclear if the apparently widespread defaulting on loans can be reduced to one cause, it was part of a larger political phenomenon that had serious repercussions for the consistory. A number of wealthy Jews of Oran expressed their anger at the consistories by withholding their contributions to the communal treasury.[71] This tax strike was a serious obstacle to the consistory's ability to make charitable disbursements. This, as we will see shortly, further embittered the local population, many of whom relied on communal philanthropy.

The events of 1848 also provided the context for some of the early battles in the long triangular struggle between Algerian Jews, reformers who would naturalize them as French citizens, and other, less sympathetic colonial authorities over marriage customs and personal status laws. As I will discuss in more depth in Chapter 5, personal status laws in the colonial context rendered Muslims, Jews, and Europeans governable by three respective codes regarding family and inheritance laws. At the same time, France saw citizenship as incompatible with anything but the French personal status, so Muslims and Jews (until 1870) were effectively excluded. Given this structure, consistorial reformers strove to encourage Jewish couples to be married in the presence of an officer of the *état civil* (public registry of names, births, deaths, and marital status) and thus be governed by French family law. From their inception, consistorial officers forbade unapproved local rabbis from contracting marriages. In the early months of 1848, however, many local Jews rejected consistorial authority in part by contracting clandestine marriages. On July 13, for example, the French grand rabbi of Oran, Lazare Cahen, reported that "during the . . . week . . . Rabbi Mimoun, in the name of an assembly meeting in Keroubi's store, came to demand that I renounce my rights to celebrate marriages in favor of the former rabbis."[72] On June 26, it was reported that a Rabbi Sénanès performed a wedding without authorization, and a week later, a Rabbi Aharon Amoiel performed another—a marriage, insisted the French rabbi, "that he knew should have been blessed by me." As we shall see, this was but an opening salvo in what was to be an ongoing battle that would place personal status laws and marriage laws at the center of discussions over civilization and citizenship in colonial Algeria.

By March 29, President Nahon, worn down by the events, wrote to the director of civil affairs to tender his resignation. "The execution of the ordinance of 9 October 1845 seems to be excessively difficult in the current circumstances,"[73] he wrote. Perhaps in consultation with Nahon, his colleague Sénanès chose to officially resign the same day, referencing, by way of explanation, "this ungrateful population."[74] Their sense of impotence was disregarded by their superiors; the director of civil affairs (concerned about maintaining public order), insisted that the men stay at their posts.[75] In mid-May, local Jews wrote to *l'Echo d'Oran* and accused Nahon of dishonesty and a host of other faults. This apparently had such an impact on Nahon that he felt obliged to reaffirm to his superiors at the Directorate of the Interior his honesty and devotion to the cause of regeneration.[76] Despite Nahon's impassioned plea and the directorate's own initial resolve, the colonial administration's desire to retain Nahon and Sénanès in the face of their unpopularity endured no more than a few weeks. In this, concern for the director's own responsibilities played a role. Because of the cessation of funds to the consistory, poor Jews who depended on the effective operation of the consistory's charity had become, in the words of the director of civil affairs, "turbulent."[77] Thus, the director began to voice his doubts about retaining Nahon and Sénanès, and on May 27 he made his opinion known to the new governor general, Nicholas Anne Théodule Changarnier, informing him that since tensions had recently translated into "material disorders," a policy change was in order.[78] To this end, the director would meet with representatives of Oran's Jews and, in collaboration with them, produce a tentative list of new candidates.

The new list represented a victory for elite Jews with local roots. The civil authorities of Oran were forced to admit to the consistory wealthy local merchants and property owners who often supported certain rabbis through their ownership of private synagogues. Their wealth, combined with their claim of upholding religious custom through patronage, had provided them with an influential role in the institutional life of the pre-consistory community with which they were not eager to part. Ultimately, the financial dependence of the consistory on this native elite put the institution in a vulnerable position. When members of this group (who were by no means united on all issues) withheld their financial support of consistorial activities, they played an important role in ousting most of the members who were categorized as French in the organization's original incarnation. The civilizing mission, it would seem, was less easy to suture to the Algerian-Jewish landscapes than its shapers had imagined.

The director informed his superior of the new candidates for the consistory with some trepidation. According to him, these men participated in the "turbulent opposition" to the current consistory.[79] The minister of war agreed to appoint the new representatives conditionally, waiting for the pair to prove their fidelity to the administration before offering their confirmation. By August, two new members of the consistory had been appointed: the local notables Mordechai Darmon and Abraham ben Haim. Two original members (both local Jewish elite), Abraham El Kanoui and the French Rabbi Lazare Cahen, would also remain. What happened in Oran was true elsewhere; consistorial members in the provincial city of Mostagamem changed, as well. On May 26, the Moroccan rabbi Salomon Sarfati and his colleague Isaac ben Oliel tendered their resignations to the civil commissioner of Mostaganem, and their opponents were installed in their place. It appears that a similar trial period was accorded in Mostaganem, for there was no official act of instatement for nearly six months. Nevertheless, the administration produced a list of new deputies that included those previously active in the opposition: Jouda Smadja, Maklouf Troudjman, and Moshe ben Jacob

Abou.[80] In both cities, local notables serving on the consistory were maintained, while those who had clearly entered the administration as a consequence of their previous French military service were expelled.[81] By dint of
their vocal and persistent opposition to colonial rule, the Jews of Oran had
made some progress in molding the consistory to reflect the previously existing communal hierarchy.

Local Jews were clearly determined to reshape the consistory to conform at least partially to preexisting models. Exploring the language of their
struggle, as well as the forms it took, reveals some important characteristics
defining the interaction between the French administration of the consistories and the local communities. Perhaps most obviously, the struggles of 1848
in Algeria concerned the religious integrity of local Algerian-Jewish communities. Rabbinical authority and the right to lead prayers quickly emerged as
points of conflict. In February 1848, local Mostaganem Jews complained in
their petition that Salomon Sarfati had, during the high holidays the year
before, forced the venerated Rabbi Mordechai Obadia out of his functions
and replaced him with a rabbi of his own choosing. In another instance,
Sarfati allegedly interrupted the prayers when he noticed they were following the local, not the Moroccan, rite to which he insisted they conform.
Later, it was reported that the same community had forced his appointee
out of the main synagogue and into a smaller local meeting place, because
they wished to choose their own religious leader.[82] Sarfati himself confirmed
that his actions had made him enemies among the established rabbinate of
Mostaganem. This opposition, he wrote "[acts] entirely in concert with the
former chiefs who support it energetically."[83] Furthermore, he complained,
his local opponents constantly changed the times of prayer to evade him and
the other consistorial representatives.

The religious character of the movement against consistorial rabbis
was also manifest in its appeal for the support of the dead. Opponents of
Sarfati, soon after being summoned by him for a discussion, organized into
a group and left for the Jewish cemetery of Mostaganem. There, according
to the embattled representative, "They swore upon the tombs never to make
peace with us."[84] It is impossible to know the exact nature of these activists'
oath, but one can imagine that it was taken on the grave of a departed rabbi
(or rabbis) whose spiritual strength the opposition hoped to capture for
their cause.[85] In a related episode, opponents of Sarfati claimed that he was
dangerously negligent of local customs and beliefs; a petition submitted to
the director of civil affairs at the prefecture noted that Salomon Sarfati had
invited catastrophe upon Mostaganem by mishandling old holy books that,
according to many in the community, protected the city.[86] The consistory's
offence to Mostaganem's local Jewish populace, it would appear, was at once
political, spiritual, and rooted in local loyalties.

Jews from the city of Oran also articulated their protest in religious terms, mostly in the form of complaints about the imposed French rabbinical leadership. They criticized Cahen for being ignorant of local customs, for not speaking Arabic, and consequently for being "completely incapable" of fulfilling his religious functions. That he was a functionary of the state also unnerved the local population.[87] Opponents sarcastically noted that the government could save money by terminating Cahen's position. They pointed out further that Cahen's previous official appointment included duties at the prison in Nîmes. The Jews of Oran, less impressed than the Ministry of War with this professional experience, insisted that while he may have been well suited for the prison job, he was "totally out of place" in Oran.[88]

Compounding their poor opinion of French religious authority was the corruption Oran's Jews saw in the manner in which community funds were managed. For example, President Nahon took money out of the charity funds to pay his own salary. Comparing this practice to the previous system, many saw this as stealing from the community resulting in less money being available for the destitute.[89] Rabbi Cahen's practice of accepting money for performing marriages compounded the problem. The community was also disgusted by the consistorial officer's willingness to offer communal buildings as collateral on loans used to pay expenses. When it came to locals' opposition to the French imposed consistories, issues of religious and financial management converged.

The 1848 disputes did not hinge on resistance to innovation per se, nor did they reflect a simple colonizer/colonized binary. Rather, they show how multi-polar the colonial dynamic quickly became, as France's occupation opened up a new field of conflicts between various actors. Supporters of established institutions and locally respected rabbis rejected the financial and religious conceptions of the French—and, equally important, of the Moroccan Jewish—leaders who had been installed to oversee them. The conflict between Abou and Sarfati, for example, was not simply a conflict between a representative of colonial power and a representative of the local community, but an episode in which colonialism helped turn marriage into a political and social battlefield between different groups of North African Jews.

The revolution of February 1848 also added a republican element to the language of the Jewish opposition in Algeria. Many European colonists organized in support of the new republican government in Paris and included in their demands the replacement of military rule with civilian rule in the colony.[90] The Jews of Oran applied the democratic ideals of the movement to their struggle. In their letter to the republican General Cavaignac, Oranais Jews insisted that "[we] welcomed with happiness the rise of the Republic," and that they now would take advantage "of the liberty of thought acquired with this Republic, and [we] dare hope that you will accept our requests and carry them out."[91] Their demands included references to the widespread call for universal suffrage in France. For instance, they wished for a new grand rabbi, "who will have obtained a majority of votes in elections held for this purpose, and in which only native Israelites of Oran will have had the right to participate," and for alternative consistorial officers, who would also be selected "by means of election." The consistory reported petitions in which local Jews demanded "the abrogation of the ordinance of 9 November 1845 and the liberty to govern themselves as it had been during the times of the Regency."[92] Finally, the petitioners demanded the elimination of the office of the president of the consistory. If Algerian Jews viewed the consistorial officers as committing a variety of religious and social abuses, their response was both to refer back to the "self-governing" days of the Turks and to call for a "republican" consistorial administration. Algerian Jews used the French language of liberty to express their opposition to the French regime that claimed to be its champion.

Jewish opposition also seems to have borrowed organizing techniques from the European colonists' republican movement. According to President Nahon's report to the director of civil affairs, the Jews of Oran were coordinating their actions with other communities, using print media, and organizing into groups. Furthermore, he had learned that "tumultuous meetings have taken place, and flyers have been sent to Israelites of all the localities of Algeria in order to ensure that the rebellion is similar everywhere, and that this uniform character gives it more power. These communications have been fruitful. In the . . . communities of Tlemcen and Mostaganem, they have reignited the discord that we had extinguished through patience and persuasion."[93] It is unclear whether the Jews of Oran regarded themselves as a political "club," as did many organized groups of workers in Paris and Algeria during this period. But the evidence does suggest that they achieved a certain degree of coordination. In addition to distributing flyers, they published posters that appeared in synagogues throughout the province and published defamatory articles about the consistorial president in a local paper.[94] These strategies suggest that the political movement of indigenous Jews was not isolated from the political agitation that surged among the wider urban population at the time.

The petitioners also drew on the French political language of freedom of religion. The 1848 letter from Mostaganem included, for example, "These acts infringe upon our beliefs, our habits, our customs, and upon the free exercise of our religion." Thus, using the stated principles of liberalism, the Jews criticized the consistory for not respecting promised freedoms. Similarly, Mostaganem's Jews challenged the basis upon which consistorial officers were to be chosen in the consistory's own reformist language. They insisted that Sarfati's chosen rabbi "cannot exercise any influence upon our co-religionists" since "he merits neither respect nor consideration." In the wake of the aforementioned dispute over the displaced holy books, the petitioners made a point of adopting the voice of the civilizers, stating that Sarfati's actions were poorly conceived because they offended the community's "superstitious" members. They warned that "the consistory of Oran does not achieve results that one has the right to hope for from enlightened administrators" while the Mostaganem Jews directly challenged Sarfati on the same grounds: "all these facts that appear to be of little importance to you, Mr. Director, nevertheless have a great deal of influence over the spirit of our co-religionists. After all, what must they think of such brutal behavior from a man who should, on every possible occasion, provide an example of gentleness and moderation?"[95] In their letters to higher authorities, the Jews of Mostaganem and Oran used the rhetoric of the consistory and of the civilizing discourse more generally, in order to criticize the consistory. If the Jews were to be "attached to France," the petitioners insinuated France would have to find better local representatives.

"Among Almost All of Them, It Is Ignorance"

The liberal language of civilizing also provided the terms by which officials could dismiss the demands of the Jews of Oran and Mostaganem. Algerian-Jewish republican language made the consistorial administration uncomfortable, and they quickly dismissed the unrest as a primitive rebellion among people who did not fully understand the motives behind their own actions.[96] Despite the fact that consistorial correspondence was headed with the republican motto "liberty, equality, fraternity," the Ministry of War did not democratize the colonial consistories. Nor did the new political climate help local consistorial officers appreciate the substance of local Jews' complaints about their new community structures. When the members of the consistory described events to their superiors, they made it clear that in their estimation no Algerian Jew could fully understand the meaning of his own words. For example, in a note to the director of civil affairs, the consistory noted, "these words—*liberty, republic*—that have reverberated so strongly in French hearts recently, have also been heard by the Jewish population of Oran." The problem, in their mind was that this population does not "wish to understand the true meaning or importance [of these terms], and it has misinterpreted them."[97] The consistory consequently equated Algerian-Jewish protest with a rejection of authority in general "for [Algerian Jews], [republic] signifies the abolition of all existent laws, the ability of everyone to do what he pleases, or to not do that which does not please him, the absence of any brake and of any authority, that is to say, anarchy and license."[98] When the governor general ordered that posters be put up in synagogues in response to the unrest of May 1848, the language he used was similarly dismissive. As Michael Shurkin has noted, the posters themselves demonstrated the paradox of an administration inspired by liberalism but deeply convinced of its subjects' inability to appreciate or profit from it. Below the republican motto, the posters announced: "the authority of the consistory will be maintained intact. France does not intend to let either its laws or its functionaries be insulted by men who, held for a long time under a yoke from which it has freed them, misunderstand its benefits and mistake an unbridled license for a liberty which they do not comprehend."[99] Such notes provide a rare insight into the reality of mid-century French colonial republicanism, and the profound disconnect between rhetorical and material realities. As we have seen, at the height of official tolerance for freedom of expression in the first half of 1848, even favored colonial subjects slated for civilizing were regarded as incapable of participating in representative politics and were quickly denigrated for being insufficiently French and politically immature.

Like Arabs and Kabyles, Algerian Jews became the subject of colonial mythologies; in this case, the narrative simultaneously justified their preferred status and their exclusion from power. To this end, the notion of ignorance and contempt for civilization was particularly important. Algerian Jews' alleged ignorance was the official justification for the consistory's existence; the trope of ignorance also explained why these Jews rejected French efforts to enlighten them. As President Nahon explained to his superiors in the department of civil affairs, the Jewish revolt against the consistory is laid to two major factors: "Among some of the perpetrators, it is jealousy against those whom the consistory accorded its confidence; among almost all of them, it is ignorance."[100] Were the native Jews enlightened or civilized enough to know what was in their best interest, went Nahon's reasoning, their opposition would dissipate. As it was, their rejection of authority was nothing less than a rejection of civilization itself. Grand Rabbi Cahen insisted, "this anarchy, these threats, and this hostility [are] fomented by lies and greed, by jealousy and hatred for every civilizing institution."[101] The comment underscores how various actors used civilization to advance their competing claims to authority; Cahen argued that native Jews' fidelity to local (non-French) institutions was due to ignorance and "hatred" of civilization, while the objects of his fury justified that very fidelity through the Enlightenment-rooted French ideal of liberty.

Given the centrality of emancipation in France's colonial ideology toward Jews, it follows that reports that Algerian Jews "rejected civilization" were accompanied by reiterations of a Jewish mythology that both explained their behavior and offered hope for the civilizing mission. To ease the concerns of the military authority, officials such as Nahon assured the department of civil affairs that the consistory would continue the difficult but feasible task of enlightening. Furthermore, comparisons to the domestic French movement for Jewish regeneration served to collapse metropolitan and colonial histories, and were wielded as proof that the effort of civilizing Jews would work. Just as the origins of French Jews' purported degeneracy lay in the oppression of medieval Europe, the Algerian-Jewish failure to respond "correctly" to colonial institutions lay in its history under Islamic rule. "For eons crouched under Turkish despotism, brutalized by a government of oppression," Nahon argued, "the Israelite population of Mostaganem is still, it must be said, incapable of appreciating the advantages that they accrued as a result of the royal ordinance of November 9, 1845."[102]

Consistorial officials therefore linked Jew's ignorance and their rejection of the consistory's civilizing mission. As President Nahon grew frustrated with the unrest in Oran, he again blamed the degraded society from which the opposition came: "this population that we wanted to raise to the heights of our French co-religionists, requests today to squat in the mire (*fange*) of ignorance and superstition."[103] The usefulness of this formulation lay in the certainty of its conclusion. Reformers imagined that the inevitable march of history would eventually lead Algerian Jews to submit to consistorial tutelage, thereby becoming French. In the short run, however, their ignorance would have to be overcome by coercion. "Fortunately for it [the Jewish population], it is forced to accept . . . and submit to the process of regeneration."[104] It would be difficult to produce a clearer example of how the language of Jewish emancipation in France saturated the ideology of civilization and justified colonial power.

The metropolitan press was not unaware of the disturbances among Jews in Algeria, nor was it inured to the fact that the authorities' response seemed to challenge many accepted truths of republican colonial ideology. Parisian publicists also sought to attribute indigenous resistance to irrationality, lack of education, and superstition, thereby echoing the consistory's critiques. The *Archives Israélites*, for example, published a piece on Algerian Jews, reporting: "The Israelites of Oran, after seventeen years of contact with the French, have hardly made any progress in civilization." The explanation offered was that the population in question was ignorant and superstitious: "in the Israelite community of this city, we have been assured, they still do not know how to read or write in French. It is difficult to find several who can mangle a couple of words. To change this state of things, we will need many more years, and above all good schools, and they still are lacking. Additionally, ignorance and fanaticism continue to reign supreme. It is in the interest of morality that a quick and effective remedy be brought to this terrible situation."[105] The report argued further that Algeria's Jews were still "medieval" and required medieval methods of enlightenment: "In the Middle Ages, it was the Catholic clergy that spread instruction. The Israelites of Algeria are still in the Middle Ages. We therefore must give them good rabbis and good schools."[106] Like the official correspondence, then, the press linked a resistance to coercive policies to a resistor's ignorance and fanaticism. Failure to accept or even welcome outside dominance of their institutions, it seems, could only be indicative of irrationality. Such commentators naturally concluded that Algerian Jews would only arrive at modernity—and attachment to France in the colonial arena—through force.

While the consistories hastened to insist on the feasibility of their mission in their notes to the local civil authorities, these authorities did not need much convincing that the consistories should continue in their task of civilizing. Indeed, the civil authorities were generally anxious to reestablish order in the colony, and saw the consistories as a tool in this effort. In response to the incidents in Mostaganem, the director of civil affairs of the province told the local authorities to use "moderate firmness" to assure respect for the deputies of the consistory and to continue their civilizing task. As for the opposition leaders, the civil authorities ordered the commissioner to "repress severely the spirit of insubordination that has possessed several agitators." The same letter asked the local authorities to "please continue, through the combined effort of persuasion and force, to enlighten (éclairer) the Israelites."[107] As noted above, enlightenment was by no means coterminous with rights of representation.

Algerian-Jewish resistance to French institutions and laws did not end with the brutal repression of Parisian workers in June of 1848 that ended the Republic's phase of radical free expression.[108] Indeed, native Jewish resistance to French colonial institutions outlived the Second Republic's fall in 1852, remaining a central component of the relationship between the French authorities and the local Jewish community throughout the years of the Second Empire. Resistance to the consistory's efforts, often justified with terms such as progress and enlightenment, continued even after local Jews succeeded in constituting the majority of consistorial members.

The French republican language of emancipation, a concept associated with civilization in the colonial context, could also function as an exclusionary or even repressive ideology. The previous chapter suggested that by isolating elements of the Algerian population for their civilizing campaign, the French advanced the wider project of colonial consolidation. The incidents described here suggest another dimension to this dynamic; when it came to the reform of Algeria's Jews, the discourse of civilizing also housed an effective logic of exclusion or even repression. Indeed, terms such as "regeneration" and "enlightenment," like the term "civilizing" (all of which had historic associations with French republican discourse and the notions of emancipation and freedom), were deployed in the colonial context to justify the exercise of force against even those Jewish subjects whom the French had decided to place on the path of civilization. The same Jewish subjects, conversely, quickly justified their resistance in the same flexible, polyvalent lexicon.

Parisian Parallels

The civilizing mission in Algeria, as part of a colonial venture, differed significantly from reform efforts in France, but this should not veil its ideological kinship to the French movement for Jewish regeneration. If the Ministry of War made civilizing the Algerian Jews an element of colonial strategy, this strategy was based on the model of the Jewish consistory system in France.[109] Interesting similarities also marked French and Jewish responses to consistorial policies during the events surrounding 1848. The existence of these parallels does not imply that reform in France was the same as colonial civilizing. It does suggest, however, that Oran's Jews felt a reasonable level of security and confidence in their privileged position within the colonial context. Notably, they rejected consistorial authority in ways similar to Jewish citizens of France did in their own struggles with the consistory in Paris.[110] Before concluding, let us turn to a single Parisian episode of Jewish activism, using it to understand the wider imperial context of the civilizing mission towards Jews in Algeria. As we shall see, the Enlightenment-derived ideology of civilizing justified both the exercise of state power and the language of resistance in multiple locales in France's mid-century empire.

Over the first half of the nineteenth century, Jews had steadily emigrated from Alsace in northeastern France to other parts of the country. Paris, like Oran, experienced Jewish immigration that both augmented and diversified its community in the years before the July Monarchy passed legislation (in 1844) to increase official oversight and control of Jewish religious practice in France. As in Oran, Parisian consistorial efforts to control the Jewish community had angered many of its members. Particularly irksome for many poor Jews of the capital were the tax on kosher meat, attempts to repress unauthorized prayer meetings, and the institution of controls on the practice of circumcision.[111] Many religious Jews responded critically to the 1844 ordinance, often expressing their criticism in the journal *l'Univers Israélite*. Following the revolutionary events of February 1848, a group of working-class religious Jews also organized along the same model as many of their non-Jewish neighbors, forming a republican political club through which they could express their grievances.

The Club Démocratique des Fidèles was led by a merchant named Abraham ben Baruch Créhange, who for years had been a vocal opponent of various consistorial abuses. By early 1848, his outspoken opposition to the consistory had earned him some prestige. The organization's meeting notes mention that his club attracted more than 1,000 members to its first gatherings. Official circles, too, were paying heed; the club's demands for a democratic Jewish community were mentioned not only in the *Univers Israélite* but also in correspondence between the Ministry of Religions and the central consistory.[112] Much like the Jews of Oran, the members of the Club Démocratique vigorously defended existing community structures with republican language of democracy and free expression.[113] For example, the club's leader insisted that the prophets Moses and Samuel were both republicans, and that such a form of government was the only one truly blessed by God.[114] Like their counterparts in Oran, for club members in Paris the manner of choosing consistorial officers was a pressing issue—Créhange complained of elitism in the existing system and argued that voting notables should not be determined purely on a basis of wealth. Finally, the colonial and metropolitan groups focused their political activities on the democratization of the Jewish community and the defense of religious orthodoxy. At the beginning of April 1848, the club decided to address its complaints about the consistory to higher authorities.[115]

Thus, it came to pass that on April 9, 1848, the same month the Jews of Oran sent their petition to the French authorities in Algeria, the Club Démocratique sent a petition "to the citizen members of the Provisional Government of the French Republic." The letter summarized the provisions of the May 1844 reform decree that dealt with the "notability"—those permitted to vote for consistorial officers. It pointed out particularly that the list of notables eligible to vote was so exclusive that in 1847, only 111 people were allowed to vote for members of the Parisian consistory. "A consistory named like this," declared the petition, "is not the expression of the mass of Israelites of the [department] because it is precisely this mass that is not permitted to vote."[116] The Parisian petition, much like the petition of Oran, called for the dissolution of the local consistory and its reconstitution by universal male suffrage.

As in Oran, the movement behind these complaints won some gains. The consistories in France were briefly and partially democratized. In the longer term, however, official reaction to the June 1848 workers' rebellion led to increased restrictions on suffrage. Ultimately, neither in Paris nor Oran did consistories become truly representative organizations. They were, however, altered by the political actions on the part of those they were officially charged with reforming. In the two cases, French subjects (in Algeria) and French citizens (in France)—both of which had been denied representation in official Jewish organizations due to their social class or colonized status—responded in parallel fashion to comparable institutions. This similarity was not lost on observers. In a report on the uprising in Algeria published in *Archives Israélites*, the writer jokingly commented that as of yet, there was no report of a Club des Fidèles being formed in Oran.[117]

As noted above, the Algerian civilizing mission was not a shadow of reform efforts in France. French metropolitan models notwithstanding, Jewish reformers in Algeria targeted colonial subjects whose assimilation to France was viewed as important for colonial domination. As such, the Jewish civilizing mission in Algeria can just as usefully (and with a similar degree of caution) be compared to the civilizing mission aimed at the subjects of French West Africa in later decades. Like consistorial officers in Algeria, officers under the Third Republic who interpreted and justified their colonial presence via the civilizing mission often expressed an Enlightenment-rooted faith in progress and human perfectibility. And while the civilizing mission may have had a significant influence on French policy in West Africa, it did not lead to citizenship rights for the vast majority of colonial subjects.[118] In contrast, the effort spearheaded by men such as Altaras and Cohen (also indebted to Enlightenment ideas of progress and human regeneration) *did* lead to the naturalization of Algerian Jews in 1870, a fact attributable in part to Jews' presence in France and the revolutionary-republican legacy of Jewish emancipation.[119]

Oranais Jews' confidence and eventual success in changing the face of civilizing institutions brings into relief the most important way Jews and Judaism influenced French colonialism. French or Algerian Jews were not central actors, but French discussions of emancipation and citizenship had been (at least partially) forged in struggles over Jewish civil equality in the late eighteenth century. Much like a preexisting Orientalist intellectual and artistic tradition helped form attitudes and policies toward Muslims, the revolutionary past continued to resonate in the debates over colonial policy toward Jews in colonial Algeria.[120] Violent Jewish responses to the consistories did not seriously derail efforts to grant Algerian Jews full citizenship. This stands in startling contrast to other subsections of the Algerian population, none of which would be granted citizenship en masse. Colonial administrators, though at first inclined to dismiss Algerian-Jewish demands as expressions of ignorance, later felt obligated to accept and implement a portion of them. Due in part to a specific French republican tradition in which "The Jews" figured prominently, Jews could influence the course of reform in Algeria; the parallels between Parisian and Algerian-Jewish responses further highlights the contrast between the treatment of Jewish and Muslim subjects. In both Paris and Oran, men drew on Enlightenment ideals both to forge exclusionary mythologies and to justify resistance to them.

Conclusion

The events of 1848 in Oran suggest that the received history of the Algerian-Jewish encounter with French colonialism needs dramatic revision. Algerian Jews were not passive recipients of the French civilizing mission, and the meaning of civilizing these Jews offered by French reformers and officials cannot be taken at face value. Many Jews in Algeria at the time of the conquest were highly ambivalent about French colonial institutions.[121] Often, Algerian Jews regarded the consistory not as an emancipatory institution but as an intrusive and impious force that usurped power in their communities. In addition to their clearly expressed sense of religious impropriety, the Jews of Oran often articulated their protest in republican terms. Their demands to be rid of consistorial control appealed to the rhetoric of the republic, to their right to vote for their leaders, to progress, and to guarantees of religious freedom.

Blending a French republican political language with graveside oaths and rabbinical support, Jewish protests therefore point to the complex encounters engendered by colonialism in Algeria. In this sense, the story of 1848 makes problematic not only older scholarship hailing the emancipatory effort of the consistories, but also adds a layer of complexity to later scholars' classification of the consistory as "Jewish colonialism." The consistories were not only ingrained in the larger (not specifically Jewish) French colonial structure, they were deeply influenced by their charges. Furthermore, local reactions against them did not always target French personnel, such as Cahen, but also Moroccan rabbis, such as Sarfati, whom the consistory invested with power. Further illustrating the interconnectedness of French and Algerian histories—and the dynamism of Algerian-Jewish modes of rebellion—are the parallels between events in Oran and Paris.

The civilizing ideology framed a claim to authority and a campaign to control and dominate in the colonial arena but did not necessarily succeed in its stated goal. Moreover, civilizing also proved to be a pliable discourse quickly adopted and transformed by Algerian Jews hoping to resist certain colonial policies. Algerian Jews, like French Jews, were represented as degraded and immoral because of their history of persecution. Colonial officers thus understood indigenous resistance to an emancipating and enlightening France as necessarily stemming from Jews' extreme state of ignorance. Even as Algerian Jews adopted French themes and discourse, their protests were still interpreted as the anarchic passions of uncivilized and fanatic men. The truly enlightened, implied consistorial officers, would welcome the institutions of colonialism. At the same time, resistance to the consistory of Oran not only adopted post-Enlightenment themes of civilization, liberty, and republicanism, but it succeeded in dramatically remaking the institution. By the end of 1848, a number of local Algerian Jews sat on the consistory, many of whom the French officials had initially character- ized as ignorant members of the opposition. Certain reforms such as the closing of private synagogues were temporarily abandoned by the French while at the same time favored French officials were pushed out of power. Due to their own activism and appropriation of the consistory's own prin- ciples, Algerian Jews were destined to help shape France's Jewish civilizing institution in Oran.

3

Synagogues, Surveillance, and Civilization

In March 1848, Emmanuel Nahon of Oran's consistory requested financing from the director of civil affairs to support the construction of a "large and unique" synagogue that could unite the entirety of Oran's Jews. Nahon framed his request as an urgent response to the social unrest that had recently gripped Oran. The owners of the city's private synagogues, he explained, were "convinced that the articles of the ordinance of November 9, 1845 . . . cannot be applied to them due to recent events."[1] Currently, "a spirit of revolt has surged amongst them" and the consistory was doing its best to suppress it. At the same time, explained Nahon, these efforts could not be effective until a large communal building was built that would justify closing all the other synagogues of Oran. The director to whom Nahon addressed his request readily agreed, and, in turn, made a formal request of the governor general of Algeria to build a large synagogue that could "replace the private synagogues whose existence and use for private profit are entirely contrary to the spirit and letter of the ordinance of November 9, 1845."[2] Though the community would only receive the funds to construct the synagogue years later, this incident marked the beginning of a long struggle over control of Jewish social and religious life in the Province of Oran.

The private synagogue, which was a central feature of Algerian-Jewish life during the period under discussion, garnered the particular interest of French reformers in Algeria. These synagogues provided centers of community, schools, charitable foundations, and rabbinical councils that frustrated centralizing efforts. Meanwhile, members of the same Algerian elite who owned these synagogues entered into the consistory. These men could then help determine which local practices and institutions would be supported or suppressed. In some cases, this involved protecting their synagogues or those of their allies. In other cases, the Moroccan ethnic loyalty of consistorial members took precedence over the colonial administration's goals. Therefore, efforts to submit these (and other) Algerian-Jewish religious spaces to surveillance had the unintended consequence of strengthening, rather than weakening, local elites. Once again, the civilizing ideology proved malleable as both local and French actors justified their actions as efforts to advance progress, emancipation, or civilization. The social and religious landscape of colonial Oran ended up making a significant mark on the goals and activities of the consistory; as the consistory struggled to penetrate and monitor Algerian-Jewish domestic and religious space, local Algerian Jews in turn penetrated and helped shape the direction of these civilizing institutions.

Nahon's request to the director of civil affairs also marked an early episode in a wider campaign to monitor other Algerian-Jewish interiors, not only synagogues, but homes and schools as well. Strikingly, this campaign was interlaced with a discourse of health and hygiene. As others have noted, French discussions of disease and hygiene developed in interesting ways during the decades following the initial conquest. In the metropole, health professionals focused increasingly on private dwellings and morality after the 1832 cholera epidemic.[3] In Algeria during the same period, the military medical corps helped construct the taxonomy of races upon which the logic of colonial domination rested.[4] It follows that the conquest of contagions and disease reinforced the ideology of civilization throughout the colonial period.[5]

Of course, medicine in early colonial Algeria was first and foremost a military effort designed to limit the devastating toll disease took on occupying troops—not help the local populace. Muslims' experience of French medical genius has been described as "an insignificant fringe of a crushing military action."[6] Yet Algerian Jews, as privileged colonial subjects in mid-nineteenth century Algeria, found that in important ways, their bodies, homes, schools, and synagogues mattered. A special concern for hygiene echoed through discussions of Jewish schools in Algeria; administrators often justified interventions in religious schools with the imperative to safeguard children's health. This recalls Michel Foucault's observation that it was the body and private life of the bourgeois, rather than that of the proletariat, that first became the locus of discourses of sexuality during the articulation of modern power/knowledge in the eighteenth and nineteenth centuries.[7] While most Algerian Jews were far from bourgeois, they were part of a relatively privileged urban society over which French law claimed increasing jurisdiction. The effort to civilize Algerian Jews involved integrating their educational, spiritual, and domestic lives into a regime of increased monitoring that was less invested in their Muslim neighbors.

Civilizing Domestic Interiors

The Algerian home preoccupied French-Jewish reformers. In the case of Algeria, the explosion of interest in the Muslim family, polygamy, and the place of the woman rendered Jewish domestic spaces a sort of battleground of representations. As Julia Clancy-Smith has argued, French scientific and popular descriptions of Muslim gender roles and marital behaviors fed into French arguments about Arab suitability for French citizenship during the nineteenth century. The existence of prostitution, polygamy, and divorce among Algerian Muslims not only supposedly distinguished them from the French, but many French observers used them as indices of Muslim intellectual, cultural, and moral degeneracy.[8] In addition to taking an interest in women and the structure of Algerian-Jewish families, which we shall explore in Chapter 5, Jewish reformers in Algeria, as in France, became particularly concerned about Jewish domestic and private space.

The famous 1842 report of Jacques-Isaac Altaras, discussed in previous sections, offers an example of this focus. Altaras noted that the "interior of the Jewish family remains expansive." Their homes, he insisted, feature French furniture, journals, and other signs of the "penetration" of "our society." Altaras predicted that the "domestic reform" of Algerian Jews was nearly "complete." He cheerfully noted how Algerian Jews were abandoning the "indigenous costume" and learning French to "instruct themselves in the customs, laws, and overall organization of this France that has torn from them the yoke of slavery and to which they owe love, devotion, and active service."[9] Altaras's rosy prognosis of Algerian Jews' susceptibility to French assimilatory efforts noted how the homes and bodies of Algerian Jews were assimilating; they were open, available, and visible for inspection.

Joseph Cohen (who accompanied Altaras on his trip to Algeria) also assured his readers that Algerian-Jewish homes and their women were already productively exposed. In an 1843 article, he celebrated unveiled Algerian-Jewish women, noting that their status was markedly superior to that of their Muslim counterparts. Cohen implied that women's physical exposure indicated the wider Jewish community's readiness to be fully civilized, and suggested that the Muslim woman's sequestration and unavailability served as a metaphor for how Muslims more generally resisted the French conquest: "Our contact has troubled their peaceful domestic existence. Our indiscreet eye is often plunged into the closed houses where the Arab woman could once unveil without fearing foreign gazes. Our modern homes, which dominate the low houses of the indigenous, have thrown families into [a state of] fear and cautiousness."[10] Cohen did not criticize the investigative, scientific aspect of the French colonial project. His language, nevertheless, laced the unquestioned obligation to monitor domestic space with terms that suggest sexual violation. In this, he was not unique. The mid-century French general and scholar Eugène Daumas, author of the study *La Femme Arabe*, insisted similarly that France must "tear off the veil that still covers the morals, customs, and beliefs" of Arab society before its pathologies could be cured.[11]

For Cohen, violent metaphors regarding Muslim women and their homes usefully highlighted, by contrast, the open and accepting Jewish home. He noted, "The interior of the Israelite family is more expansive and open than the domestic interior of the Muslim." Indeed, nothing "besides the laws of modesty and the demands of virtue prevent Jewish women from developing more or less intimate relations (*connaissances*) with the French."[12] Lazare Cahen, the French grand rabbi of Oran introduced in the previous chapter, similarly reported on Jewish homes and their morality. In an 1850 report, he noted that Jewish women "are admitted to the table," and that the Jewish woman "is permitted to make herself visible to the stranger and to speak with him."[13] These comments echo non-Jewish liberals who also used exposure, surveillance, and domestic policing as a mark of contrast between civilized and Islamic society. Gustave de Beaumont, as mentioned in the first chapter, argued that France's "developed and effective policing which penetrates everything, even domestic space," was a primary reason why Muslims were fleeing French-held cities in Algeria.[14] If the demands of domination required force to penetrate Muslim homes, the Jewish interior represented an inviting contrast. It would not have to be taken by force but was, instead, acquiescent and inviting.

Unsympathetic portrayals of Algerian Jews also located their immorality within the home. In an 1840 report published in the reformist journal *Archives Israélites*, a Jewish army doctor by the name of Goldscheider made much of the "disorder" that reigns in the Algerian-Jewish home.[15] The article invited the reader to "penetrate their quarters," where one is besieged by "miasma" and "uncleanness" and sees the Jews' "sicknesses" that "they owe to the extreme negligence of their domestic needs." Furthermore, asserted the article, French "stables are cleaner" than their synagogues, while by "visiting the interior of their residences," the observer bears witness to "disorder," "neglect," and "filth." They do not effectively care for the children who are permitted to play on the floor that "they have helped soil." Hygiene and disease helped trace the border between Jewish behaviors and French civilization. Of course, Goldscheider, like Thomas-Robert Bugeaud and other military men, also noted Jewish "immorality" in public spheres such as trade. But themes of the home and body clearly played an important role in transcripts by advocates of Algerian-Jewish civilizing and its legal end-point, naturalization. As Samuel Cahen, who published Goldscheider's report in his journal *Archives Israélites*, insisted in the same issue, with a "good consistorial administration, we should be able to civilize the Jews of Algeria."[16]

The Struggle with Private Synagogues

Like the home and the family, French observers and policy makers associated private synagogues with separateness, immoral practices, and even indecency. As mentioned in the previous chapter, consistorial authorities expressed the view in the 1840s that the privately held synagogues of Algeria were purely commercial enterprises that compromised the dignity of religious practice. In fact, the example of Jacob Lasry's synagogue (discussed in Chapter 2) suggests that private synagogues provided support for those crafting or maintaining independent or centrifugal religious and social forms.

At the same time, cliques formed around different synagogues and schools that often had representatives in the consistories. Even synagogue owners joined consistories, while consistorial delegates in smaller towns often owed allegiance to one local group or another. In other words, despite original plans to close all private synagogues, consistorial authority was increasingly colored by Algeria's highly textured and fractured Jewish communal landscape. The consistory continued to measure its success through the surveillance and control of religious space, but local Jews ultimately forced the consistory to integrate private local religious institutions into its operations.

So why did the French grand rabbi of Oran and the city's civil officials attach such importance to houses of prayer? Most contemporary readers familiar with Jewish religious practice might assume that synagogues do not necessarily represent the most important institutions in observant Jewish life.[17] In the context of colonial Algeria, however, synagogues were situated at the crux of a number of contesting power dynamics. They offered a public sphere in which local Jews formed opinions, met to discuss issues, and planned appropriate actions to take in response to the consistory or rival groups.[18] They were urban real estate investments from which local, elite Jews profited and through which they established their social influence. They employed Algerian rabbis who may or may not have cooperated with the new colonial consistories in their efforts to monitor and control religious practice. They often offered economic competition to consistorial synagogues, attracting local Jews who subsequently did not help defray consistorial expenses. Of course, even consistorial synagogues were not beyond conflict, as debates there raged regarding which rabbis or clans held sway. In these respects and others, the synagogues of colonial Oran represented another arena in which imperial policy provoked or sustained local rivalries, rivalries that were in turn shaped by (or expressed through) the civilizing ideology.

Moroccan Jewish immigration provided another complication in the effort of consistorial officers to penetrate and regulate synagogues. The diversification of Oran's Jewish population led to conflicts—notably, when the consistory appointed "foreign" (that is, Moroccan) rabbis or delegates who subsequently attempted to impose their own customs and rules in the synagogues. The resulting intra-communal conflict was central to the way in which Algerian Jews responded to the consistory, and consistently helped shape opposition to it. To this end, conflicts engendered by French colonialism in Algeria's cities often took the form of conflicts between groups of North African Jews, as opposed to between local Jews and French Jews. Furthermore, by appointing delegates from rival groups, consistorial efforts to penetrate and govern local communities produced the sorts of conflict that French administrators would interpret (and therefore dismiss) as petty divisions or "intrigues." To explore these points, we turn to a series of narratives that illuminate how colonial conflicts unfolded in religious space.

One of the earliest examples of how the efforts of French authorities inadvertently encouraged internecine Jewish conflicts occurred shortly after the provincial consistory was installed in Oran. Among the delegates appointed for Jewish communities in outlying towns, Cahen and Nahon chose the Moroccan rabbi Salomon Sarfati in Mostaganem. According to Cahen, Sarfati was particularly "intelligent" and capable of "pushing the community on the path of progress."[19] Sarfati's appointment may have also reflected Moroccan communal biases of Nahon and Sénanès. On October 14, 1848, a local merchant named Shimon Cohen-Solal planned to present his newborn child to the community. The assembled group would then bless the new member, and its name would be made public. Upon being informed that this ritual would take place, Sarfati ordered Rabbi Moses Abou, a representative of the charitable committee and delegate in charge of ordering the services, to prevent Cohen-Solal from mounting the *bima* (the platform in the synagogue from which the Torah is read). Members of the local community protested, explaining that what Mr. Cohen-Solal intended to perform had been an accepted custom in Mostaganem for years. According to witnesses, Sarfati responded, "I alone am chief here, and no one [else] can give orders. You are all women and dogs."[20] For this crime and others, including removing the locally revered rabbi Mordechai Obadia from his functions and installing a crony, Aaron Sidon, Jews petitioned the consistory and secular authorities to have Sarfati removed. The petitioners demanded in addition that local Jews have the power to elect a leader. While it is impossible to affirm the veracity of the accusations these petitioners launched, the event suggests that the consistory's appointment of an "enlightened" Moroccan

Jew to govern a synagogue composed largely of local Jews of Mostaganem did little to ease whatever communal tensions may have previously existed. It also suggests that resistance to consistorial attempts to control private synagogues could indelibly alter the colonial landscape; in this case, the petitioners' appeals were at least partially met, as Sarfati (temporarily) stepped down from his post.

The consistory's Moroccan delegates occasionally expressed communal loyalties that extended beyond the walls of the synagogue. One episode in the town of Sidi-Bel-Abbes indicates the extent to which delegates could act according to family or clan loyalties rather than honor those of the consistorial or even military authorities. In early 1853, the French forces in Sidi-Bel-Abbes arrested a Moroccan Jew from Tetuan for several thefts. The Jew in question had been employed by the French military, but was apparently living among Kabyle tribesmen in Morocco. Officers of the local bureau arabe were leading him and several of his Muslim accomplices through the town of Sidi-el-Abbes when the suspect saw other Moroccan Jews and called out for help. Upon hearing his calls, the locals approached the officers and attempted to liberate their fellow. A brawl ensued. The officers of the bureau responded by arresting some of the locals—including a second Moroccan Jew, named Jacob Sénanès—and thereby quieted what they later described as a "small riot."[21] Upon learning of the event, the town's consistorial representatives, themselves of Moroccan origin, contacted their counterparts in Oran about the case, complaining that it was standard procedure for the local authority to handle Jewish suspects, not military authorities such as the bureaux arabes.[22] The members of the consistory of Oran subsequently wrote to the general of the province, asking that the military relinquish Sénanès to the local command of Sidi-Bel-Abbes.

The commander of the military's Oran division dismissed the request. He informed the president of the consistory in Oran that his "co-religionists of Sidi-bel-Abbes gave you false information" about standard procedure, and that Sénanès had been imprisoned by order of the commander of the subdivision. In a revealing piece of advice, the officer informed the president that "delegates of the consistory, as well as the consistory itself, too often occupy themselves with business that is not within their authority, in a word, temporal affairs as opposed to spiritual ones." Furthermore, the officer confided, "they believe themselves to be civil authorities, and consistently cause problems for us in their relations with indigenous people." In a comment suggesting that the local consistory had come to reflect the influence of one group of local Jews, the military commander informed the Oran consistory that its representatives in Sidi-Bel-Abbes "present themselves falsely as the protectors of Jews from Morocco, so the latter [Moroccan Jews] do not believe themselves to be under our authority." He ominously warned their overseers that "if, in the future they overstep [again] . . . they will be forced to recognize our authority."[23] Local forces clearly had a way of shaping the consistory; the consistory's choices of officers and delegates in the province of Oran influenced their efforts to penetrate and control Jewish life in the colonial context.

In the first half of the 1850s, the issue of private synagogues took on a renewed importance, as they raised questions about colonized subjects' rights to administer and control urban property. In 1853, the prefect of Oran, in cooperation with certain consistorial officers, produced a report concluding that it was of the utmost importance that the consistory control local synagogues. The decree establishing the consistories in Algeria, the prefect reasoned, assumed that "the indigenous Jewish population was not sufficiently advanced with regard to civilization to enjoy rights accorded to Jews of France."[24] Therefore, the consistory needed authority to shut or control unofficial synagogues regardless of whether or not they constituted private property. Referring back to an earlier report that held that seventeen synagogues existed in the city of Oran, the prefect decided that "synagogue" really meant "place of prayer" for there was only one official synagogue. The remaining institutions, "improperly called synagogues" should therefore be considered annexes of the central institution and hence subject to "the constant surveillance and administration of the grand rabbi and the consistory." The prefect explained that without constant surveillance, it would be impossible to ensure that local rabbis conform to the law of 1844 that forbade "any instruction or explanation of the law that does not conform to the responses of the general assembly of Israelites converted into doctrinal decisions by the Grand Sanhedrin." The necessity of this surveillance was all the more important, he emphasized, given that "the indigenous [Jews] are less advanced [than French Jews] regarding education, and are thus more susceptible to fanaticism."[25]

The lack of adequate surveillance, read the report, had led to "serious abuses" that demanded rethinking the urban landscape of religious institutions. Fretted the prefect: "Order and decency are lacking in these private establishments," and "even fights (rixes) are not rare."[26] The prefect insisted further, "it is important that the authorities intervene to make [these abuses] disappear." The report concluded that to simultaneously provide adequate space for all of Oran's Jews and eliminate the problem of private synagogues, the consistory would have to build a large structure that could house the entirety of the city's Jews. With a single, communal synagogue meeting the needs of the entire Jewish community of Oran, the logic went, private synagogues could be closed, and surveillance, order, and decency assured. Such a synagogue would not be established until 1918. Nevertheless, the civil authorities used the notion of civilization to justify policies

FIGURE 3.1. Consistorial officials faced considerable obstacles in their campaign for the construction of large, open synagogues that they hoped would replace smaller, private houses of worship. The main synagogue of Oran, pictured here, was not inaugurated until 1918. From the personal collection of Stephanie Comfort.

intended to compromise legal protections for private property, to increase surveillance of interior spaces, to control religious practices, and to reduce Algerian Jews' ability to sustain or reshape their public sphere.

The Consistory, the Army, and Synagogues in Tlemcen

Tlemcen, a town about 68 miles to the west of Oran, near the Moroccan border, presents an interesting case of how synagogues could serve as loci for a number of competing dynamics. About 2,000 Jews lived in Tlemcen at the time, many of whom had roots in Tetuan and possibly other cities of Morocco. In 1852, Cahen wrote to the prefect to request help in closing down the town's several private synagogues because, in his view, "the Jewish community of Tlemcen has a sufficient number of public synagogues to hold all the faithful inhabitants of this city."[27] Furthermore, Cahen signaled, there was a synagogue belonging to an individual "that has served for some time as a meeting place for those Jews who do not want to contribute to the expenses of the community and who are an eternal source of disorder and anarchy." The rabbi then requested that the prefect give the orders that would close the El Medioni synagogue, thereby ending the "secession" within the Jewish population. Cahen urged further that, in keeping with the decree of November 9, 1845, the civil authority should order "no religious assembly be permitted outside of the public synagogue." Later that month, the prefect informed the consistory that he had given the necessary orders to close the El Medioni synagogue and repress the "disorders which some of your co-religionists of this city are guilty of provoking."[28] In this instance, it would seem, the synagogue was seen as important terrain in the consistory's effort to control the Jewish population of Tlemcen, and the prefecture of Oran was quick to recognize the importance of the mission Cahen proposed.

The contrasting story of Abraham Djian's synagogue involved an exchange that suggests the extent to which consistorial efforts to control private space inflamed disputes that already existed in Algerian-Jewish society. After the shuttering of the El Medioni synagogue, local delegates in Tlemcen provided the consistory in Oran with a list of complaints about a group of local Jews. According to their letter, a different synagogue, this one belonging to Djian, served as the meeting place for a group of dissidents led by Moshe Bliah and Saïd Sigsig. After being notified, the prefect asked the civil authorities in Tlemcen to close Djian's synagogue, in which "serious disorders" occurred "daily." Upon reviewing the list of complaints and conducting an investigation, the commissioner in Tlemcen realized that local consistorial delegates had exaggerated the crimes, perhaps for personal reasons.

According to the Tlemcen's civil commissioner, the disorders mentioned in the prefect's letter had occurred *before* he had closed El Medioni. The only recent "crime" was that Jacob Kalfon, a consistorial delegate, had brought a "foreign" rabbi by the name of Moshe Koubi to Djian's synagogue in Tlemcen. The rabbi had come in order to collect money, presumably for charity or to support a school. When the rabbi made his plea, a number of attendees who rejected Kalfon's sponsorship of the charitable request walked out of the synagogue in protest. Djian's synagogue, the civil commissioner clarified, had been open for years, and though it served as a meeting place for dissident Jews, such as Bliah and Sigsig, no disorders had been produced there. The only real complaint that the delegates of the consistory in Tlemcen could fairly make against the dissident group was that they did not want to give contributions to Kalfon's rabbi, not in itself a punishable offense. Taking "special action against the synagogue of Mr. Abraham Djian," the commissioner advised, would be to "make [French] authority into an instrument of persecution, satisfying individual hatreds and reducing a section of the Jewish population to hopelessness."[29] The commissioner affirmed that he did not sympathize with the dissidents, but they were guilty of nothing serious, and nothing more than private rivalries lay at the root of the complaints. In the absence of an order from superior administrative authorities, the commissioner insisted he had no justification to close Djian's synagogue. The absence of a response from the consistory or the prefect regarding the

Djian affair would lead us to assume that Abraham Djian and the faithful who prayed in his synagogue were granted a reprieve.

The affairs of the El Medioni and Djian synagogues of Tlemcen provide two lenses through which one may view the multipolar power contests that the civilizing mission in Oran uncovered and provoked. As for the El Medioni synagogue, the nature of the disturbances that warranted its closing is unclear. Members may have been fighting or engaging in other raucous behavior. They may have been engaging in forms of prayer regarded as indecent by outside observers. Perhaps the civil authorities closed the synagogue for offensive behavior performed by members outside the synagogue itself; members of one synagogue in Oran were sanctioned by the consistory (and condemned to the police) for going through the Jewish quarter at night, yelling and hitting doors with a baton in an effort to call the faithful to prayer.[30] In other instances, Jews condemned their fellows for public drunkenness. In any event, the civil authorities of Tlemcen, in cooperation with the consistory in Oran and its local delegates, found reason to close a privately owned house of prayer that presented alternative religious spaces for Jews not wishing to submit to Cahen's orders.

While the Djian synagogue survived, the debate surrounding it offers another view of the fraught attempt to legislate the civilizing mission upon Algeria's Jews. Rabbi Cahen and the prefect were French officials whose education, institutional support, and lines of loyalty were deeply rooted in metropolitan France. The consistory, however, consisted of a number of local and Moroccan elements whose own loyalties, sensibilities, and even family ties were not subsumed by their consistorial positions and duties. The frictions that arose from the encounter between these realities were typical of the early 1850s, when consistorial officials were feverishly compiling lists of local notables who would be entitled to make decisions for their communities.[31] It was from these lists of local notables that local delegates to the consistory were selected; unsurprisingly, many did not command the unanimous support of the communities they were to represent. Thus, for example, while Jacob Kalfon may have had local ties in Tlemcen, and while his selection as delegate for the consistory may have seemed natural to French officials, his duties as consistorial delegate (collecting money for charity, synagogue upkeep, supporting schools, and official rabbis' salaries) may have enflamed preexisting rifts—or created new ones—within Tlemcen's Jewish community.[32] To put this another way, the French project of civilizing Algerian Jews was a colonial strategy that though devised in France, was deeply hued by the actions and reactions of those it was designed to transform.

Another drama worthy of note unfolding in the arena of Tlemcen's private synagogues involved the military authorities. This case also involved questions of private property and the ability of Algerian Jews to shape civilizing institutions. A decade before the consistory asked the prefect to close the El Medioni synagogue, the French military under the command of General Bedeau had occupied Tlemcen. When the French army marched into the desolated town, it found that Abd al-Qader had taken its largely Moroccan Jewish community with him when he evacuated.[33] Thereafter, the military took over the entire stock of buildings that had belonged to the town's inhabitants, a prerogative the French army used when cities were taken "by force of arms."[34] The French designated one of the town's synagogues to holding women and children seized by French soldiers in the war. Later, military engineers undertook renovations of the building, turning it into a Catholic church, presumably for military personnel. In April 1852, Shemtov Bliah (perhaps a relative of Moshe Bliah, mentioned above), one of the town's newly selected consistorial delegates, took it upon himself to retrieve possession of the building for the use of local Jews. To this end, he wrote directly to Prince Louis Napoleon III, at the time president of the short-lived Second Republic.[35] Samuel Karsenty, a local rabbi, also signed Bliah's request to have "the largest and most beautiful of [the Jews'] synagogues" returned to them."[36] Bliah noted that the Jewish community of Tlemcen had yet to receive the same financial help the Muslim and Christian communities were receiving, and asked that Napoleon III order the return of the building or a suitable indemnity. Despite Bliah's status as delegate, he did not secure the consistory's approval for the request.

The members of the Oran consistory were horrified. Upon learning of this infraction (and perhaps others), they denounced Bliah's actions and removed him from their list of local delegates. In June 1852, Rabbi Cahen and the consistory wrote to the prefect to inform him that Shemtov Bliah had "abused the functions" with which he was entrusted.[37] Furthermore, Cahen cautioned, Bliah "and his party are a constant source of troubles in the Jewish community of Tlemcen." He then invited the prefect to recognize the new list of delegates and use whatever means at his disposal "against these agitators." In other words, against the wishes of officers in Oran, elements of the local population that had been drafted into the consistory attempted to acquire a synagogue for their community's use. Obeying the consistorial request, the prefect ignored the request and asked local officials in Tlemcen to repress the "disorders."[38] Local consistorial delegates, it would seem, could act according to their personal convictions even if these did not conform to their superiors' plans or desires.

The affair of Tlemcen's synagogue-turned-church also shows how the civilizing ideology was used to establish the racial/religious hierarchy in colonial Algeria. As it turned out, the consistory's condemnation of Bliah and Karsenty's request did not mean they did not hope to acquire possession of the synagogue in question. In fact, with Bliah's dismissal, the consistory renewed the request for the restitution of the building. The prefect conducted an investigation into the building's legal status, asking for help from the local commissioner in Tlemcen, as well as from the Domain Registration Service for the Province of Oran. One of the principal questions asked was whether "buildings belonging to the Jewish population can be seized by a decree ordered against the Muslim population." While on the face of it, the governor general's decree to seize the property appeared to "make no distinction between property of Jews and that of Muslims," there was an additional provision. This second article, noted the prefect, prohibited "Jews and Europeans" from effectuating any property transfers, orders that seemed to assimilate Jews with Europeans. If this were indeed the case, the Domain Registration Service suggested, the governor general's intention was that sequester orders were aimed "only at Muslims."[39] The implications of this conclusion were clear. The military should return the inappropriately sequestered Jewish property. The story indicates that consistorial officials and their allies in the civil administration charged with civilizing Algerian Jews could divorce the authorities' treatment of Jewish property from colonial directives aimed at disenfranchising Muslims.

The Registration Service went on to acknowledge that Tlemcen had been taken by force and that the Jews of the town had fled with Abd al-Qader, lending some credibility to the military's possession of Jewish property left behind. The logic, of course, was that if the town's inhabitants had been inclined to follow their leaders, they should be regarded as enemies whose homes could be seized. It cautioned, however, that the absence of the town's Jewish population was not voluntary, as the emir had forced the Jews into service with him. Now, however "almost all of them returned" and they wished to have their property back. This created the bedrock for the report's final conclusion—the punishment of seizing property was aimed at those who resisted the French occupation, not the Jews. Clarified the authors of the report, such "resistance [was] entirely beyond, as everyone knows, the customs and habits of the Jewish population."[40] According to the report, Jews in Algeria, even those classified as Moroccan, were protected from military rules concerning the seizing of indigenous Algerian property. The synagogue, both the Registration Service and the prefect reasoned, should be returned to the control of the community or an indemnity paid to the consistory.

It is unclear whether the army returned the contested building to this town's Jewish population. Regardless, the case of Tlemcen's synagogue suggests that the consistory and prefecture occasionally engaged in a delicate tug-of-war with military authorities over Jewish property. The seized synagogue in question was first and foremost terrain contested between local factions and the consistory. At the same time, this space came to reflect and manifest the divisive colonial hierarchy with which the civilizing mission was interwoven. The myth of Jewish customs rendering Jews friendly to the colonial authorities while Muslims remained hostile was translated into differing rules over property sequestration.

Local Resistance and Compromise

Interestingly, while the consistory in Oran struggled to close Tlemcen's synagogues and submit assemblies of prayer to their surveillance, Oran's private synagogues remained open. While these events unfolded in Tlemcen, Oran housed the same number of private synagogues (seventeen) as it had when the consistory was founded nearly a decade before. The endurance of private synagogues in Oran and elsewhere brings into relief a number of important aspects of the consistory's effort to submit Jewish communities to their control. Notably, the local divisions within the Jewish community manifest themselves within the consistory itself. The endurance of private synagogues in Oran in the mid-1850s also uncovers the extent to which urban Jewish notables of Oran shaped the consistory and protected their interests by entering into the institution.

In 1855, the consistory of Oran looked a good deal different from when Rabbi Lazare Cahen, Emmanuel Nahon, Amran Sénanès, and Abraham El Kanoui took the helm eight years earlier. While Cahen remained grand rabbi, the president since October 1854 was the local property owner and notable Abraham ben Ichou.[41] The lay members were also locals, Abraham ben Haim (a close associate of ben Ichou) and Messaoud Karoubi, who was the son-in-law of the original member Abraham El Kanoui.[42] Meanwhile, efforts to gain control over local synagogues were running into a number of complications. The map of Jewish religious spaces in Oran was, indeed, far from simple. Abraham ben Haim, the consistory president's ally, had recently built a new house for his family featuring a private synagogue on an upper floor.[43] Meanwhile, Jacob Lasry, the merchant and private synagogue owner we met in the first chapter, continued to operate his own religious foundation. Indeed, when internal divisions would force Abraham ben Ichou to step down as president later that year, Jacob Lasry would assume the presidency of Oran's consistory, all the while continuing to operate his own synagogue.[44] Furthermore, the consistory did not own, but rather rented, the large communal synagogue on Rue Ratissebonne in Oran from the wealthy Darmon family (among other partners). Efforts to purchase this crumbling and often swelteringly hot synagogue ran into snags when some of the owners refused to sell their shares. The community meanwhile rented a smaller synagogue from Mr. Kanoui and tried to rent a second synagogue from the

Cohen-Scalli family.[45] (The second transaction, however, was delayed when the parties disagreed over the cost of rent).[46]

Divisions within the consistory affected how members of the consistory attempted to manage the city's private synagogues. According to Rabbi Cahen, each time he attempted to address the lingering contradiction of consistorial members who were profiting from institutions they were meant to suppress, ben Haim and ben Ichou blocked discussion of the matter.[47] The synagogue issue was one of several leading to Rabbi Cahen's isolation in the consistory. Private correspondence between Cahen and the prefect suggests the president and ben Haim, whom Cahen referred to as "his enemies," consistently insulted him and subverted his plans.[48] Between internal divisions, the decrepit condition of the consistory's main synagogue, and the personal investments some members maintained in private synagogues, it is not surprising that so many remained in operation despite a decade of consistorial operations in Oran. The factors that differentiated the attempt to civilize Jews in Oran and Tlemcen could, it seems, be highly idiosyncratic and personal in nature. As a result, attempts by French reformers to control this population as a homogenous whole were doomed to fail.

As plans progressed to secure a large enough building to hold all the Jewish faithful of Oran, members of the consistory integrated, though sometimes resentfully, private synagogues into the normal functioning of the community. Private synagogues, for example, could sometimes be taxed for consistorial programs. Before Abraham ben Ichou stepped down from the presidency, he successfully proposed an extraordinary levy on all the private synagogues in the city to finance the repairs necessary on the large consistorial synagogue on Rue Ratissebonne.[49] At other times, individual notables within and outside the consistory seized on rivals' private synagogues to deflect efforts by the consistory to target their own investments. Reflecting this de facto acceptance, on the eve of the naturalization decree of 1870, the governor general turned down an unexplained consistorial request that Abraham ben Haim and his brother Isaac's private synagogue be reopened.[50] By the second half of the 1850s, local dynamics had forced the consistory to function in uneasy tandem institutions previously defined as obstacles to civilizing the Jews of Algeria.

The example of Jacob Lasry once again provides illustration of these broad historical trends. Upon assuming the presidency of the consistory on October 22, 1855, Jacob Lasry walked into a firestorm. In letters to the Prefecture of the Province of Oran, the grand rabbi accused President ben Ichou of inventing lies about him, opening his mail, and insulting both him and Karoubi.[51] In turn, the (Algerian) president again adopting the discourse of civilization as a claim to authority insisted the (French) grand rabbi was consistently "in agreement with the enemies of progress and civilization."[52]

This latter remark probably reflected ben Ichou's contempt for the rabbi's decision to protect a school instructor by the name of ben Ayoun, whom we shall discuss in the following chapter. In the presence of a committee of inquiry, their mutual antipathy led the president to ask the rabbi, "Mr. Rabbi, I ask you to cease speaking to me as to a *décrotteur* (shoeshine boy)."[53] Ben Ichou, ben Haim, and many others also saw the rabbi as hopelessly out of touch with the population he was intended to administer. Notably, Rabbi Cahen did not speak Arabic, which rendered his relationship to his community "nonexistent." He was incapable, for example, of monitoring the progress of children in the schools, understanding the plight of the poor, or providing "the abundant words of consolation that God has placed in the hands and mouth of the clergyman."[54] As for his Hebrew, his pronunciation was so different "from that of the land" that he could not deliver sermons comprehensible to local Jews.[55]

The division that brought Lasry into the consistory reflected a larger divide in the city's Jewish population that private synagogues helped sustain.[56] According to a report ordered by the Ministry of Public Instruction and Religions, ben Ichou and Abraham Kanoui were at the head of rival factions of Jews in the city of Oran.[57] Their mutual contempt was visceral, but unlike Mostaganem's Moroccan-Algerian rift, it did not reflect ethnic, religious, or even family divides. Indeed, the two Jewish notables were brothers-in-law, having married two sisters. In early 1855, despite the friction in their relationship, the two would be in attendance as El Kanoui's daughter (and ben Ichou's niece) was married in a grand ceremony in Oran. Given the economic weight the two families carried and the prefect's desire to keep the peace, El Kanoui ensured that the notable members of the European population of Oran were present at the ceremony.[58] The rivalry, however, endured, and by the middle of 1855 the apparently cantankerous and brusque ben Ichou was the subject of numerous personal attacks from within the Jewish community.[59] According to the city's officials, selecting Jews for membership in the consistory always risked favoring one clan over the other and provoking discord. Supporters of both sides met and worshipped in rival synagogues.

Oran was not the only city of the province to host a Jewish community with highly visible rivalries. In 1856, for example, the civil commissioner in Mascara was able to name the individual leaders of the mutually hostile camps that divided the local Jewish community and purportedly turned its synagogues into battlefields. The consistorial delegates represented in turn one opposing clique and then the other. "These internecine divisions have escaped the attention of the European population," noted the civil commissioner. "They reveal themselves in meetings [composed] exclusively of Jews."[60] According to the report Rabbi Shlomo ben Aïli, formerly the synagogue's principal spiritual leader, interrupted the reading of the Torah to announce his receipt of a letter from the consistory supposedly permitting him to choose the community's next delegates. Some worshipers insisted that he read the letter aloud, while others demanded that the Torah reading be completed. The resulting commotion forced an end to prayers for the day.[61] Sharp divisions in the Jewish communities of Mostaganem and Tlemcen were also reported.[62] Synagogues served as the arena in which opposition to consistorial direction, communal rivalries, and official efforts at surveillance were all played out. At times, these spaces could function—both in the eyes' of members and reformers—as rather less spiritual than political meeting halls.[63]

Upon taking the reins of the consistory, Lasry asserted his hope to make peace and reconciliation a guiding theme of his administration.[64] One of Lasry's first acts of power was to intervene into Oran's synagogue map. He emphasized the need to speed the construction or purchase of a new communal synagogue capable of uniting the entire community. To this end, he proposed new measures that taxed certain private synagogues and encouraged the purchase of a site capable of housing a large new synagogue. In 1856, for example, he instated a policy that rotated responsibility for charitable drives, charging different owners of private synagogues each week. In concert with the prefect, he proposed establishing a commission of ten Jewish notables responsible for deciding on the consistorial budget. To this end, he forwarded a list of 20 possible candidates to the prefecture. Numerous owners of private synagogues were featured, including David ben Haim, Joseph Medioni, David Taboul, Mordechai Darmon, and Elghali Guenoun.[65] Lasry thus worked to co-opt private synagogue owners, giving the institutions a role in the execution of consistorial duties. His work with these institutions reiterates the extent to which Lasry defied easy categorization in the colonial binary; he was neither entirely insider nor outsider, neither a dogmatic reformist nor an obstacle to colonial policy.

At the same time he recognized them by enlisting their help, Lasry also moved to close a portion of Oran's private synagogues and submit the rest to surveillance. With Lasry's cooperation, the Ministry of Pubic Instruction and Religions decreed in late 1856 that five local synagogues were to be shuttered, including that of consistory member Abraham ben Haim.[66] The decree also rendered the remaining synagogues dependent on the approval of the consistory. The synagogues were not chosen at random. According to ministerial decree, the first to be shut were those that had been "enemies of order" as attested to by the police or other authorities.[67] Lasry's effort extended to the smaller cities of the province, as well; he called on local authorities to force a synagogue owner in Mostaganem by the name of Saoud Djian to rent his private synagogue to the consistory.[68] As in Oran, the divisions in Mostaganem were deep; the sub-prefecture noted that Djian was doing the bidding of clan leader Mr. Cohen-Scalli, and that his synagogue was "often the home of intrigues [conducted] under the cloak of religion."[69]

The fact that Lasry himself owned a private synagogue did not escape the notice of Abraham ben Haim, whose synagogue was slated for closure. While Lasry cooperated with the Ministry of Public Instruction and Religions to draft the decree, ben Haim set to work producing a brochure in an effort to subvert the cause. Publishing under the name of his brother, Isaac (who was not a member of the consistory), ben Haim accused his fellow consistory member of distributing misleading information about the charitable functions of his synagogue in an effort to shelter it from his own policies. Furthermore, insisted ben Haim, Lasry was not directing his synagogue's proceeds toward charity, as he had claimed.[70] The brochure caused a sensation in Oran, attracting not only the attention of local Jews, but the prefect, as well. The latter was called upon to investigate the allegations against Lasry's synagogue and charitable trust, toward which end he appointed a commission of investigation. The commission then examined the accounts of Lasry's synagogue to check for irregularities. While the investigators determined that Lasry's "acts of charity were not numerous," the receipts of the synagogue had indeed gone to the foundations' stated purposes.[71] Lasry and his synagogue survived the inquiry, and ben Haim left the consistory the following October.[72]

The investigation of Lasry's synagogue and the larger effort to close private synagogues in which it was enmeshed shows how the civilizing mission provided both a language and an institutional structure through which local contests were played out. Both Lasry and ben Ichou justified their actions in the same terms as their European counterparts, as part of the campaign to spread progress and civilization. The fact that Lasry himself had North African roots underlines how the profoundly colonial character of the civilizing mission does not mean participants in its drama could be mapped along a straightforward French/Algerian axis.[73] Men of Algerian or Moroccan backgrounds were often in charge of executing the French ideology of civilizing. Lasry, ben Ichou, and even Moroccans like Nahon and Sénanès strove to submit fellow Jews to a preferential regime requiring increased surveillance, but interpreted their duties in unforeseen ways. The consistory reflected the imperial civilizing mission of its founders, as well as its colonized Algerian context. Many of Oran's independent synagogues, unsurprisingly, persevered.[74]

Local animosities and divisions found expression in the consistory, and these feuds were articulated within the official civilizing lexicon. In most cases, the intrigues and scandals frequently associated with private synagogues in colonial transcripts were often vaguely described. Certainly, episodes of cursing and scuffles were real and occasionally detailed in reports, as suggested in the Mascara episode mentioned above.[75] The extent to which these fights were a regular feature of spiritual life in these buildings, or how frequently they were of a religious nature, is unclear. Questions of saint worship, ecstatic prayer, or other forms of practice that may have struck reform-oriented French Jews as problematic are not discussed in the archives, but remain an interesting subject of speculation. In at least one case however, it would seem that communal divisions sparked by the consistory's efforts at centralization overlapped quite clearly with religious perspectives and preexisting chains of authority.

Consistory, Colonialism and *Kashrut*

As we have seen, the consistory's role as a governing body over the Jews of Oran placed it at the nexus of a range of communal, colonial, and religious struggles, with private synagogues serving as the institutional site of religious conflicts in colonial Algeria. The consistory, then, could be understood at once as a colonial and a religious institution, and while its legitimacy was derived from the colonial chain of command, it was nonetheless entangled with more local hierarchies. These networks, private synagogues among them, were less respectful of modern political boundaries than was the colonial administration, and they occasionally forced consistory members to participate in regional discussions of religio-communal authority they might rather have avoided.

Algerian Jews continued, for example, to seek the advice of rabbis who were not affiliated with the consistory or, indeed, who lived outside of France's colony altogether. In so doing, Jewish rabbis and legal theorists subtly undermined colonial authority and signaled the persistence of preexisting hubs of power in and outside of colonial Algeria. In the following pages, we explore an episode that illustrates the complicated relationship between the consistory, private synagogues, and the religious and social divisions that fissured Algerian Jews, an ostensible community the consistory both provoked and hoped to master. As we shall see, these dynamics were intertwined with the wider Mediterranean Jewish world.

In 1858, a rabbi in Mascara by the name of Abraham Enkaoua (who may have been a descendent of the previously mentioned Spanish immigrant to Tlemcen) published a religious book concerning the laws of *Shechita*, or ritual (kosher) slaughter. The book was first entitled *Zevachim Shleimim* (Peace Offerings) and later supplemented and renamed *Zevachim Shleimim veKesef Aher* (Peace Offerings and Other Money). Examining the medieval philosopher and rabbi Maimonides' *Mishneh Torah*, a widely accepted compilation of law, Enkaoua sought to discuss the laws dealing with the supervision and certification of kosher slaughterers (*shochetim*). While all shochetim should be supervised, Enkaoua argued, a shochet trusted in one place should be authorized to practice his trade in another.[76]

At the beginning of the year following the publishing of Enkaoua's book the Oran consistory's Abraham ben Ichou, who also happened to be the rabbi's brother-in-law, complained to the prefect of insults and humiliations to which Enkaoua had been subject. These condemnations may have been related to Enkaoua's published opinions on kosher slaughtering, but his precise offense is unclear. So great was Ichou's concern that, with Enkaoua, he appealed to respected rabbis in Algiers, Tunis, Paris, and Jerusalem for aid. Their pleas were rewarded with letters of support for Enkaoua and his work. These letters were supposed to be posted in the synagogues of the Jewish quarter.[77] Lasry, president of the consistory at this time, had at first agreed to allow letters that supported Enkaoua to be posted, but when he read them, he grew concerned, for some condemned those who opposed Enkaoua, proposing even that a *herem* (ban from the community) be imposed upon them. "Today the consistory received these [legal] decisions," wrote Lasry to the prefect, "but they contain a form of excommunication," so he "hesitated to publish them in the synagogues" because he did not know if the consistory could "do so legally."[78] Lasry's confusion, it seems, stemmed from the fact that he did not know the extent of the consistory's authority when it came to enforcing or dismissing a herem imposed by rabbis, in this case rabbis outside of Algeria. Perhaps his concern was particularly acute because hostility to Enkaoua's writings emanated from two private synagogues, those of Moshe Karsenty and Mordechai Darmon. In other words, the ban was in all likelihood directed at, among others, two powerful figures in Oran's Jewish community.

The prefect took the dispute over the book on kosher slaughter seriously, and his earnestness is worth demonstrating in some detail in so far as it signals the hesitation (indeed, inability) of this relatively high ranked colonial official to undercut the authority of the trans-Mediterranean religious elite. In response to Lasry's appeals, the prefect suggested that the letters concerning Enkaoua be published only in censored form, omitting the call for a herem. Specifically citing the authority invested in the rabbis of Jerusalem and Tunis (who penned letters in support of Enkaoua), the prefect expressed the desire to give Enkaoua and ben Ichou satisfaction, but at the same time to avoid unrest in the community which these letters threatened to cause. Clearly, the prefect took Lasry's warning of potential social unrest seriously, going so far as to assure him that "If, as you seem to fear, you encounter resistance in any of the synagogues, I am informing the chief of police that he may place as many officers at your disposal as required."[79] On the same day, the prefect, in keeping with his promise, wrote a memo to the chief of police in Oran. "I have just authorized the publication of two letters in all the synagogues of Oran," he warned. "The president of the consistory has forwarded them to me and I fear they might encounter resistance on the part of several leaders of the Israelite population." The police chief was then ordered to make available as many officers as necessary to prevent disorders.[80] The prefect of colonial Oran, sensitive to the weight of rabbinic authority in other Mediterranean cities, preventatively deployed police to keep the peace among Jewish groups organized around private synagogues.

The letters written by the rabbis in Tunis and Jerusalem themselves give some indication of how vituperative the conflict had become. The rabbis lamented the "bad things that occurred in your holy country: the great scorn that was produced for a new book entitled *Kessef Aher* and *Zevahim Shleimim*, composed by the Rabbi Abraham Enkaoua." They went on to accuse Enkaoua's critics (presumably Karcenty, Darmon, and their followers) of being motivated by jealousy, noting that "they have mocked it, they have torn it apart, page by page, they have used it for lighting their cigarettes and all forms of use." Furthermore, they wrote, "We have knowledge of this fact both by witnesses and written testimony."[81] Finally, the authors insisted that public apologies be made to Enkaoua, and warned that those who failed to do so would "suffer their own ban herem and punishment from God."[82]

What does the dramatic local and regional controversy sparked by Enkaoua's writings tell us about Jewish life in colonial Oran or, indeed, the relationship between this urban center and the wider Jewish Mediterranean? First, that the Enkaoua controversy resulted in the exchange of letters from rabbis as far afield as Tunis, Jerusalem, Paris, Tetuan, and Livorno that demonstrate clearly that the dispute in Oran was not a purely local affair.[83] While this study frames nineteenth-century Algerian-Jewish history in its colonial context, these events suggest how one could also situate it as part of a larger regional narrative.[84] At the same time, the story suggests how local colonial authorities were forced to confront rabbinic decisions made not only within but also outside of Algeria. Finally, the story points once again to the sustained social significance of private synagogues and their leaders' ability to test the limits of consistorial authority.

On a different register, the struggle over Enkoua's work highlights how Algerian Jews, and notably owners of private synagogues, could mobilize colonial ideology in their favor. In opposition to the herem pronounced against him from abroad, private synagogue owner Karcenty attempted to reduce the impact of foreign authorities in Oran, whom he accused of inappropriately challenging the very local authority to which he was complaining. He did so by taking issue with the authenticity of one of the letters the authorities republished for local readers. "It has been affirmed," he wrote to the prefect on January 21, "that you have just authorized the publication of a piece attributed to the rabbis of Tunis and Jerusalem in the synagogues of Oran, for this Saturday, the 22nd of January. If this is correct, we are led to believe that a complete and faithful translation has yet to be submitted for your examination."[85] A synagogue owner, Karsenty apparently had received a copy of the rabbis' letter from the consistory, despite the fact that he was one of those vilified by its authors. In response, Karsenty insisted that no authentic letter would have been so vitriolic, nor should anything so hateful be published.[86] Karsenty then mobilized a discourse of science and progress to convince the authorities to block the publication of the letters, arguing that members of his faction should have freedom of expression: "religious works, like all other intellectual productions, are subjected to review and exposed to [the evaluation of] men endowed with a certain expertise. Criticism is free, and the success of the book depends as much on its true value, as on its style for the elevation of thought. These have been the professed and applied principles in France for several centuries. And yet discussion will not be granted to the Israelites living in French possessions . . . violent and arbitrary measures deny them one of the principal advantages of an advanced civilization."[87] Karsenty accused the consistory of turning its back on France's civilizing mission in Algeria.

On January 22, the first day of its publication in the synagogues, Karsenty and Mordechai Darmon, both private synagogue owners, issued a summons to Lasry, delivered through the local court, demanding that he produce Tunisian and Palestinian rabbis' original letter within twenty-four hours.[88] The consistory discussed the demand, and eventually forwarded the note to the prefect for his consideration. Their demands not met at this level, they petitioned the minister of Algeria and the colonies in Paris for intercession. The minister turned to the prefect of Oran for more information about the affair. He noted that he had received a petition from a group of "property owners and merchants (*négociants*) of the city of Oran [presumably including Karsenty and Darmon]," who objected to the fact that the prefecture had commanded the publication of a work by a non-Algerian rabbi in the synagogues.[89] The Parisian minister's involvement in the affair appears to have ended with whatever explanation he received in reply.

The Enkaoua affair demonstrates that private synagogues were at once loci of resistance to consistorial policy and agents charged with disseminating its orders—orders that in this case came to the consistory from Tunis and Jerusalem. Because of their power, colonial authorities occasionally had to reckon with religious authorities in Algeria and beyond. In addition, we learn from this episode that owners of private synagogues were patrons of larger communal factions that occasionally expressed themselves along religious lines. When subject to rabbinical condemnation, as were Darmon and Karceny in the late 1850s, these notables could invoke colonial authority to help shield themselves from the fallout of putatively religious disputes, drawing upon a post-Enlightenment language of free expression, critical thought, and scientific progress to support their case. Finally, and perhaps most remarkable, Algerian Jews occasionally invoked France's colonial sovereignty to neutralize potentially damaging rabbinical decisions made outside French possessions.

Schools and Synagogues: Experts and the Interior

In addition to hedging against scandals, civil administrators wielded concern for health and hygiene as a method of penetrating, mapping, evaluating, and closing interior religious spaces. This was particularly the case with Jewish schools, which were often located within private synagogues. We shall have more to say about efforts to close or monitor Algerian-Jewish schools in the next chapter, but the thematic parallels between official efforts to control both types of institutions merits discussion here. At the beginning of 1855, a new law on *midrashim*, or local Algerian-Jewish schools, coincided with efforts to close synagogues. Among the results of the measure were increased statistical monitoring, architectural inspections, and the production of tables to guide policy toward Algerian-Jewish schools. The imperative to safeguard the health of children was thus intertwined with efforts to police the interiors of homes and synagogues.

In 1846, French Rabbi Michel Weill wrote an article in the journal *Archives Israélites* about the state of his Algerian co-religionists. Weill was serving as schoolmaster in one of the first French Algerian-Jewish schools for boys, but would become grand rabbi of Algiers in November of the same year. Given his position, it is not surprising that he took a serious interest in the state of Algerian-Jewish education. He reported that hygiene was a serious problem in local schools and would be "the first reform to carry out in the indigenous schools," and "the first amelioration to introduce in the name of religion." The filth amidst which Algerian Jews lived and studied, according to Weill, was less an innate characteristic than attributable to Muslim oppression, for "no religion in the world insists upon the duty of cleanliness more than ours. If occasionally habits contrary to this have prevailed, one must attribute them to the discouragement and social degradation into which centuries of oppression have plunged them."[90] Weill's remarks were emblematic of consistorial and civil administrators' attitudes toward Jewish schools and synagogues over the following several decades. Hygiene and health created a new medical imperative to intervene. Yet accusations that Jews were hostile to civilization never crystallized into a mythology of an immutable or ontological trait.[91] Rather, Jewish dirtiness tended to be linked to a past from which they were permanently in the process of being emancipated.

After 1855, fathers of school-age children were required to register their children in the municipalities' *état civil* and to document their children's age and name, and provide proof of vaccination.[92] The decree also required the consistory to monitor sick children and prevent them from attending school until their condition improved. The decree quickly produced results, and forty students were sent away from the schools in the first months of the year due to "contagions." Based on reports of skin disease, a similar number of students were sent away at the beginning of 1856.[93] Increased statistical monitoring led attendance of the various midrashim to become a standard matter of discussion at consistorial meetings.[94] Whether more children were being kept from schools is impossible to know. More evident is how schools—both communal and independent—were brought into a system whereby Jews were increasingly registered, documented, and monitored by the colonial administration.

In response to the prefect's request, the sub-inspector for the rector of the Academy of Algiers soon produced a report on the students and teachers of the midrashim. It included names of rabbis directing unofficial schools, their age, place of birth, number of dependents, number of students for whom they were responsible, names of adjunct instructors, and an evaluation of the cleanliness of the surroundings.[95] Several weeks later, Grand Rabbi Cahen produced his own report on the schools. The report accompanying it provides an image of early attempts to quantify the problem of midrashim in Oran. The chart was accompanied by Cahen's assurance that the instructors were both moral and capable. Cahen also included recommendations about how to increase enrollment at the official school. He did not neglect health conditions. The new policies toward midrashim also drew more attention to documenting birth dates and to regulating the ages of children attending schools. This increased rigidity led Algerian-Jewish women to make official requests for leniency so that they could continue to work. One woman whose husband worked far from home as a military interpreter asked that her five-year-old child receive special permission to attend the local school despite his young age. "I have the honor of informing you," she did not hesitate to add, "that this child was vaccinated and [already] had chicken pox."[96] Despite the health of her child, her request was denied. Similarly, schools themselves were ordered to keep registers of students, including birth dates and medical records. The grand rabbi's 1856 report described schools' registers, noting with disapproval, "one only rarely finds [records of] when the student began his studies, and almost never is their date of birth [recorded]."[97] By the middle of 1856, school inspections included charts of how many students had documents of identification filed with the municipality.[98]

TABLE 3.1
The Midrashim of Oran, 1855

Name of school	Name of schoolmaster	Number of children, 1/2/1855	Number of children, 2/11/1855	Sent home for reason of contagious disease 2/11/1855	Remainder	Observations
Ben Ayoun	Zarka, Salomon, Ben Ayoun, Joseph, and Enkanuoua, added	200	164	10	154	Many children are not yet the minimum age of six. Once their age is officially established, I shall endeavor to execute the regulation regarding student admission.
Ben Sadoun	Ben Sadoun, Isaac	50	45	2	43	
Haziza	Haziza, Abraham	45	45	6	39	
Nissim	Reubeni, Nissim, and Taboul, Messaoud	45	59	8	51	
Metat	Metat, Isaac	35	39	8	31	
Hazan	Hazan, Abraham	30	24	6	18	
Total		405	376	40	336	

Source: Cahen to Prefect, 13 February 1855, CAOM, fol. 3U/1.

TABLE 3.2

Health Conditions of Jewish Children in Oran's Midrashim, 1855

Schools	Vaccinated students	Marks for smallpox	Total
Ben Ayoun, Zarka and Taboul	96	37	133
Reubeni, Nissim	20	15	35
Haziza, Abraham	27	16	43
Hassan, Isaac	19	5	24
Ben Sadoun, Isaac	15	9	24
Bentoto, Isaac	17	10	27
Totals	194	92	286

Source: Cahen to Prefect, 13 February 1855, CAOM, fol. 3U/1.

Algerian-Jewish schools' unhealthy, miasmic, or otherwise dangerous conditions also concerned numerous inspectors. Experts in medicine and architecture increasingly attempted to determine the number of students that could attend a given school. To this end, the prefect engaged a "chief architect of the service of civil buildings" to determine that "the locale of Ben Sadoun can accommodate from 18 to 20 students."[99] Such information was transmitted to the rector in the process of determining whether a midrash was over-enrolled. In the case of a different school, the chief architect was requested to judge "the salubriousness and surface area of a locale situated on impasse Wagram, currently used for the school, known as a midrashim [*sic*], directed by a Mr. Sadoun, Isaac." The reason was that the prefect had ordered the school "closed for being too narrow for forty-seven students and having a difficult and dangerous means of access."[100] The demands of health, as perceived by consistorial authorities, required securing access to interior spaces in order that experts could judge the safety of children.

In keeping with the concern for healthy air then preoccupying French scientists, determining the potential for miasma and contagion occasionally involved far more detailed descriptions.[101] Some included measurements of the cubic volume of "breathable air" in a given space, as well as estimates as to how many children could safely breath it. "I visited the places and here is a description," read one report. "This school is attached to the synagogue belonging to Mr. Eliaou Karsenti, forming the gallery. It is installed on the second story in a room of Moorish construction . . . the area of breathable air is . . . 34.339 cubic meters and would be enough for eleven students maximum, assuming it could be replaced every hour or so, or if it were renewed perpetually by opening the four windows."[102] In Isaac ben Sadoun's case, the prefect ordered the previously authorized schoolmaster to close his school following the architect's report. He had concluded "the place wherein he holds his school is very narrow . . . it is even dangerous for the students . . . and ought to be closed." Cahen was thus required to advise ben Sadoun that he could continue operating his school only "on condition that he presents a suitable property that fulfills all the conditions of surface area, ventilation, and salubriousness required by the law of January 1, 1855."[103] In other cases, it was Cahen himself who offered advice: "The worst school is that of Isaac Hassan. The dirtiness of the children, the master, and the class, [as well as] the disorder and lack of discipline, render this school unworthy of the name."[104] The effort to control the midrashim, therefore, involved an increased presence of medical/architectural experts authorized to intervene and monitor the Algerian homes and synagogues. This involvement reveals that reformers in Algeria were motivated by contemporary understandings of health, space, and bodies that were shaped in France.

Conclusion

The mission to civilize the Jews of Algeria was a multipolar and multidirectional process. Administrators and reformers followed the army into the cities of Algeria, hoping to spread progress and attach the Jewish community to France. Men such as Lazare Cahen and Emmanuel Nahon believed that by gaining access to interior spaces, subjecting Jewish families to French law, and closing their synagogues, they could improve the likelihood of their naturalization. Their vision was not groundless; it reflected a larger colonial legal framework by which citizens were increasingly identifiable by their subjection to intimate official interventions. At the same time, the struggles over synagogues reveal how Algerian consistories were quickly transformed by the colonial social landscape. Elite Moroccan and Algerian Jews occupied key positions in the consistory, and their interests, perspectives, and loyalties accompanied them. In the peripheral towns, such as Tlemcen, Mascara, and Sidi-Bel-Abbes, consistorial delegates reflected local groups, bases of power, and rivalries. Local ethnic divisions, notably between Moroccan and Algerian Jews, were exaggerated by the power the consistory conferred on its delegates. Meanwhile, the influence produced by the consistory became instrumental in local contests. France's civilizing mission, having justified the consistory's establishment, was by the 1850s at least partly reflective of the North African Jewish landscape that its original framers, such as Crémieux and Altaras, had hoped to transform.

Synagogues were sacred spaces and meeting halls, urban investments, charitable trusts, and loci of resistance to religious centralization. They were power bases for rival clans and locations of rabbinical tribunals. Consistorial officers, even when they themselves owned synagogues, identified private synagogues as crucial strategic terrain in the effort to bring Jewish communities under control. When schools were located in them, they used emergent notions of hygiene, miasma, and contagion in their efforts to close or control their operations. Importantly, the fact that men such as Lasry, ben Haim, and Karsenti owned synagogues did not preclude their mobilizing the discourse of civilization—or even believing in it—as they sought to close private synagogues or harness their revenues for consistorial projects. Progress and civilization were themselves malleable terms that were adapted to various interests and situations. Civilization simultaneously provided Ben Ichou with ammunition against Rabbi Cahen, justified Lasry's effort to shut five private synagogues in concert with the minister of public instruction and religions, and figured in Karsenti's arsenal against the publication of a herem against him.

Private synagogues also affected the ways in which the consistory supported itself and carried out its mission. Local notables who owned them belonged to a larger community with networks of patronage that extended into the membership of the consistory. Any effort to close an institution had to contend with personal ties and devotion to institutions that predated the French conquest. As we shall see in the campaign to reform Jewish schools explored in the following chapter, the strength and endurance of local Jewish community networks and sensibilities continued to influence religious, social, economic, and institutional life in colonial Algeria.

4

Teaching Civilization

French Schools and Algerian Midrashim, 1852–1870

It was the beginning of January 1859 and Mr. Fredja ben Sadoun was furious. The Tlemcen Jew had been sending his ten-year-old son to the Jewish school that Oran's consistory oversaw in his town. One day, his son came home upset about having been punished in school. The boy told his father he had misbehaved in class, but the school supervisor agreed that he had committed only a minor fault. In response to the infraction, an adjunct teacher named Nerson beat the child severely and locked him in a room for some time. Understandably, ben Sadoun complained to the school director about the teacher's violent attack on his child. News of the episode was then communicated to the local sub-prefecture. One can imagine ben Sadoun's frustration, then, when he learned that prior to assuming the post in Tlemcen, Nerson had occupied a teaching position in Oran from which he had been transferred in the wake of a judicial censure for mistreating children. When he discussed the affair with his superior in Oran, the sub-prefect noted that instead of "moderating the violence of his character" since arriving in Tlemcen, Nerson had already been the subject of a number of complaints. The official requested that his superior urge Rector Delacroix of the Academy of Algiers (the local educational administrative district) to punish Mr. Nerson "severely" by dismissing him and obliging him to leave Tlemcen. "I believe it to be unnecessary," noted the sub-prefect, "to explain fully the consequences" if no action were taken. "Parents will prefer to keep their children with them rather than expose them to mistreatment," causing great damage to "the prosperity of the Jewish school of Tlemcen."[1]

Just why did ben Sadoun's complaint strike such a chord in this bureaucrat? The sub-prefect's letter omitted the major issue that framed his anxieties over the future of Jewish education in Tlemcen—the formidable competition local Algerian-Jewish midrashim were posing to communal schools. Local Algerian rabbis ran these Jewish schools in private synagogues and homes and, interestingly enough, accusations of corporal punishment were a staple of official attacks on these ostensibly clandestine Jewish institutions. Ben Sadoun's complaint disturbed the authorities so because it threatened French civil officials' recently constructed opposition between the supposedly enlightened education offered by French-Jewish communal schools and the supposedly backward local pedagogy. This story is one of a series of episodes where efforts to civilize Jews by way of French-supervised religious education ran up against local cultural and institutional obstacles. Polemics against the competition that midrashim offered to consistorial civilizing efforts, as well as the barbarity of corporal punishment were counterbalanced by political support (even within the consistories) and parental preference that local rabbis and teachers could mobilize in their defense. Because of the potency of these issues, the intersection of competition, violence, and parental involvement offers a suitable starting point for a discussion of Algerian-Jewish education in the years of the Second Empire (1852 to 1870).

Consistorial efforts to monitor, control, and alter indigenous Jewish education in Algeria resulted in substantial compromises with local institutional and cultural forms. Such efforts also bring into relief how education, like synagogues, represented a battleground on which the civilizing effort bent to conform to the wishes of local Algerian actors, including those charged with its execution. The events that follow also provide a window into mid-century educational campaigns that were justified by the cause of civilization, yet carried out well before the adoption of the civilizing mission as a semi-official colonial ideology under the Third Republic. The early period during which this process unfolded suggests we revisit some common notions about education's role in the colonial civilizing mission.[2] While French administrators held education to be vitally important, continuity with preexisting educational forms—rather than the transformation or deracination of colonial subjects, as has more often been proposed—distinguished civilizing policies in the Algerian-Jewish context.

This discussion builds on three distinct bodies of historiographic literature. First, there is the significant scholarly work on nineteenth- and twentieth-century efforts to civilize Jews of the Muslim world through education. The discourse of the consistorial officers discussed below foreshadowed in important ways the moralizing agenda outlined in Aron Rodrigue's study of teachers of the Alliance Israélite Universelle (AIU) schools in the late nineteenth and early twentieth centuries.[3] The Algerian consistories explored here differ in that they predated the AIU (Algeria did not receive an Alliance school until the early twentieth century), and were established in territory that was legally integral to France. Furthermore, while Jews in the Ottoman east (as in many coastal communities in Morocco) tended to welcome AIU schools to their communities and send their children to them, Algerian Jews seem to have been unimpressed by real or imagined opportunities provided by a French education, and often avoided new French-Jewish schools.[4] Indeed, Algerian Jews often forced French educators to fit existing pedagogical institutions into their system rather than allow them to create new schools according to their original plans.[5] Furthermore, most campaigns under examination here were nominally entrusted to the consistory and local civil administrations, rather than rely on a private institution such as the AIU.

A second body of scholarship explores how schooling was part and parcel of colonial dominance.[6] Consistorial campaigns to educate Algerian Jews were not divorced from the colonial ideology that held that education could effectuate what many called the "moral conquest" of the natives. At the same time, scholarship on Indochina, Algeria, and South Asia all suggest that consistorial programs featured a level of incoherence and compromise that also characterized other colonial educational programs. Colonial educators in Egypt and India, for example, also hoped to stem the influence of native religious teachers and instill loyalty to the mother country. Like the French administration in Algeria, they too "outsourced" education to local actors and, as a result, often saw their schools shaped by the religious influences whose power they hoped to curtail.[7] As much as French administrators may have hoped to contain religion by defining it as Talal Assad has called a "new historical object . . . expressible in belief sentences" and "practiced in one's spare time," religion appears to have remained a structuring epistemological lens in consistorial schools.[8] Furthermore, the emphasis that administrators in Algeria placed on French language education in the 1850s and 1860s was not isolated from the ideology underlying the nineteenth-century effort to integrate the multiple linguistic communities of metropolitan France, even if Jules Ferry's educational laws, so instrumental in spreading free, secular, and obligatory education, remained many years off.[9]

Finally, scholarship on Algerian Muslim education must be considered in order to highlight the contrasting experiences of colonialism encountered by Algeria's Jewish inhabitants. Jewish schools did not suffer the crushing blows that the French delivered to Islamic education through the sequestration of the *habous* (charitable endowments) that supported the schools.[10] When France established three official Muslim schools, called *médersas*, in 1850, they were subject to significant material and ideological controls that reinforced the colonial regime, while their student bodies remained small.[11] Subsequent legislation further compromised their pedagogical independence. Despite reforms intended to expand attendance and the efforts of a number of individual educators, the Third Republic consistently denied the vast majority of Algerians the resources to obtain any formal education.[12] This would only begin to change in the interwar period as both reformist Muslim *Ulema* (religious scholars) and colonial reformers began to construct an educational infrastructure for Muslim youth.[13] Jews of early colonial Oran, by contrast, though subject to increasing intervention and controls, did not find their access to a basic education blocked.

It would seem paradoxical that the school attended by Ben Sadoun's son operated under the auspices of the municipal authorities, given that corporal punishment was the chief accusation French administrators leveled at Algerian teachers. Reformers had insisted, even before the installation of the Jewish consistories in Algeria, that France had an obligation to rescue young Algerian Jews from the mire of their native educational milieu. Altaras and Cohen, for example, argued that any successful transformation of Algeria's Jews would require closing their existing schools, which often resorted to corporal punishment for lack of any moral authority.[14] Yet when it came to actual interventions, neither the consistories nor the Ministry of Public Instruction and Religions could ignore existing institutions and practices. When the consistory was established in Oran, the city already featured a network of religio-educational institutions that served the community, provided rabbis with employment, and held the trust of many parents. Thus, the consistory's campaign to fulfill its educational mandate quickly sparked an enduring contest among colonial officials, Algerian rabbis, and different factions within the Jewish community and the consistory.

What ben Sadoun's son was learning at school was probably not terribly different from what ben Sadoun himself had been taught. Whatever innovations the communal school featured were the sole responsibility of a single French instructor, so the child's school featured several hours a week of French and perhaps some geography and history.[15] In contrast to the metropolitan Jewish communal schools that emerged over the course of the early to mid-nineteenth century, the colonial French Israelite schools established during the 1850s and 1860s do not appear to have given much attention to secular subjects besides the French language, and no mention is given to the vocational skills emphasized in the metropolitan Jewish schools of the same period.[16] Religious education in the French-Jewish schools remained in the hands of local Algerian rabbis. The French component, meanwhile, was often limited to a single French instructor. In the approximately two decades of the Second Empire, teaching the French language was the only obvious curricular innovation of putatively civilized schools. If the French instructors taught other subjects, all mention was omitted from the extensive administrative discussions about reforming Oran's Jewish schools. Regardless, in the 1850s administrators began drawing a clear contrast between the two by accusing indigenous instructors of obstructing progress and civilization. By the second half of the decade, however, the municipality hired a number of Algerian rabbis to teach alongside French instructors in communal schools. The result was a policy of compromise that leads one to question whether early French administrators actually understood the civilizing mission to be tied to a tangible body of real educational changes.

Unlike Muslim schools, Jewish education was not under direct French military control. While both European and Jewish schools were technically under the direction of the Ministry of Public Instruction and Religions, they were directed separately. Notably, the consistory had a say in the organization of Jewish schools and offered advice to civil authorities as to which Jewish schools should be permitted to remain open. Despite the unique status of Algerian Jews and Algerian-Jewish education, the discourse surrounding the process suggests that the question of educating Algerian Jews was not divorced from debates surrounding the education of other colonized groups.

Jewish Pedagogy in a Colonial Context

French colonial efforts at educating Jews and Muslims began inauspiciously in the 1830s and 1840s. In 1832, for example, the government established a special French-Jewish school in Algiers, to be replaced the following year with a mixed Muslim and Jewish primary school.[17] In its first years, the school attracted up to 200 students, of whom 50 were Jewish, but both Jewish and Muslim students ceased attending as the Catholic prejudices of the schoolmasters made themselves felt. In 1836, a "French Moorish" school opened for Muslim children, featuring a curriculum of four hours of French study followed by four hours of Qur'anic study. In 1837, the municipality of Algiers allocated funds for the establishment of a school for young Jewish girls, under the direction of a French-Jewish woman, Héloïse Hartoch. Three years later, the municipality created a school for Jewish boys under the direction of M. A. Lepescheux, the inspector general of Algiers.[18] By the end of 1840, there were three French-sponsored schools open to native Algerians in the capital, far from a comprehensive effort.

Attendance patterns belie the limited scope of these projects. At the beginning, the French-Muslim school taught 57 students, the French-Jewish school for boys 75, and the school for Jewish girls 65.[19] But after several years, student enrollment at all these institutions dropped precipitously. Many families demanded that their children work to supplement the family income, while others were alienated by the impiety or perceived conversionary intent of schoolmasters. By 1843, only eight to ten girls regularly attended Hartoch's school; M. Lepecheux's Jewish boy's school lost students, as well; at least 42 of them had returned to study with native rabbis by 1842.[20] In contrast, 298 Muslims and 315 Jews attended locally directed institutions in Algiers.

Oran had a communal French-Jewish school in 1849, but not without considerable challenges from the local population. According to an 1850 report by Grand Rabbi Lazare Cahen of Oran, the school managed to achieve some stability after a year or so, despite "its struggles against the intrigues of the indigenous teachers, the fanaticism of some, the prejudices of others, and the indifference of everyone."[21] While it had counted 100 students several weeks before the time of Rabbi Cahen's 1850 report to the Ministry of Public Instruction and Religions, attrition posed a threat. Fluctuating attendance was to prove an enduring challenge for French colonial civil administrators, and other cities of the province, such as Mostaganem and Tlemcen, were not to have French-Jewish schools until several years later. In Tlemcen, Rabbi Cahen singled out native resistance as the primary reason for the military's previous failure to establish a school. Combined, the number of students attending religious schools deemed indigenous in Algiers, Oran, Bône, Mostaganem, Bougie, and Philippeville came to 1,172, including 406 Muslims and 766 Jews.[22] In contrast, the popularity of French schools among Jews and Muslims made few advances over the course of the 1840s.

The situation was different for Algeria's European settlers. During the same period, the Service of Public Instruction (a local civil agency, as opposed to the ministry of a similar name in Paris) established increasingly popular public schools geared toward the diverse (but overwhelmingly Christian) population of European settlers. By 1848, 9,000 students attended roughly 110 of the resulting schools. These institutions were geared toward assimilating the European settler population in Algeria's cities. By the early 1850s, the population included French, Spanish, Maltese, Italians, and Germans, and both Protestants and Catholics. These schools were open to Algerians, but, by the second half of the 1840s, only 7 percent of the students were Muslim or Jewish.[23] The small numbers can be explained by the exclusive social climate that prevailed in the schools and by a curriculum laden with Christian overtones.

The Second Republic's policy of assimilation in Algeria affected Muslim education as well, receiving the support of General Randon who believed in the gradual assimilation of Muslims to French civilization.[24] Education, Randon believed, would eventually permit the "*rapprochment* of the two races" necessary for successful colonial rule. In 1850, Randon established three French-run médersas in Constantine, Blida, and Tlemcen, before becoming governor general in 1851.[25] These schools were designed to undercut schools in Fez and Tunis that trained Muslim clergy. While these schools had attracted about 140 students by 1862, the numbers began to trail off in the 1870s and 1880s as many *mahkamas* (juridical circumscriptions for qadis, or judges, which employed their graduates) were suppressed under civilian rule. Among French colonial administrators, few saw the use for these supposed schools of fanaticism. By 1885, there were only 55 students in all three médersas.[26] Starting in the 1850s, unofficial indigenous Muslim schools also began worrying the French authorities. Various administrators complained of the enduring fanaticism and of the competition such schools created for French schools, and began taking measures to control them. In 1850, for example, the military administration required Muslim *tolbas* (religious teachers) to acquire special authorization to teach in approved Qur'anic schools.[27] An 1857 circular instructed local authorities to make frequent inspections of Muslim schools, and announced the decision of the prefect of Constantine to close half of the 24 religious schools operating in the city.

The 1845 decree that established the consistories in Algeria also included provisions for educating and assimilating the Algerian-Jewish population. A combination of subsidies from the consistory, tuition fees and, if need be, special subventions from the government would support these schools. According to Article 25, the curriculum was to include both "religious instruction and the study of the French language."[28] The director of civil affairs soon specified that the grand rabbi of Algeria, whose office had been established by the same decree, would supervise the institutions. He was thus responsible for "ensur[ing] that in all these establishments, [the instruction] will conform to biblical spirit and morality" and would "not allow any part of the instruction [to] degenerate into fanaticism."[29] To encourage assimilation, the proposed law would require students to recite a Hebrew prayer for the longevity of the king, and the schoolmaster was to consistently remind his students of their duties toward France and her king.[30] Similar to proposals for Muslim education, curbing fanaticism and cultivating loyalty were also chief motives in early discussions of Jewish education.

Despite the ideological parallels between the plan of the director of civil affairs and those directed at young Muslims, French administrators were in the process of giving Jewish education in Algeria a unique institutional condition. When the Second Republic brought more Algerian agencies under civilian rule in 1848, it brought French and Jewish schools under the Ministry of Public Instruction and Religions. Muslim schools, however, remained under the Ministry of War's authority. Several months later, the government established the position of rector and his jurisdiction—the educational-administrative district of the Academy of Algiers.[31] From 1848, the military's role in Jewish education ceased to be one of making policy decisions.[32] The *rectorat*, prefects, and consistorial grand rabbis were charged with determining where, when, and how to establish Jewish schools.

The Shaping of a Reformist Agenda:
Algerian Realities and Metropolitan Visions

The hope of solidifying the conquest motivated most educational projects in early colonial Algeria, including those directed at the Jewish population. But to what extent were the plans and resulting schools the products of social and pedagogical realities on Algerian soil, and to what extent were they shaped by discourses emanating from the French metropole? Before returning to the practical effects of colonial pedagogy in Algeria, let us explore the inspirations for these reforms.

Again we find that Altaras and Cohen's celebrated tour of Algeria at the beginning of the 1840s charted the rhetorical map for later policies toward Algeria's Jews. The reformers noted, for example, that the Jews of Oran had only one small school under French supervision; other cities in the Province of Oran, including Tlemcen, Mascara, and Mostaganem, featured no French-Jewish schools prior to 1851. Oran's school featured a French teacher, an Algerian teacher, and roughly a dozen students. Foreshadowing some of the critiques consistory members and colonial officials would level at local schools in the 1850s, Altaras dismissed the ability of such an establishment to effectuate real change among Algerian Jews. Supplies were practically nonexistent, the teachers were negligent, and parents were suspicious of the institution. Particularly important, classes were held in a low, narrow room in a synagogue. When a rumor spread through Oran that French-Jewish schools would soon become obligatory, concerned parents sent their children to study with rabbis in Tlemcen or Mascara to avoid what they feared would be a Christian education.[33] Rather than welcome French pedagogy into their communities (as did so many Jews in Ottoman Turkey and Southeastern Europe), numerous Jews in Algeria viewed French-Jewish schools as unwelcome guests. From early in the conquest, reformers faced a colonized population resistant to their educational endeavors.

Men like Altaras and other shapers of early colonial educational ideology toward Jews were influenced by contemporaneous French discussions about teaching Muslims. Notably, many officials emphasized mutual education geared toward the elite of both populations. Léon Roche, a cavalry officer and translator who worked closely with both Abd al-Qader and then Thomas-Robert Bugeaud, suggested that France use schools "to assimilate the aristocracy of the country."[34] This could be done through pairing (*jumeler*) native and French schools so that the students could be in contact during recreational times. Through this "mutual education" (*éducation mutuelle*), the children of the Arab elite would be exposed to French customs and habits and ultimately come to serve the colonial administration. Bugeaud agreed that while common "Moors" were of no

use to France, well-trained sons of great chiefs could "serve us as intermediaries between us and their co-religionists." He was opposed, however,
to the prospect of the institutions serving as stepping-stones to military
schools. Referring to the second-century B.C.E. Libyan king who made
war with Rome after having been aided by it, Roche noted, "Jugurtha was
trained in the Roman army."[35]

Minister of War Soult also supported educating the North African elite,
noting that schools had the potential of delivering important political
benefits. Any educational program the French administration undertakes
must, insisted the minister, have well-conceived goals, since even partial
"cohabitation" of the student bodies carried with it the risk of "denation-
alizing" the native students. In other words, Algerian education must not
render colonized students overly ambitious—rather, it would have to focus
on the French language and serve vocational ends. In 1845, the inspector of
primary education also proposed French schooling for young Muslims, who
would then return to rural areas and teach in religious schools. This way,
he argued, they could neutralize the current tolbas, who were "imbued with
their false principles, animated by an implacable hatred against Christians,
and blinded by fanaticism."[36] The putatively civilizing project of destroying
fanaticism and superstition through education was justified as a tool to
weaken Algerian resistance.

Along the same lines, the Service of Public Instruction proposed a
teacher training institute (école normale) that would train religious teachers
"who would be devoted to us" and "appropriately remunerated, [they] would
teach their children in the tribes to love the French and bless the name of
the king."[37] On the eve of the declaration of the Second Republic, Governor
General duc d'Aumale lamented how French policy since 1830 had left native
education in ruins. He insisted that "the direction of public instruction has
always been a powerful political tool (levier)" to destroy fanaticism.[38] These
words led to few serious efforts to educate Algerian subjects, but they provide an idea of how education in Algeria, a mainstay of the civilizing project,
was conceived as part and parcel of colonial domination.

Those reporting on Algerian-Jewish education, such as Altaras and
Cohen, also hoped reforms would solidify colonial hierarchy. An 1843 report
composed by military doctors suggested that native schools taught their
students "all the vices of misery, all but how to learn."[39] Progress, they suggested, would first require education to "topple . . . the edifice of fanaticism"
that these schools had constructed. The report added that erudite, upright
men must control the new schools, men who were "religious without fanaticism." People whose intelligence the French had conquered through instruction, the authors insisted, would be forever safe, reliable, and eventually lead
the intellectual progress of their co-religionists.[40]

Progress was generally understood to be reducing local aversion to French institutions deemed fanatic. Echoing the generals, Altaras advocated a form of mutual education that brought students of multiple faiths together in the same school, but in different wings. The students would study French and spend recreational time together, and then return to their religiously specific domains for meals and religious instruction. This controlled cohabitation would "bring about the birth of that equality of science and mutual sympathy that engenders assimilation of mores and principles."[41] When Joseph Cohen published modified elements of the report in the pages of the *Archives Israélites*, he insisted on the importance of maintaining religious instruction while introducing reforms designed to counterbalance native fanaticism and hostility. It would be more sensible to reduce the control of the native rabbinate over the Algerian institutions by inserting French instructors, who could "initiate the children to the pure doctrines of the religion"[42] rather than to native superstitions.

Altaras hoped to educate all classes of Jews, but his vision was also deeply elitist. "Children of the elite," he wrote, could be brought to France to acquire useful skills. Once they had studied for several years and adopted the cultural forms of the bourgeoisie, they could "exercise a salutary influence on the spirit of their co-religionists of the inferior classes."[43] Foreshadowing the call of the Alliance Israélite Universelle after 1860, Altaras envisioned trained educators returning to work "for the emancipation of their co-religionists of Africa." Perhaps consciously echoing Bugeaud's paternalist social vision and anti-urban biases, Altaras also warned against educating poor Algerian Jews out of their element. Secular metropolitan schools had given many "unfortunates" in France the "gilded dreams of power and glory" resulting in "the depopulation of our fields, the abandonment of agricultural labor, the invasion of our cities by a jobless mob who believe themselves to have talent because they completed some studies." Altaras went so far as to blame the ideas of "modern socialists" on the fact that "the lowest rung" of French society had been educated to have "exuberant ambitions."[44] Colonial education could attach Algerian Jews to France, but if poorly planned, Altaras warned, it could lead to calls for equality.

Education for the poor, therefore, ought to remain primary, religious, vocational, and agricultural. The latter would assure that many took up a profession "as honorable as it would be useful for the colony." To deal with the problem of poor families deprived of the income their children would otherwise provide, Jewish schools could house workshops in which students would serve as apprentices, earning an income as they learned useful trades. Altaras saw education as a potential source for security and order in the new colony. At the same time, Altaras was already cognizant of the resistance of local populations to French pedagogy, and integrated this knowledge into his early plans. In Algeria, he warned, the populations have "barely left the state of ignorance and barbarism, and . . . do not know how to appreciate the value of instruction," so they might "oppose it with blind resistance." To eliminate the "ignorance and barbarism" that weakened France's control over the colony's Jews, Altaras emphasized the need for close governmental surveillance of their future schools.

Judging from such reports, 'ignorant' and 'fanatic' implied physical as well as pedagogical characteristics. Algerian-Jewish schools were threatening for preaching intolerance of the French as well as for being cramped and dangerous sources of contagion. In a report published in the *Archives Israélites*, the author insisted that the answer to educational backwardness was government-financed and well-monitored popular instruction that would take place in "two spacious and well-ventilated buildings."[45] This author was not alone in focusing on the physical environment of education. Altaras's report included the following description of an Algerian midrash: "Let us imagine narrow rooms painfully overcrowded with numerous children, dirty and disorganized. Unhealthy exhalations spread in the fetid, miasmic air, while the children's dirtiness engenders contagious diseases among them. . . . everywhere it is the same, in Algiers, Bône, [and] Oran. With rare exceptions, we have seen the same disorder, the same uncleanness, the same germs of serious diseases . . . the health of the children is constantly threatened by the impure atmosphere in which they breath in these narrow places."[46] The author concluded that it was "in the interest of civilization" to close the schools.

In 1846, Albert Cohen, the French-Jewish Orientalist and reformer introduced in the first chapter, issued a report to the director of civil affairs of Algeria that similarly emphasized the unsanitary nature of Algerian-Jewish schools.[47] Rabbi Lazare Cahen, several years after arriving in Oran, described indigenous schools as "very dirty, poorly laid out, poorly ventilated, some are even too narrow, so the children are packed together from morning until evening."[48] While these observers often criticized the incompetence of the teachers and the use of corporal punishment, the theme of miasma, contagious disease, and dirt proved particularly enduring. Indeed, the risk of contagion for students was often the primary justification for closing or controlling Jewish schools in Algeria.

In sum, early reports on Jewish education echoed much French thinking about Muslim education, while providing ideological groundwork for an evolving policy of civilizing. French supporters of both Jewish and Muslim education hoped to weaken resistance, in part bringing colonized youth into contact with members of other religious groups, part of a process of weakening "national" attachments. Yet officers also struggled to balance the desire to pull young Algerians from the influence of supposedly fanatical teachers, with worries that improved education would breed demands for independence or social mobility. Those reports concerned specifically with the Jewish schools also highlighted the unsanitary and unhealthy environments in which Algerian children languished. Despite these conditions, French observers acknowledged that Algerian Jews would hesitate before sending their children to any French-sponsored educational institution. Such ideas and constraints would form the kernel of French-Jewish educational ideology, even if colonial realities would soon force further changes in the policy it engendered.

French-Jewish Education in Oran

The history of the French-Jewish school in Oran deserves further examination. Initially, a communal school under the direction of a Protestant schoolmaster, it extended free, French-language instruction to approximately 60 Jewish boys in the city who, according to a later report, attended classes irregularly.[49] In June 1851, however, Rector Delacroix of the Academy of Algiers, who oversaw French education in Algeria, hired a man by the name of Stieffel to direct the school catering to Jews. By hiring a local rabbi and limiting his involvement to teaching French for several hours a week, he increased enrollment to 170 by 1853. The school for girls, established in 1852, counted as many as 80 students a year later. In 1854, the municipal council of Tlemcen also voted for the establishment of a French-Jewish school, and by early 1855 Rabbi Cahen reported that the new French-Jewish school of Mostaganem offered adequate places of instruction for all the Jewish boys in the city.[50] In 1855 and at the beginning of 1856, the municipal council of Mascara chose to devote the funds necessary for establishing a Jewish school.[51]

Almost immediately, most officials agreed that the official schools needed significant improvements. The school for boys had an acceptable building, but there were not enough qualified teachers for the number of enrolled pupils. Despite the French adjunct, the majority of students were still not conversant in French, an important measure of their success. As for the girls' school, the building was too narrow, and it was across the street from a house of prostitution. "In a country such as this one," the rector insisted, "this proximity cannot be tolerated for an extended period without posing a danger for public morality."[52] A new space would have to be found if it were to continue its mission, more money would be necessary to run the schools effectively, and more students would have to be brought into the system.

In late 1854, a report by the sub-inspector for primary instruction noted that the state of the official schools in Oran had worsened perceptibly. Fully two-thirds of their students had disappeared and were attending midrashim.

The report noted in particular that a local rabbi, Joseph ben Ayoun, had become a powerful opponent of the official communal school. Over the course of 1854, for example, ben Ayoun had managed to attract more than 200 students to his school; at the same time, the official school's attendance had slipped to 50. In the eyes of the sub-inspector, parental confidence in local rabbis was due to their "excessive severity toward the children."[53] Ben Ayoun, like the teacher of Fredja ben Sadoun's child, had already been imprisoned for several months for brutality toward his students. (The punishment consisted of the *phelatto*, fixing a child's ankles between two dowels and then hitting the balls of the immobilized victim's feet with a baton.[54]) And yet, despite the advice of the inspector, who hoped to close the school, the prefect allowed it to remain open on condition that ben Ayoun cease his offensive behavior.

Anxiety over ben Ayoun's school was but one example of how civil authorities in Oran increasingly monitored the competition presented by indigenous midrashim. Efforts to limit ben Ayoun's influence also show how the link between fanaticism and hygiene noted in the reports of the 1840s evolved into policy by the 1850s. In 1853, the rector, under orders of the prefect, produced a report on Jewish education in Oran. He concluded that despite the progress of the city's two Jewish schools, local rabbis continued to exercise undo influence on Algerian schoolchildren. According to the report, eight rabbinical schools continued to draw more than 350 students. While "the law does not tolerate schools in Algeria wherein the French language does not constitute one of the subjects of study," the schoolmasters in these schools continued to neglect its study. Furthermore, allowing "these veritable homes of ignorance and filth" to continue unhindered would be to "sacrifice the future of a public establishment that costs the commune 4,300 francs per year."

Faulting schools for being foyers of ignorance, fanaticism, and brutality toward the children was central to the articulation of civilization in these discussions. The sub-inspector, for example, felt that local schools' ability to train an increasing share of Oran's Jewish schoolchildren constituted an attack on civilization itself carried out "for the profit of several rabbis who are ignorant as they are fanatic."[55] In a different context, the prefect attributed the popularity of local teachers largely to the fact that they were hostile to "civilization."[56] This fanaticism could be tempered, however, if the administration could expose Jewish children to French instruction. This would "allow the student to remain faithful to the beliefs of his fathers," offered the sub-inspector, "[while French would] soon partly destroy prejudices and religious fanaticism."[57] As it stands, the ill treatment local Algerian instructors meted upon their students supplemented an impoverished pedagogy that "had no object other than chanting biblical verses which the students translate into Arabic." The actual meanings of civilization and progress were often less clear than the strategic purpose they served, which was to criticize local institutions and practices.

Paradoxically, officials such as the sub-inspector all the while decrying the competition local schools dealt the official institutions admitted that little value for civilization would be accrued unless a more developed system of French-Jewish schools took their place.[58] They noted, for example, the economic role they played in the Jewish community. The desperate material conditions of many of Oran's Jews, including many teachers, made suddenly closing all of them a bit dangerous. Beyond the economic ramifications, the report acknowledged that political reasons prevented closing all midrashim immediately. Instead, its author advised severe regulations and limitations on attendance that would eventually lead all of Oran's Jewish children to the French-Jewish schools.[59]

Why did midrashim survive? Why did Jewish parents avoid French-inspired schools in this context, in contrast to their contemporaries in the Ottoman lands? In important ways, the conflict over schools in Algeria ran parallel to the struggle over private synagogues discussed in the previous chapter. Local rabbis, such as ben Ayoun, were members of a larger community and of networks of patronage that extended into the consistory itself. Within the consistory, personal ties and devotion to the institutions that had existed before the French conquest continued to influence religious life and education. The sub-inspector inveighed, for example, against the "enemies of progress and civilization" among the leading Jewish notables of the city. "The gentlemen [Maclouf] Kalfoun, [Abraham] Kanoui, and others" had taken ben Ayoun as their protégé. Indeed, ben Ayoun had even managed to attract Rabbi Cahen's children as pupils. We must remember that the division in Oran's Jewish community discussed in Chapter 3 saw ben Ichou and ben Haim arrayed against Kanoui and Cahen. When one father had decided to bring a complaint to the police, Kanoui and Kalfoun encouraged him to drop his complaint. These men were now hindering the authorities from taking appropriate actions against ben Ayoun.[60] Local schools survived in part because of the protection they enjoyed in the consistory.

One drama in the larger saga surrounding ben Ichou's term as president of the consistory suggests how personal rivalries, consistorial influence, and the discourse of civilizing intermingled to preserve rabbinical schools in Oran. The episode began in January 1855, when Faris ben Ichou (a relative of consistorial president Abraham ben Ichou), complained to the police about Rabbi ben Ayoun.[61] According to ben Ichou, the instructor beat her son so severely that his life had been put in danger. Ben Ayoun was arrested following the testimony of several witnesses and a medical report. Soon after, however, the witnesses withdrew their testimony, insisting that the child had not undergone any beatings, and that his poor state was, instead, due to a disease. Faris ben Ichou, they insisted, had solicited (or pressured) them to make a false declaration. Upon a second medical inspection, the police were convinced by the verity of the new disclosures and released him. Police inspectors followed up with an investigation of Faris ben Ichou herself, an inquiry that necessarily implicated her relative, Abraham ben Ichou, then president of the consistory. At the time of his resignation from the consistory, ben Ichou accused Kanoui and Rabbi Cahen of supporting an "enemy of civilization," ben Ayoun. While Faris was acquitted for lack of evidence, many officials continued to suspect that ben Ichou had convinced his relative to falsely denounce ben Ayoun. This dispute was central in the decision to encourage ben Ichou to resign and to install Jacob Israel Lasry as president of the consistory of Oran.

The controversy surrounding Faris ben Ichou's child is also of interest in so far as it suggests that ben Ayoun (and perhaps other Algerian teachers) enjoyed firm consistorial support, despite the consistory's ostensible ambition of supporting official schools as replacements for these local institutions. This proved a point of contention among French officials. When the prefect received information from the sub-inspector detailing consistorial divisions, support for local midrashim, and general inaction, he was livid. At the beginning of December, the prefect sent a number of "observations" to the president of the consistory, an office still occupied by Abraham ben Ichou. "Mr. President, it is absolutely necessary that the consistory have but one thought, one motivation, and that it erase from memory the dissentions that may have existed between several of its members." He felt it necessary, in addition, to remind the members of the consistory of their duties. These included maintaining order in the synagogues, appointing and monitoring the ritual slaughterers, and making sure Jews exercise useful professions. He also demanded that the situation of communal schools be ameliorated, and made particular reference to Joseph ben Ayoun. "The good favor he enjoys among Jewish families," insisted the prefect, "is due less to any real merit than to his backward ideas and pedagogy that flatters [both] the ignorance of the fathers [as well as] their antipathy toward our civilization."[62] Furthermore, the prefect implicitly criticized the current president of the consistory by reminding him: "the consistory must not forget that the communal school, uniting all branches of teaching and requiring great [financial] sacrifices on the part of the commune, particularly deserves its interest and protection."[63] The prefect, it would appear, was well aware of the divisions within the consistory, and how these battles had led to a stalemate regarding ben Ayoun's school. Perhaps he blamed President ben Ichou for the acrimony within the consistory, despite the fact that ben Ichou was the most active partisan for closing the midrash in question. In sum, the parents who trusted ben Ayoun profited from the divisions, finding effective supporters for their school among one faction of the consistory. Despite the prefect's passionate critique of the institution, it survived.

Pressure to keep the school open and requests from his friends in the consistory led ben Ayoun to make some efforts to regularize his situation. In November, he and his fellow teacher Salomon Zarca, for example, formally requested from the prefect a state subsidy to pay for a French teacher for their school.[64] The members of the consistory, meanwhile, interrogated ben Ayoun about his methods of discipline.[65] In December 1854, worried about the schools they had implicitly sanctioned, the consistory carried out a more comprehensive inspection of this and all midrashim of Oran. The terse commentary that resulted from the investigation evaluated physical and pedagogical features of the school. Orderliness was one issue to which evaluators paid heed. One midrash provoked the following comment: "There were about forty students abandoned to the utmost disorder," as a result of the rabbi's inability to teach or discipline. "This school is well kept," another evaluation read, "but the teacher is not capable of teaching his students more than the first elements of reading."[66] Often, the commentary was simply a quick impression of the school's upkeep and the state of the children—for example: "Rabbinical School of Nissim Siméoni and Messaoud Taboul; there were forty students present. This school is well kept." Out of six rabbinic schools surveyed, only one did not receive generally passing marks. Even ben Ayoun's midrash was complimented for maintaining its students "in the greatest silence."[67] Of course, the choice to leave ben Ayoun's school intact was politically motivated; while most schools counted between 20 and 40 students, ben Ayoun and Zarca were responsible for more than 200. Divided and with social and political ties with the teachers concerned, the consistory was compelled to assume a more accommodating approach than the sub-inspector.

Ben Ayoun's experiences with Oran's Jewish notables, the civil administration, and local parents tell a larger story about the nature of the civilizing agenda in Algeria. We recall that the civilizing rhetoric in reports on schools was most obvious in its negative form; it was used to urge the elimination of schools deemed dirty and/or fanatical. Yet colonial realities impeded the execution of this supposedly civilizing step. The very consistorial administration he campaigned to install, whose legal mandate included the reform of Jewish education, sometimes ended up defending local midrashim the civil administration was ready to close. Faced with local resistance, students' needs, and consistorial divisions, the prefect, rector, and local civil commissaries had little choice but to implement their civilizing ideology flexibly, and sometimes to relinquish it altogether. When it came to the question of how Algeria's Jewish youth ought to be schooled, liberal plans often gave way to acquiescence to preexisting pedagogical norms. Regardless, civilizing remained a claim to authority.

If the consistory did little to shut rabbinical schools, they did manage to use charity to direct some children to communal schools. For example, in 1844, the widower Judah Addi was given a weekly stipend on the condition that he would send his children to the communal school.[68] When Messaoud Benarros petitioned the consistory about her "sad situation" in 1855, the consistory agreed to provide her three children with "a cap, a pair of pants, a shirt, a vest, and shoes" so that they could attend the communal school.[69] This practice was also used to encourage attendance at the girls' school. Following the first consistorial inspection of her institution, the director of this school was asked to explain the diminution in attendance. She replied that the poverty of the girls had become a problem, as they had no clothes to wear to school. In its next meeting, the consistory approved a subsidy to supply students with appropriate garments.[70] Policies like this were encouraged throughout the period, and in 1859 the consistory mentioned in a letter that its subsidies included money for tuition, clothes, paper, and books.[71] One cannot help but reflect that charity and bribery were close cousins. It may be that the poorest families of Oran were the least likely to decline free schooling for ideological reasons, and thus some poor families may have proved more willing to acquiesce to state intervention.

In response to the persistent strength of rabbinical schools in Algeria, the grand rabbi, having ascertained that approximately 500 Jewish students could be expected to attend schools in Oran, suggested limiting enrollment of all rabbinic schools to 310 students, thereby guaranteeing 190 students for the communal school.[72] This could be accomplished if individual midrashim limited enrollment to 50 students or fewer. Based on the advice of the prefect, children of eight years or older would be required to spend several hours a day at the communal school, where they would be given French instruction. The consistory took up Rabbi Cahen's suggestion again, asking the prefect to insist that native schools, which in everyone's opinion were capable of teaching religious subjects, would remain open with limited enrollment.[73]

The competition rabbinical schools offered communal schools constituted a resurfacing theme in official correspondence, despite a new decree to limit enrollments. In 1855, Rabbi Cahen visited all the private schools, explained the implications of provision to the nine instructors, and accorded the required certificates to all. He hastened to inform the prefect that he had certified ben Ayoun as well, based on the fact that he was a capable teacher. It was up to the civil authorities, concluded Rabbi Cahen, to judge whether he deserved an additional certification of morality. Within weeks of Cahen's visit, the rector had received requests for the required authorization from eight midrash instructors (not including ben Ayoun), and furnished the necessary certificates of morality to all. The decision about whom to accept, the rector noted, belonged to the prefect. As if to explain his generosity, the rector noted that no locality should be deprived of an educational institution. He nonetheless added, "It is important to avoid multiplying these establishments and to ensure the prosperity of French Jewish schools." He requested further that the prefect make use of the new measure, writing: "I am also convinced, Mr. Prefect, that in demanding the rigorous execution of the conditions imposed by Article 8 of the law, you impede the excessive development of midrashim in which the children hardly receive religious instruction, and which must, one day, cede their place to institutions that are more complete, and above all, more French."[74] The day when French education triumphed was evidently not yet at hand. Competition remained a central theme in the struggle of the civil administration to exert control over local educational institutions.

The Ministry of Public Instruction and Religions' decree of early 1855 provided local administrators with tools to control Algerian-Jewish teachers and stem competition to communal schools. It thus invested civil administrators with the right to approve or close rabbinical schools, wresting this responsibility from the consistory as laid out in the 1845 ordinance. The decree also provided the (French) grand rabbis with a new measure of influence. According to the decree:

> No rabbinical school can open without the permission of the rector.
> This authorization will only be accorded after the advice of the prefect
> and the mayor, and on the presentation of
> 1. A certificate of morality, delivered by the municipal authorities
> 2. A certificate of capacity, delivered by the grand rabbi of the Algerian consistory or by the rabbis of the provincial consistories.[75]

From the beginning of 1855, municipal authorities of Algerian cities were thus officially charged with guaranteeing the morality of Algerian rabbis.[76] At the same time, the (French-born and -trained) grand rabbis were given more oversight of Jewish religious teaching in the colony. Following Rabbi Cahen's suggestion to the authorities, the decree limited enrollment to 50 students per instructor. Algerian teachers were forbidden from teaching subjects outside the traditional religious curriculum; only Frenchmen were permitted to teach modern subjects. The new requirements also specifically outlawed corporal punishment. In sum, the 1855 reforms gave a legal framework to the processes by which midrashim and their pupils were monitored.[77] The state's reach over Jewish pedagogy was extending, albeit with a flexible approach.

Crucially, the reforms charged municipal officials, rather than the consistory, with enforcement. This perhaps explains why the tenth article of the decree officially entrusted supervision of Jewish schools to the Academy of

Algiers and municipal authorities—a departure from the original decree of November 9, which provided for the creation of schools under the aegis of the consistories. Letters were sent not only to the mayor of Oran but also to the civil commissioners of Tlemcen and Mascara, informing them of their responsibilities and requesting that each "vigorously take in hand the execution of this law in their administrative circumscription."[78] In the following months, correspondence concerning schools circulated among civil commissioners and mayors of cities, officials of the Academy of Algiers (such as the rector and sub-inspector) and higher authorities (prefect, governor general, and ministers).

The move to give civil officials and the French grand rabbi more influence had some unintended consequences. For instance, Cahen intervened with the authorities in favor of local rabbis and their midrashim on several occasions. Despite their limited power, local consistorial delegates also continued to make requests to local officials asking for temporary or permanent authorizations for local teachers so that they could stay in business. Cahen, for example, defended ben Ayoun against efforts to close his school, supported by the civil administration and his consistorial rival, Abraham ben Ichou. In Mascara, the rector asked the civil commissioner to shut schools run by Mordechai Atouaty and Ichouda Karsenty in July 1855.[79] Soon after, numerous fathers of children attending these schools complained to local delegates of the consistory, demanding that Karsenty and Atouaty's school be reopened. Abraham ben Ichou, as committed as he was to closing ben Ayoun's school in Oran, in this case asked both the civil commissioner and the prefect to allow the instructors to open their doors.[80] Cahen, agreeing with his enemy ben Ichou, warned the prefect that the children risked being left to "vagabondage" were the schools not reopened.[81] Thus, it was decided that the schools would reopen on the condition that they close upon the founding of a communal school, projected for the following year. The prefect permitted the schools' reopening, and advised the rector to accept the instructors of closed midrashim as adjuncts to the future French-Jewish establishment, if they proved morally fit.[82]

Furthermore, civil administrators' new influence over Jewish schools in no way guaranteed their funding. While local Jews were responsible for paying wages to teachers in midrashim, instructors in communal schools expected adequate governmental salaries. This issue arose in Mascara, when in 1856 the rector informed the municipal council that while it had done well to authorize a new Jewish school, it had failed to provide for the religious instructor's salary. After a quick debate over the amount, it was soon approved, at six hundred francs per year.[83] One thousand francs had previously been voted to support the French director of the school.[84] When the religious instructors at the French-Jewish school of Tlemcen claimed that the small portion of tuition fees allocated as salary left them in poverty, the municipality was asked to augment their wages.[85] The story suggests lack of adequate resources was another complicating dynamic in the story of Jewish education in colonial Oran.

Despite the campaigns of local parents and the occasional intervention of the consistory, officials continued to try to stem the number of students attending midrashim. If most rabbis were begrudgingly authorized to keep their midrashim open, civil authorities used Article 8 of the 1855 decree to limit enrollment to 50 students. Thus, in addition to the oppositions framed by the notion of civilization, competition became a structuring principle of the French colonial effort to channel students toward French teachers. The issue was not limited to the city of Oran where large operations like ben Ayoun's operated. In 1855, for example, the rector informed the prefect that the "grand rabbi of the Algerian consistory informed me that the authorized midrash in Tlemcen receives 140 students, contrary to Article 8 of the law of January 1, 1855." The midrash in question was run by Rabbi Aaron ben Ichou. Furthermore, "a Mr. Abraham Chouraki maintains a rabbinic school without authorization."[86] Later that year, a distressed civil commissioner complained that while he had "always devoted all my efforts to these schools and . . . constantly invited the Israelites to send their children there," his success at bringing in 80 students to Tlemcen's French-Jewish school was short lived. According to the commissioner, "Little by little, the teacher saw the number of his students reduced to 40. This decline can be traced to the opening of rabbinic schools."[87]

In some cases, the prefect denied the request of native schools to remain open, even if a communal school had yet to be established. Once again, competition was cited—a rabbinical school could eventually compete with a communal school, were one to be established. After several teachers of midrashim in Mascara were issued certificates of morality, for example, the prefect lectured local civil authorities. According to the prefect, allowing the creation of "a purely rabbinical school" was dangerous if a French-Jewish school was slated for the near future. The midrashim were "always more sympathetic to the prejudices of the indigenous Jews" than French institutions. "We have in Oran a disturbing example of the midrashim's antagonism toward instruction of a more advanced degree. The communal Jewish school, which counted nearly 150 students, has seen this number reduced to 70, through the influence of the rabbis on the fathers of the families."[88] Such anecdotes suggest that local Jews harbored an enduring mistrust of French-Jewish institutions, while local teachers provided considerable competition.[89]

Officials took a similar approach to competition throughout the province. The prefect notified all the mayors and civil commissioners of Oran,

Tlemcen, Mascara, and Mostaganem of the new decree to ensure that communal schools, if they existed, were not to suffer competition from midrashim. In May 1855, the rector gave permission to a Mr. ben Sadoun of Oran to operate his midrash on the condition that he limit enrollment to 20 students.[90] In Tlemcen, the rector advised the prefect to allow one midrash to remain open, but to close the rest. At the same time, he recommended approving the request of several local Jews associated with the consistory to open a French-Jewish school in the city. The prefect dutifully denied permissions to other instructors who wished to remain in operation.[91] There was little reason to approve these "purely indigenous schools," declared the prefect, when they would just compete with the French-Jewish schools.[92] The prefect's concern was well founded; Aaron ben Ichou's school, approved to teach 50 students, hosted more than 140 a month later. Furthermore, an unapproved midrash had reportedly refused to close.[93] By September, the official school had been reduced to 40 pupils.[94]

Civil officials continued their efforts to reduce competition by limiting enrollments and closing unauthorized schools for the remainder of the decade. When Nissim Reubeni attempted to reestablish a midrash in Oran after having worked as an adjunct to the French-Jewish institution in Mostaganem, he was refused permission.[95] The rector noted that it was a narrow space that was "only accessible with difficulty, even dangerous" where "tens of students" were in a room "hardly large enough for fifteen."[96] The prefect closed the institution, however, to reduce the number of midrashim and to protect the communal school.[97] In 1859, the prefect closed another rabbinic school run by Isaac Hassan, probably a member of the prominent Livornese Moroccan family by the same name.[98] Even when a father hired a private instructor to give religious lessons to his children, the authorities intervened, viewing their mandate as extending beyond the walls of the midrash and into the home. In one such case, it was eventually decided that the lessons could continue, if no other children were present in the father's home while the lessons were conducted.[99]

Administrators also closed schools run by Moroccan immigrants. Messaoud El Kannoui probably came to Oran from Morocco sometime in the 1840s or early 1850s. First he worked as a teacher in Joseph ben Ayoun's midrash and received a certificate of morality at the time of the 1855 decree. Perhaps after a dispute with ben Ayoun (who sided with Lazare Cahen, Abraham El Kanoui, and Jacob Lasry in the community division described in Chapter 3), he relocated to the town of Sidi-Bel-Abbes to work as an instructor. While he obtained authorization to teach at Sidi-Bel-Abbes, it was conditional on renouncing his authorization in Oran. Despite this, after a year or so, he returned to Oran and taught students at the provisionally tolerated private synagogue of Abraham ben Haim (a partisan of the opposing clique led by ben Ichou). Rabbi Cahen vigorously opposed the reopening of this synagogue, noting that the community of Sidi-Bel-Abbes was "unsatisfied with [Messaoud El Kannoui's] services" and that "we already have more than enough of these midrashim in Oran."[100] The rector was less convinced, noting that there were no complaints against him, and thus no evidence that the community of Sidi-Bel-Abbes had asked him to leave.[101] The prefect, for his part, noted that El Kannoui was an honest family man, and that he had only heard good things about him. Nevertheless, official policy was to diminish the number of midrashim, "these houses of ignorance," he continued, "that will be obstacles to progress for as long as they exist."[102] Messaoud El Kannoui was forbidden from offering classes in Oran, but exceptions appear to have become more common by the early 1860s.

From "Enemy of Progress and Civilization" to "the Best Rabbi in Oran": Compromise, Co-option, and the Midrash of Joseph Ben Ayoun

As the stories related above suggest, the civilizers were forced to compromise a great deal with Algerian rabbis, teachers, and parents. As much as one consistory member might have wished to close a school, another member might have organized to keep it open. In many cases, local Jewish parents affected policy by writing petitions and sending their children to teachers of their choice. The story of Joseph ben Ayoun's popular midrash illustrates both the compromises consistorial officers, Rector Delacroix, and the prefect made with Algerian teachers and parents in the 1850s, as well as the fine line that divided Algerian and French schools in officials' imaginations. Thus we find, for example, that a year after the decree concerning rabbinical schools had passed, the prefect alerted the rector that ben Ayoun continued to teach without a certificate of morality. As noted above, ben Ayoun had suffered legal consequences for beating his students. The rector had hoped for a final arbitration on this case, but the situation proved too complicated for quick results. For one thing, accusations that ben Ayoun had continued to mistreat students had been proven false. Furthermore, ben Ayoun was extremely popular. The year before "a considerable number of [his] co-religionists" had petitioned the authorities to maintain the school, the prefect noted, "regardless of [the fact that] he had been refused a certificate of morality by the municipality." The petitioners had also offered "to support at their cost a French instructor, certified by us to complete the school, and to bring it closer to our ideas."[103] The prefect opted to maintain ben Ayoun's school, but to take steps toward making it French.

Most officials appeared to agree that it would be impolitic to simply close the rabbinical school despite a year having passed since the law designed to restrict schools of that nature had been adopted. Ben Ayoun's popularity and effectiveness were well known, and the community would protest such a move. They agreed, however, that ben Ayoun's strengths could be harnessed for French education. If Rector Delacroix had severely criticized ben Ayoun several years earlier, in August he encouraged the municipality to hire ben Ayoun as a teacher at the communal school. If this proved impossible, the prefect could hire a French instructor for ben Ayoun's midrash, producing a sort of private school on the model of the French-Jewish institutions. Whether the local Jewish petitioners had given the French administrators the idea for a private school, or it had emerged in official circles first, is difficult to determine. Yet the rector and prefect were clearly bending their initial ideas to suit the environment. Delacroix's change of heart was particularly radical; after visiting every rabbinic establishment in his jurisdiction, he told the prefect that it would "insult justice" and "upset a considerable portion of the Jewish community of Oran" if the school were closed. Furthermore, upon studying the situation, he determined that "ben Ayoun is the best rabbi in the Province of Oran."[104]

These ideas engendered a conversation among the civil officials of Oran. The mayor of Oran preferred the first option.[105] The consistory first agreed with the mayor, noting that ben Ayoun must work at the communal school, for indigenous schools were by the 1855 law forbidden to teach secular subjects.[106] Later, they changed their opinion to support a private school that would have communal status.[107] The reason for the change was indicative of the larger dynamic of compromise at work. Director Stieffel of the French-Jewish communal school was so unpopular among the Jews of Oran that bringing ben Ayoun under his wing could backfire.[108] Furthermore, the physical constraints of the communal school's building were such that it could not admit that many more students. On November 13, the rector informed the prefect that he had authorized a M. Léon Lévy to open a new private Jewish institution, employing Joseph ben Ayoun as adjunct director. Algerian teachers Salomon Zarca and Haim ben Ayoun were also hired as instructors.[109] By the end of the month, the experiment in private education was in operation and had an enrollment of 200 students.

Civil administrators in Oran also tried co-opting other popular Algerian rabbis. The prefect noted in 1855, for example, thanks to the agreement of several indigenous rabbis to teach as adjuncts in the French-Jewish school, that the institution continued to function. "For this population," noted the prefect, "prefers the midrashim."[110] In 1857, the consistory supported Stieffel's initiative to hire a Moroccan teacher at the communal school to counteract his own unpopularity. By the end of the year, school attendance had grown to 140 students.[111] When the communal institution began losing students to the midrashim once again at the end of the 1850s, the consistory proposed that a popular instructor, Abraham Haziza, merge his private school into the communal one, bringing in his 50 students.[112] Nissim Reubeni, who had held one of the original midrashim of Oran, was hired as an adjunct to the French-Jewish school of Mostaganem.[113] These measures were justified as bringing the students under the civilizing influence of French instruction while better monitoring the Algerian teachers. When Oran established ben Ayoun in his new school, the rector noted that any future wrongdoing on the instructor's part would be easier to notice and correct. The consistory, in the end, was charged with monitoring and controlling ben Ayoun's conduct.[114]

The story of ben Ayoun's school reveals the controls, compromises, and contradictions bound up in the civil administration's effort to civilize Jewish education in Oran. Civil authorities first identified the Algerian-Jewish teacher as a brutal and retrograde example of local pedagogical practice. The rector and sub-inspector had found that in addition to his incarceration for beating students, his pedagogy was fanatic and catered to local parents' hatred of civilization. Nevertheless, his popularity, effectiveness, and eventual pull with the grand rabbi soon influenced official opinion. The eventual compromise brought ben Ayoun into a communal private school with French instruction. Officials' improved ability to monitor his behavior partially justified the move. Regardless of the French civilizing ideology, communal schools increasingly conformed to their Algerian surroundings.

Immigration and Negotiation

At first glance, 1860 appeared to be a turning point in the effort to control Algerian-Jewish education. Civil commissioners and the prefect were taking fewer actions against midrashim, and the consistory published a report in 1859 boasting that many of them had been closed. According to the consistory, only a few continued to operate in the city of Oran.[115] Furthermore, the system of French-Jewish education seemed to be stable, with two French-Jewish schools in Oran, and one each in Mascara, Mostaganem, and Tlemcen. Remarkably, the French-Jewish school in Mostaganem boasted having no competition from local midrashim. Either the consistory's report exaggerated the success of French-Jewish schools, or the moment was fleeting.

Soon, civil officials were again concerned with the spread of midrashim. The likely spark was the influx of Moroccan refugees to the Province of Oran. As mentioned earlier, western Algeria had long been a destination for Moroccan Jewish immigrants, dating at least from Muhammad al-Kabir's reconquest of the city from the Spanish in 1792. The new Ottoman authorities had invited neighboring Jews to settle in the decimated city to revive commerce, and along with the Jews from Gibraltar, Tlemcen, Mascara, and Mostaganem, came many from Tetuan. With the outbreak of the Spanish-Moroccan War of 1859 to 1860, however, a new flow of Moroccans reached the area.[116] On October 30, 1859, for example, French citizens and protégés were ordered out of Tetuan, the same year the city's Jewish quarter was attacked. Refugees went to Gibraltar, Spain, Peru, and Argentina, as well as to cities and towns in western Algeria such as Tlemcen, Oran, Sidi-Bel-Abbes, Aïn Témouchent, and St. Denis du Sig.[117]

The story of Rabbi Salomon Nahon sheds some light on how the Spanish-Moroccan War affected rabbinical education in the province of Oran. In 1859 or 1860, Nahon came to Oran from Morocco with his wife and five children. In a letter to the mayor of Oran written in May 1860, Nahon begged the official "to take [his] sad situation in consideration," and authorize him to teach several students so that he could earn a living.[118] At around the same time, the mayor received notice that Moroccan immigrants Isaac and Moshe Kalfon were teaching students at an address on Rue Ratissebonne in Oran. Joseph ben Chetrit, also Moroccan, meanwhile had opened another unauthorized midrash on Rue de Naples.[119] Without mentioning Salomon Nahon, the prefect ordered the mayor of Oran to immediately close the two other midrashim taught by Moroccan immigrants.[120] The consistory, however, stepped in to defend the teachers by highlighting their miserable plight. At the time, a number of charitable drives were organized to help the Moroccan refugees in Algeria and elsewhere. For example, Albert Cohen, the Orientalist who campaigned for Algerian consistories in the 1840s, made a well-publicized tour of Jewish refugee communities in Morocco, Spain, and Algeria in 1860 to raise funds.[121] Lasry told the prefect that Cahen had already visited the unauthorized schools and informed them of the rules pertaining to private midrashim. The rabbis, he insisted meant no harm, and were teaching students to avoid depending on community funds. The consistory had chosen to accept their promise to request authorization, and Lasry asked the prefect to allow them to continue operating in the short term.[122] Given both Lasry and the prefect's silence, we may assume that Nahon, ben Chetrit, and the Kalfon brothers continued to operate their schools.

Nahon and his compatriots were not the only North African schoolmasters to find themselves with more leverage in the 1860s. The diversification of Algerian Jewry, fueled by migration and regional violence, only further thwarted the officials' ability to realize their vision in an idealized form. In 1863, for example, the director of the consistorial school in Oran wrote to the prefect to complain about competition. Aron Lévy, the school's director, noted that the number of clandestine schools had risen to eleven in the past several months. This was a problem because "these schools (of which one is next to one that I [Lévy] direct) do immense damage to the consistorial school." Audaciously, wrote Lévy, "the rabbi directors of these midrashim come take students from me, even at my school."[123] In an 1867 report, the new grand rabbi of Oran, Mahir Charleville, noted that eleven still existed in Oran. Furthermore, there were three in Tlemcen and twenty-five in the province.[124] According to Oran's new grand rabbi, midrashim now existed in such towns as Aïn-Témouchent, Nedroma, Nemours, and Saida, which had not even received consistorial delegates in the early 1850s.[125]

Interestingly, the prefect noted that even if eleven schools continued to operate in Oran and twenty-five in the province as a whole, efforts to control Algerian-Jewish schools could be deemed successful. In a note to the governor general, the prefect championed "the spirit of progress that reigns among the Israelites of the Province of Oran." Yet out of 2,214 students attending classes, 1,249 were in midrashim and only 965 were in the French-Jewish establishments.[126] Sixty-seven additional children, too young to be attending normal classes, had been placed in French-Jewish preschools. The prefect's characterization of such figures as markers of success underlines the French colonial regime's complicated and contradictory approach to Algerian-Jewish education. The consistory encouraged Jews to attend communal schools, but also defended independent local teachers. A number of factors influenced their policy—pity for refugees, fear of supporting those whom they deprived of a livelihood, and sometimes the existence of personal ties or animosities. Furthermore, we must remember that the primary distinction between authorized and unauthorized schools was the presence of a French-language instructor. Little else distinguished the supposedly civilized schools under the rector's surveillance from those characterized as clandestine.

The official campaign to control midrashim during the Second Empire period did not shut many schools, but it significantly extended official surveillance, inspection, and medical control of young Algerian Jews. The regulation of January 1, 1855, nominally intended to ensure the morality of instruction, marked the beginning of an explosion of official correspondence regarding the health and hygiene of colonized Jews. Similar to efforts directed at synagogues and circumcision rituals, French officials in Algeria echoed medical discourse in France that described physical interiors as dangerous sites of dirt, immorality, and contagion. The following pages demonstrate that, in the eyes of the state, Jewish homes and schools required inspection because they were privileged sites where civilization served as a vehicle to evaluate, critique, and intervene. Attention to the physical and moral state of Jewish schools represents another example of governmental interest and control of a population many civil officials expected to see naturalized.

Conclusion: Compromise and Conquest

The story of Oran's midrashim adds new complexity to our history of the civilizing mission in Algeria. On the one hand, Algerian teachers of midrashim often played an important role in the French-Jewish communal schools. On the other hand, members of the consistory and civil officials consistently portrayed the same midrashim as obstacles to enlightenment. Jacob Lasry, for example, when proposing that ben Ayoun be hired by the communal school, described how "the large majority of our co-religionists still stagnate in the ignorance that centuries of slavery and persecution have dropped them." This explained the continuing popularity of schools that offered exclusively religious instruction. Lasry also insisted, "civilization is dependent" upon public instruction and "the education of the youth." Yet, for strategic reasons, he hoped to bring the most popular representative of the schools he criticized into a communal school. In sum, Lasry mobilized the civilizing ideology both to criticize Algerian-Jewish teachers as ignorant and simultaneously transform them into allies by hiring and controlling them. Nominally, civilizing involved learning French, but the term was most meaningful as justification toward increased control over Algerian teachers.

Corporal punishment also emerged as an important metaphor for understanding and deploying the notion of civilization. For this reason, the prefect insisted that schoolmasters cease to use batons in school not only to stop corporal punishment, but also to "remove all substance from accusations that present rabbinic instructors as hostile to our laws, morals, and the progress demanded by civilization."[127] Other examples also point to a concern for public appearances.[128] Yet the example of Fedja ben Sadoun with which we opened this chapter, as well as ben Ayoun's move to a communal school, suggests that reality did not align with French officials' mapping of civilization; corporal punishment existed in French schools as well. The term was far more important as a rhetorical claim of authority than as a description of a set of behaviors or perspectives.

Comparing early reports of Algerian education with the actual policies the administration pursued in the late 1850s and 1860s brings into relief the fluidity of the concept of civilization. In the earlier period, reformers were inclined to paint stark contrasts between Algerian-Jewish education and the French philosophy, as an article published in the *Archives Israélites* clearly illustrates: "As for their principles, they are diametrically opposed [to ours]. Between us, there is a struggle between prejudice and liberal education, between blind intolerance and the alliance of reason and faith, between superstition and the true spirit of religion."[129] In addition to such lofty (if vapid) oppositions of platitudes, rabbis were portrayed as possessing a near-total power over young minds. As one report phrased it, the community "marched with fanatic obedience to the orders of a rabbi."[130] Reformers described the antagonism between French and Algerian sensibilities in warlike terms. For example, Rabbi Michel Weill, who also served as schoolmaster of the first French-Jewish school in Algiers, reported: "the indigenous rabbis are adversaries of our school" and "before the foundation of the French school, they alone enjoyed the monopoly on instruction," giving them a power that was "exorbitant" and "dictatorial." In an 1846 report, Joseph Cohen warned that alongside the several French schools, there were a "crowd of others" in which the students were completely "absorbed by the rabbis, following the Hebrew course professed by their indigenous teachers."[131] As late as 1854, the sub-inspector for the Academy of Algiers accused Algerian teachers who had attracted parents away from the communal school of being "enemies of progress and of civilization."[132] In 1855, the rector attributed the decline of attendance at the French-Jewish school to "the war that rabbinical teachers wage against it."[133] As these quotations suggest, until the middle of the 1850s, the struggle to close local schools and bring young Jews into communal institutions was frequently seen as a war for civilization.

Yet, by the end of the 1850s all this would change. By this point, numerous Algerian rabbis had allied with reformists to shape an institutional (if not pedagogical) middle ground. This dramatic shift was strategic on the part of the consistorial leadership that simply lacked overwhelming power over their urban charges. Hostile confrontations with parents of school-aged children, as well as with powerful heads of local midrashim, had shown these officials that they could ill afford to antagonize Algerian Jews by micro-managing their educational system. Leniency toward midrashim was also inspired by shifting social realities, such as the war that generated an expanded refugee population. When it came to the question of how Algeria's Jewish youth would be educated, civilization sacrificed none of its rhetorical salience despite being quite adaptable to historical exigency and tactical compromise.

The colonial administration's campaign to civilize Algerian Jews through the control of midrashim is best understood in dialogue with efforts to close private synagogues, explored in the previous chapter. In both cases, the ideology of civilizing demanded increased surveillance and intervention into interior spaces. In neither case, however, was the policy implemented without significant compromise with the preexisting social and institutional landscape. Oran's Jewish elite were represented in the consistory and in municipal councils, and frequently succeeded in transforming the various demands of civilization to fit their own perspectives or financial imperatives. Civilizing did not engender the creation of an entirely new system.

Jewish schools in Algeria were considered French by virtue of having a French instructor present for several hours a day. This understanding was based on a belief in the French language, but also on the perceived necessity of conforming to local beliefs and habits. French authorities, responding to attendance patterns and petitions, simply feared closing all the midrashim. The authorities, therefore, chose to work within the preexisting institutional infrastructure, rendering a number of local teachers and schools "legal" according to the new code. In both Oran and Mostaganem, municipal authorities took advantage of the popularity of indigenous and Moroccan rabbis by bringing them into French schools. It follows that the scathing critiques of local institutions and methods tended to soften over the course of the period anterior to the Third Republic.

The processes by which French-Jewish schools were established and developed were intertwined with other important institutions of control. Education provides a lens through which we can explore an important chapter in the pre–Third Republic history of the civilizing mission in Algeria, as well as the history of the legal assimilation of Algerian Jews to France. Efforts to educate included a range of small but real controls over the lives of colonized subjects. The period was marked by the confrontation between the colonial authority's appropriation of important cultural institutions and Algerian Jewry's transformation of colonial efforts to conform to local standards. This confrontation produced a form of education that maintained a significant Algerian-Jewish religious component. This very fact suggests that when the Algerian Jews were naturalized en masse in 1870, they remained a population with distinct institutions and traditions and had by no means embraced a widely accepted French model of assimilation—however broadly defined.

5

From Napoleon's Sanhedrin to the Crémieux Decree

Sex, Marriage, and the Boundaries of Civilization

In the early 1870s, a wealthy Algerian Jew named Sasportès, married for more than thirty years to a certain Kamra Karsenty, entered into a polygamous marriage with Messouda ben Jehou.[1] Sasportès took a second wife hoping to have a child, which his union with Kamra had failed to produce. It had been a lengthy search, a number of his proposals having been rejected by prospective wives or their families. Word soon spread that he had not only remarried, but had also backdated his *ketuba* (wedding contract) to 1869, the year before Jews were granted citizenship. In so doing, Sasportès planned to make it appear that his second marriage was contracted before Algerian Jews became French citizens, and were consequently obliged to observe French family law, by which polygamy was illegal. Sasportès was arrested and a trial was set for 1875. When the date of the trial arrived, it was presided over by Edouard Sautayra, a judge who had advanced his prestige several years before by copublishing a translation of the medieval Jewish legal text *Eben haEzer* with the French grand rabbi of Oran, Mahir Charleville.

Sasportès's examination of the defendant raised a number of issues about family status, naturalization, and morality. Early in the questioning, the prosecutor argued that polygamy was not only illegal for French citizens, but that it was immoral and not becoming of respectable people. Sasportès's justification for his actions was rooted in the morality dictated by local interpretations of Jewish law.

PROSECUTION: You know very well why [many of your proposals were rejected]. For 20 years now, has there been a single respectable Jewish family in Algeria that accepts polygamy?

DEFENDANT: That is false. Our law authorizes polygamy, and it is a violation to not take a second wife if, after ten years of marriage, the first wife does not give you an heir.

PROSECUTION: As long as you were governed by your [Jewish] personal status, polygamy was indeed authorized. But that is no longer the case since, by decree of 24 October [1870], you have become French and you are submitted to French law.

DEFENDANT: French law cannot change my religious law.[2]

The prosecutor's response revealed a certain anxiety. He was not content to simply underline polygamy's illegality, but sought to emphasize its rarity among Jews. Saportès's interpretation of Judaism's marital laws must be unusual, the prosecution's strategy seemed to imply. Sasportès responded by brushing aside any implication that another community's interpretation of Jewish law was relevant to his case, or even that he should act as a French Jew might:

PROSECUTION: But all the Jews of Europe, with only those of Poland and Hungary excepted, have submitted to monogamy, and in so doing have they abandoned the Law of Moses?[3]

DEFENDANT: They conduct themselves as they understand [the law]. I maintain that one is only a good Israelite when one practices all the precepts of our law. Furthermore, I never asked to become French.

With the naturalization of Algeria's Jews, could Jewish family law continue to contradict French law? What was the meaning of this divergence between European Jewish practices and those of their newly naturalized co-religionists in Algeria? Sasportès's response drew on the principle of religious freedom, but the prosecutor appears to have changed course. After the defendant's response, the prosecution limited itself to arguments based on the actual law in effect, not to wider questions of respectability or the variety of interpretations of Jewish law.

PROSECUTION: You became [French] in consequence of the decree of 24 October 1870?

DEFENDANT: I did not know what that required [of me].

PROSECUTION: You knew perfectly well, for the decree was in preparation for several years. The *conseils généreaux*, the *conseil supérieur* of the colony, had all approved [of the draft law]. [Had not] the government of the Empire prepared the decree and the delegation of Tours promulgated it?

DEFENDANT: I don't know about all that. I am Jewish. I want to remain Jewish. That is all [*voilà tout*].

In so responding, Sasportès expressed a sentiment that demonstrated some of the contradictions and failures of the civilizing effort. In response to questions, he guessed that 200 ketubas in Oran were similarly backdated to avoid being subject to French marriage law. Upon hearing this information, the prosecutor asked Sasportès if this meant that the Jews of Oran sought to avoid obeying the law. His response was telling:

PROSECUTION: Do the Jews of Oran, like you, aim to avoid the law?
DEFENDANT: All those who do not want to be French certainly do. We all want to be French for business, because the [French] consuls protect us, and so foreigners no longer abuse us. But for all that concerns marriage and repudiation, we want to remain Jews.

Remarkably, Sasportès was acquitted and the court transcript circulated widely in official circles. In the wake of his trial, new laws were proposed to clarify any ambiguities in the legal status of Algerian-Jewish marriage. One idea vetted by the Ministry of Justice was to require all Algerian Jews to register their ketubas, even those from before the 1870 decree.[4] The idea was dropped, perhaps because according to French law, the documents by themselves had no legal weight. Nevertheless, the Sasportès trial quickly became a matter of concern among Jews in Algeria and France.

The trial casts light on the interwoven histories of French marriage law, citizenship, and colonial difference in nineteenth-century Algeria. It suggests that marriage law and family customs played a vital role in determining the success of assimilating efforts directed toward Jews in Algeria from the beginning of colonization until their naturalization in 1870. This chapter builds on the previous chapters that have shown how civilizing, though a fluid and frequently appropriated term, often took on meaning in discussions about bodies, domestic space, and the interiors of religious institutions. The concept of civilization demanded official surveillance and control over the values, beliefs, and laws underpinning the Jewish family.

Efforts to extend French law over Algerian-Jewish families were interwoven with representations and discussions of Algerian Muslim families. Specifically, Jewish reformers and civil officials advocating Algerian-Jewish naturalization often played on prevalent stereotypes about putatively immoral Muslim family customs to accentuate Jewish cultural superiority and suitability for citizenship. Discussions about morality, naturalization, and citizenship intensified with Napoleon III's Saint-Simonian experiments with assimilation, and policies that tended toward subsuming Algeria to the same governing institutions as metropolitan France. Legists, Jewish reformers, and lawmakers all identified Algerians' supposedly debased morality, polygamous marriages, and divorce practices as basic obstacles to French citizenship. Jewish or Islamic family law would have to conform to the French code, observers argued, before naturalization could be considered. These writers often found a legal precedent in the form of Napoleon's 1806 to 1808 Assembly of Notable Israelites and the Grand Sanhedrin. These assemblies

were convened to solicit rabbinical approval of measures meant to "harmonize" Jewish law, and notably issues pertaining to marriage, with French civil
law. Some sixty years later, when France collectively naturalized Algerian
Jews, it again affirmed the centrality of family law and morality to the cause
of civilization. It did so by stripping Algerian Jews of their right to marry and
divorce solely in conformity to local customs and religious authority, and
requiring them to contract civil marriages. It did not, however, legislate a
parallel change for Muslims, who remained colonized subjects without citizenship rights. The struggle to naturalize Algerian Jews as French citizens
appeared to hinge on the successful civilization of the Jewish family.[5]

The process traced a broad chronological arc from the early Third
Republic back to Napoleon, so our story builds on the scholarship of several
periods of French and Algerian history. Scholars of the Revolutionary period
have argued that Napoleon's patriarchal 1804 *code civil* reflected a mounting
Catholic reaction to efforts made during the Revolution to introduce more
equality into the home.[6] The success of these efforts at protecting paternal
authority from any dependent's possible challenge is undeniable. Women
could no longer enter into legal agreements without the consent of their
husbands, they could not plead in court under their own names, and they
could own property only with the written consent of the man of the family.[7]
Furthermore, the French family's new hierarchy often placed the integrity
and internal hierarchy of the family over the individual's national citizenship status. This meant that the Napoleonic Code "officially fixed the relations between the *qualité de français* and the family."[8] At the same time, the
conservatism of the code civil reflected Catholicism's increasing hold on
the politics of the time.[9] This influence is also notable in Napoleon's Jewish
policy, which decisively severed any claim Jewish law might have held over
an autonomous sphere.

Napoleon's decisive subordination of religious law to civil law reverberated in colonial policy. Of course, this secular approach was historically
quite specific; it emerged in a limited number of places and in different
ways.[10] Nevertheless, colonial lawmakers pointed to the failure of North
African Jews and Muslims to accept limits on religion as a justification for
exclusionary colonial laws. Indeed, the fact that for Muslims and Jews there
was no difference between religious and civil law was a leitmotif in colonial
discussions over naturalization. Counterintuitively, colonial legislation drew
on Napoleonic Jewish policy as a model for naturalization's requirements.[11]

Another important body of scholarship has brought attention to representations of women and family customs in Algeria and Islamic society
more generally, noting particularly their increasing importance in French
colonial discussions after 1840. These representations were never devoid of
moral judgments, and by the 1870s they constituted a significant element of

descriptions of Muslim cultural differences.[12] Others have underlined how moral differences implicitly or explicitly justified the legal divide separating colonized Algerians from French settlers.[13] These ideas doubtless influenced Second Empire-era laws that allowed Muslims to apply for citizenship, contingent upon the renunciation of their personal status, thereby ensuring the endurance of colonial inequality.[14] Building on this work, the following pages trace the role of marriage law and representations of family on the process of Jewish naturalization in colonial Algeria. As we will see, French colonial understandings of Muslim and Jewish family life and marriage grew out of a parallel set of prejudices but translated into asymmetric laws.

Policing the Family

As we have seen in earlier chapters, the civilizing ideology demanded access to interior spaces. In addition to schools and synagogues, family law, customs, and morality also came under scrutiny over the course of the period of the Second Empire. This was most evident in consistent appeals by consistorial reformers and their allies in the civil administration to require Algerian Jews to register marriages with the French état civil, as well as submit them to the authorities regulating French personal status. These measures would have substituted the prevailing Jewish personal status laws governing colonized Jews' marriage, divorce, and inheritance, with standard French law. The principle was that once colonized Algerian Jews were governed by the French personal status, the most formidable legal obstacle to citizenship would be surmounted. To hasten this legal reform, consistorial reformers and civil administrators made great efforts to represent Algerian-Jewish family customs and marriage practices as already being on the path of progress throughout the period before naturalization in 1870.

To present an image of Jews as closer to the French, reformers juxtaposed an array of stereotypes about the status and sexual morality of Muslim and Jewish women. These stereotypes drew upon images of Muslim women and family life that featured prominently in French popular and scientific literature in the nineteenth century. Descriptions of Muslim gender roles and marital behaviors fed into French arguments about Arab suitability for French citizenship. The existence of prostitution, polygamy, and divorce among Algerian Muslims not only distinguished them from the French, it was claimed, but these "traits" were also used by many French observers as indices of Muslim intellectual, cultural, and moral degeneracy. Such pejorative depictions served as powerful arguments to maintain the colonial hierarchy that relegated Muslims to an inferior social and legal status.[15] Conversely, French reformers used these negative evaluations of Muslims to highlight the moral superiority of Algerian Jews.

These negative representations began to be articulated as early as
Altaras's famous report of 1842. While Muslim women and their homes were
represented as veiled, enclosed, and generally inaccessible, Algerian-Jewish
women and their homes were portrayed as open and welcoming. In a section
of his essay devoted to the Algerian-Jewish woman, Altaras contrasted the
oppression and servitude of the Muslim woman with the Jewish woman's
relative freedom and her desire for increased contact with French culture
and people.

> While Moorish women—either shut in behind the narrow walls of
> their domiciles or behind their thick veils—flee before our civilization
> or tremble when passing next to a *Roumi*, the Jewish woman goes out
> with her face exposed and does not fear hosting friendly gatherings at
> her home. By her religious principles and her cloister-like separatism,
> the Moorish girl only receives the imperfect education of the family.
> The Israelite girl, on the contrary, attends public schools where she
> finds the full range of instruction that France offers her children.[16]

Although this last comment, as we saw in the last chapter, was highly exaggerated, Altaras wished to demonstrate that the Algerian-Jewish woman,
representative of her obedient and presumably civilize-able people, was
open to the colonizer.[17]

Altaras's use of girls' education as a diagnostic of the Algerian-Jewish
woman's social superiority over her Muslim counterpart was not an isolated
case. In 1850, the consistorial Grand Rabbi Michel Aron Weill and Heloïse
Hartoch, head of the French school for Jewish girls in Algiers, sponsored a
public ceremony at which the prefect, the procurator of the republic, and
the deputy mayor were in attendance. The occasion was nominally the "religious initiation" of a group of girls at Hartoch's school, but it also served as
a form of showcase. The grand rabbi used the occasion to give a speech on
"the condition of the woman," during which he "eloquently denounced the
Muslim dogma which reduces women to the condition of a brute."[18] Weill also
presented his audience with an argument for the opening of synagogues to
women. The educated, civilized Algerian-Jewish girl, in his rendering, highlighted the difference between Jews and Muslims more generally, reinforcing
an imagined binary between civilizable/uncivilized.

Joseph Cohen published slightly modified sections from Altaras's report
in article form in the French-Jewish press. In 1843, he published a rich article
celebrating the unveiled Algerian-Jewish woman and her role in the family.
Cohen, like Weill, used generalizations about Muslim women as a foil for his
argument. The article implied both that the wider Jewish community was
ready to be civilized, and that the Muslim woman's sequestration served
as a metaphor for Muslim resistance to all that France offered. We recall

Cohen's explanation, cited in Chapter 3: "Furthermore, our contact has troubled their peaceable domestic existence. Our indiscreet eye is often plunged into the closed houses where the Arab woman could once unveil without fearing foreign gazes. Our modern homes, which dominate the low houses of the indigenous, have thrown families into [a state of] fear and cautiousness."[19] Cohen's words suggested that Arab women's invisibility was bound up with Muslim aversion to the French. The language he employed was sexualized and violent, and likened the French obligation to discover what lurked behind the veil to a form of sexual violation. As discussed earlier, Cohen's use of a violent metaphor to describe France's duty to uncover Muslim women was not unique. We recall that the French general and scholar Eugène Daumas made similar claims.[20] Cohen recycled these brutal metaphors regarding Muslim women and their homes to highlight, by contrast, what he perceived to be the open, visible, and easily monitored Jewish woman and her home. We recall once again that Cohen claimed that Jewish women kept "more open and expansive" homes than Muslim women.[21] If the demands of surveillance required forced entry into the Muslim home, the Jewish interior represented an inviting contrast.

Altaras and Cohen located the moral rectitude of Algerian-Jewish women in their supposed visibility and openness to the colonizer. This visibility, in turn, helped bolster the argument that the Jews of Algeria were so fundamentally different from the Muslims among whom they lived that these differences left them in the position to be naturalized. The moral superiority assigned to Algerian Jews was also manifest in representations of Jewish women's familiarity with bourgeois French standards. As Altaras noted, "Many [Jewish women] frequent high society and are often invited to brilliant *soirées*."[22] Lazare Cahen made a similar point in 1850 in a report to the minister of public instruction and religions to discuss the consistory's progress. He remarked that "she is admitted to [sit at the] table, she is permitted to make herself visible to the stranger (*se présenter aux regards*) and to speak with him, and she may go out and take the air along our promenades. Some of them mingle in high French society, and they have even been seen at the theatre and soirées."[23] Lower-class Jewish women were also praised for their visibility. "Nearly five hundred Israelite girls . . . work as domestic servants for French families," noted Cohen, "and through their constant contact with honorable families . . . soon take on the allure of our population."[24] Phrased elsewhere as the "forging of a gaze," colonial officials often sought to render colonized subjects, institutions, and cities observable in the interest of securing dominance.[25] It is not surprising that Jewish reformers factored the relative visibility and accessibility of Muslim and Jewish women into judgments about their level of cultural proximity to the French.

These representations of Jewish women's availability were thus framed within a deeply moralistic picture. Once again, it was the putative immorality and sexual perversity of Muslim society that provided a foil for advocates of Jewish emancipation.[26] Rabbi Cahen, for example, happily noted to the minister of public instruction and religions that "almost everywhere the most strict morality, the purest virtues, the most austere social mores are still intact" among indigenous Jewish women. Their moral perseverance was all the more laudable since prostitution, as noted in a previous chapter, was a prominent feature of the Jewish quarter of Oran. The moralistic tone suffused any mention of this fact, as Cahen's report demonstrates: "I say this with shame and sadness, in plain view she constantly has the hideous spectacle of deprivation . . . these miserable creatures whom the authorities tolerate in the city and who live for the most part in the Jewish quarter . . . [they] profane the domiciles of our co-religionists."[27] Altaras also drew a moralistic attention to the existence of Jewish prostitution. He explained that a degradation of public morality occurred naturally during sudden transitions from one civilization to another. The risk in Algeria was especially grave, as many Jewish girls were poor, and many French were drawn to "their notable beauty." Despite the fact that Jewish women were "freer than indigenous Muslim women, being able to go out without veils at any time," Altaras informed the minister of war that they were not overrepresented in the sex trade. To prove this moral rectitude, he included research on the official numbers of prostitutes classified by religion and by major Algerian towns.[28] The dissipated morals of the surrounding city had not corrupted "their moral state," he concluded.[29]

Clearly, one of Altaras's main goals was to distance Jews from prevailing stereotypes about Muslims and Algerians more generally. From 1838, the government kept track of the numbers of prostitutes in Algerian cities, and charts became available of "public girls" divided by "nationality" and race—a taxonomy that was itself organized by colonial ideology. Without demonstrating an over-representation of Jewish prostitutes, the statistics did suggest significant involvement of Jewish women in the sex trade.[30] In 1853, E. A. Duchesne, a doctor and member of the French Council of Public Hygiene and Salubriousness, published his book, *De la prostitution dans la ville d'Alger depuis la conquête*, expressing many French stereotypes and misperceptions about Muslim sexual degeneracy. His commentary on Algerian Jews hints at prevailing images reformers hoped to sanitize. "It is among the Jewish girls," Duchesne observed, "whether in Algiers or Oran, that our soldiers have the most mistresses."[31] Furthermore, "the Jewish girls easily allow themselves to be debauched. Dull, insipid, their hearts do not guide them to their choice, for if they give themselves to a man, they consult only their avarice and pride."[32] Such representations provided fuel for the brisk trade in eroticized stereotypes of Algerian women.

Occasionally combating such images, but often working in tandem with them, Altaras and other reformers mobilized a deeply moralistic civilizing discourse. "We do not wish to deny that in addition to the registered girls, there are others who give themselves over to immoral passions," but such was the "normal march of society." Furthermore, their natural weakness placed women at higher risk for corruption. It was up to (male) reformers and police, Altaras insisted, to ensure that public morality was maintained. "For as long as the words of the serpent of seduction penetrate the soul of the woman, we will be forced to lament these shameful falls that push a weak and loving sex into vice." Like other reformers in both France and the colonies, Altaras suggested that a more active pursuit of natural fathers among the Jews should be a part of recognizing the moral rot and removing it.[33]

The allegedly despised status of women in the family and the frequency of divorce were interwoven with this moralistic discourse. In 1841, an official commission charged with observing the state of the conquest in Algeria also highlighted the sad state of family morality among locals. At the same time, the writers predicted that legal assimilation would eventually lead Algerian Jews, at least, to abolish polygamy and divorce.[34] Nearly a decade later, Rabbi Cahen's report fretted about the subordinate position of the woman in the Algerian-Jewish family, linking it to divorce and other problems: "Indeed, she has hardly changed. Her education is still what it was before. The circle of her relations has not expanded, and her position in the family is still one of humiliating inferiority. She has only to displease [her husband]," he noted, "to hear resonate in her ears the fatal word *divorce*."[35] Other reports begged for some indulgence regarding Algerian-Jewish family structures. "It is important to not judge this situation with our nineteenth-century ideas, and certainly not with our French ideas," insisted Rabbi Weill of Algiers in 1850. When one reflects on the condition of the Jews before the arrival of the French, "one must consider this among Oriental mores and customs and, seen from this point of view, the condition of the Israelite woman is relatively better than that of the Muslim woman."[36] Again, the Jewish woman's unveiled and uncloistered existence rendered the Jews superior to Muslims.

Reformers gave the amelioration of Jewish women's status within the family a leading role in the discursive edifice of civilization. Weill's report of 1850 argued that local customs and culture, lack of education, and domination by men had reduced the indigenous Jewish woman to something less than human: "Raised as a brute, only the instincts and appetites of the brute developed within her. Tenderness, sensibility, devotion, modesty, reserve . . . all those qualities and naïve graces that are the halo of the young woman and the crown of the wife, have perished among the indigenous woman due to lack of care or cultivation. One might say that the woman has died, and

only the female remains."[37] Some early reformers saw the Jewish woman
as no better than the Muslim, and thus in particular need of French help.
Brutalized, isolated, and jealously shielded from the gaze of men outside her
immediate family, she represented an exaggerated example of her entire
people. Early observers concluded that if the Jews were to be civilized, the
Jewish women would be central to this effort. The process would include
educating them and submitting them to family laws identical to those governing French families.

Such perspectives provide the context for the consistory's early attempts
at combating prostitution in the Jewish quarter, an effort briefly noted in
Chapter 2. Only months after its installation, the consistory of Oran was to
take on the issue of prostitutes, who according to the consistorial deliberations dwelled exclusively in the Jewish quarter of Oran. Indeed, in late
December 1845, the *Courrier d'Afrique* devoted several articles to the arrest
of Messaouda bint Fenardj, a Jewish woman who had been maintaining a
brothel where French soldiers had access to very young girls: "The house
inhabited by this woman was the place of clandestine meetings. Two young
Muslim girls of eleven to twelve years of age were found there with a soldier,
at the moment when the arrest took place."[38] Bint Fenardj was jailed for a
year and fined 50 francs for her crime.[39] Consistorial officers condemned
proprietors of brothels who threatened the moral well being of the Jewish
community. Such concern for girls' morality may have inspired concerned
members of the municipal council of Algiers to establish the French School
for Young Indigenous Israelite Girls in 1837, several years before the establishment of the comparable boys' school in 1840.[40] A smaller girl's school was
functioning in Oran by 1850, directed by a woman from Gibraltar who taught
"fifteen or twenty" Jewish girls "several words of French."[41] As mentioned in
the previous chapter, the consistory chose to relocate this same school 15
years after it was created because of its proximity to a brothel.[42]

Jewish reformers' campaign to eradicate ostensibly unseemly relations
between men and women also required moralizing local marriage practices,
starting with the nuptial ceremony itself. From the middle of the 1850s, consistorial officers strove to put an end to "scandalous" wedding practices that
were characterized as costly, noisy, and a manifestation of Algerian Jews'
lack of civilization. In February 1856, the consistory sought to limit marriage ceremonies that "last nearly a month" and "are very costly and tiring."
Furthermore, it was noted, these events "give occasion to noise and commo-
tions in the streets, and they tend to lead to many abuses inside the homes."
Members of the consistory, "in the interest of civilization and economy,"
chose to "abolish a part of these ceremonies and to abridge the length."[43]
Because eradicating the celebrations would "interfere with deeply rooted
popular customs," members proposed a series of meetings with synagogue

owners, rabbis, and other notables in the interest of convincing them of the necessity of reform. The issue of wedding ceremonies was important enough to earn a place in later reports from the Oran consistory to the prefect. In 1856, Jacob Lasry boasted of his "abolition of numerous scandalous marriage ceremonies." He called it an "eminently moral reform" that was "a great victory of civilization over prejudices."[44] In 1860, belying his exaggerations in the earlier report, Lasry insisted that the local marriage customs were merely imitations of "Arab customs" that could be suppressed without infringing on "true" religious practice.[45]

Consistorial correspondence of the late 1850s suggests that efforts to stamp out indigenous wedding customs met with some success. In 1859, a musician by the name of Mymoun wrote to the prefect from a village in the Province of Oran to complain, "our rabbi prevents us from exercising our profession as musicians at marriage ceremonies."[46] According to the petition, "We now find ourselves stripped of the major source of our means of existence," with many musicians reduced to selling their own clothing to survive. When the prefect investigated the complaint, the consistory affirmed that civilization demanded the suppression of outdoor weddings but noted that traditional weddings were permitted indoors.[47] Beyond noting instances in which the success of this agenda may be tracked, it is difficult to know how many local Jews accorded with reformers' desires.

These events demonstrate that by the 1840s, a number of consistorial reformers deployed colonial stereotypes of Muslim women's morality and Arab family customs to argue that Jewish women's social, familial, and legal conditions were relatively more French. Especially in the reports of the 1840s, "closed" homes and concealed faces became symbolic of Muslims' wider evasion of French scrutiny, surveillance, and control. At the same time, reformers also demanded access to Jewish families, whose Arab customs and oppressed women still demanded supposedly civilizing interventions. Throughout, anxieties about sexual morality played a central role. In discussions of both Muslim and Jewish families, levels of education, social contact, and visibility became yardsticks of the social group's level of civilization.

The État Civil and Jewish Reform Efforts

Far more consequential than the Jewish wedding ceremony was the parallel effort to submit Algerian Jews to French personal status laws. As a reminder, colonial law established three personal status regimes in colonial Algeria: one French, one Muslim, and one Jewish. This arrangement gave local religious authorities jurisdiction over Algerian Muslims and Jews for matters pertaining to marriage, family, and inheritance. At the same time, in order to be governed by their faith, colonized subjects sacrificed the rights of citizenship, since only those governed by the French personal status could be candidates for naturalization. The état civil existed independently of personal status laws as the official bureau that kept records of marriages, divorces, births, and deaths, but the two were not unrelated. When Algerian Jews registered their marriages with the état civil, they found themselves governable by French personal status laws. Advocates for Jewish naturalization, however, hoped to regularize the situation by abolishing the Jewish personal status altogether and making all Algerian Jews governable by the French personal status. This reform, they reasonably believed, would eliminate the major obstacle to citizenship. What this meant, however, was that marriage, divorce, polygamy, citizenship rights, and the erosion of Algerians' legal autonomy were bound up together in French colonial Algeria.

The ordinance of October 8, 1832, greatly reduced communal autonomy by allowing both Muslims and Jews who were unsatisfied with the rulings of their qadis and rabbis to appeal to French courts. After this early ordinance, however, the legal evolution for the two religious communities diverged significantly. The majority of the Muslim population lived in rural areas where French control was more precarious. Preexisting judicial institutions were therefore harder to dismantle and replace. The *bureaux arabes* were established in 1844 to govern military (as opposed to civil) territory. In addition to acting as liaisons between tribes and the colonial state, these military bureaus oversaw the execution of justice, which though under the firm control of French officers, was nevertheless often guided by local customary and Islamic law.

The order of August 20, 1848, placed the judicial system for Europeans (and Jews) in Algeria under the control of the Ministry of Justice in Paris, leaving Muslim justice in the hands of the military. When the capricious judgments meted out by the bureaux arabes came under increasing criticism, military authorities sought to further institutionalize Muslim justice in the territories they ruled. On October 1, 1854, the government issued a decree that formally established a system of Muslim justice in the countryside, complete with newly drawn circumscriptions. From this date, a hierarchy of qadis and twenty-one *madjles* (juridical councils) were instructed to employ *shari'a* (Islamic law) to govern civil life, without appeal to French tribunals. Notably, these French Muslim courts dealt with questions of marriage, divorce, and inheritance. As Michael Brett has pointed out, Islam had come to be seen by the French colonial system not only as a source of fanatical opposition, but also an effective means of indirect control.[48]

The dismantling of Jewish civil autonomy was more swift and definitive. The population's concentration in the French-dominated cities, of course, influenced this evolution. In the summer of 1831, the highest ranking official of the Jewish community, the moqaddem, was obliged to share power with a council of three members named by the governor general. This brought control of financial affairs under the surveillance of French officers, but had little direct impact on the legal autonomy of the Jewish community and its religious courts. A year later, the colonial administration charged the royal judges at Bône and Oran with settling differences among Jews and Muslims, and after several months, the criminal courts and police tribunals took over judgments of those same crimes.

The first major distinction in colonial policy toward Jews and Muslims was legislated on August 10, 1834, when the French government divested rabbis of all legal authority except for marriages, divorces, and matters judged purely religious. Orders of subsequent years organized the system of justice throughout Algeria, and essentially confirmed the loss of Jewish autonomy.[49] According to Article 49 of an 1842 decree, for example, rabbis would be "called to give their written advice on contests relative to personal status, marriages, and repudiations among Israelites."[50] In other words, Jewish law was to guide French courts in cases involving the civil status of Jews. The decree reaffirmed the limitation of rabbinical authority to "infractions of religious law" that "according to French law . . . do not constitute a crime." All other cases were expressly forbidden to them. This law, which largely subsumed Algerian Jews to French justice, nevertheless preserved the Jewish personal status. The law extending consistories to Algeria in 1845 similarly did not affect the Jewish personal status laws. Jews were permitted to live by Jewish family law, and were not required to register their marriages before an officer of the état civil.[51]

During the Second Empire's experiments with legal assimilation, colonial administrators and consistorial members began campaigning in earnest for the subjection of native Algerian Jews to the French état civil. It was during this period that the consistory expressed its chagrin over the Courchiya case, when the court distinguished Jewish marriage from civil marriage. The court recognized that Jewish and Muslim personal statuses were different, given the clear intention of previous laws to assimilate the Jews. To the consistory's dismay, however, the ruling allowed Algerian Jews to continue neglecting the état civil and civil marriage.

Reformers' efforts to subject Algerian Jews to French personal status laws coincided with a wider movement to extend civil law in Algeria. By definition, this meant reducing the extent of military rule. Following the Doineau Affair in 1856, when a captain of the bureau arabe of Tlemcen was sentenced to death for killing a Muslim *agha* (a local governor installed by the French authorities after the administrative reorganization of 1854), the campaign for legal assimilation gained momentum. By the early 1860s, new legislation further unified the laws of Algeria and France, but nevertheless maintained exclusionary provisions toward Jews and Muslims rooted in separate personal status regimes. In 1865, Napoleon III's *senatus-consulte* (decree) gave both Jews and Muslims the choice of becoming citizens, on the condition that they surrender their distinctive, religiously defined personal status. Given that many (Jews, as well as Muslims) perceived this as apostasy, few took advantage of the law. More definitively, in 1870 the Crémieux Decree declared all Algerian Jews to be French citizens, eliminated the Jewish personal status, and required them to contract marriages before an officer of the état civil. Muslims were exempted from this law. At the same time, the newly established Third Republic enacted a flurry of assimilationist legislation.[52]

Legislating the Nuptial Bedroom: Marriage, Divorce, and Polygamy in a Colonial Context

From as early as Altaras's report on the status of Algerian Jews, reformers recognized that the French government would always make French citizenship contingent on marriage laws and customs. His report stressed juridical independence as a key obstacle to Jewish regeneration in Algeria, flagging the fact that Algerian Jews were not compelled to register their marriages with the état civil as an egregious example. The lack of government jurisdiction over the sphere of marriage, he argued, was particularly unjustified because the état civil was "perfectly established" and should by all means record the births, deaths, and marriages of those governed by French law. French authorities should not be reluctant to "disturb customs or essential dogmas" because, he insisted, family law was not a solely religious affair. If Jews chose to be married in accordance with their religious law, it was a separate affair that had to be carried out after the legally binding civil marriage.

France's failure to distinguish between civil and religious marriages for Jews constituted a "double vice" in Altaras's mind; it harmed both the interests of the state and "the moral interests of civilization."[53] First, state authority was dangerously curtailed since marriages conducted merely by rabbis receive "no type of publicity." Such lack of surveillance limited the state's ability to settle questions of legitimacy, property, and inheritance. French courts would thus encounter difficulties when called upon to settle disputes over inheritance or other matters connected to families, for "nothing legitimates the (new) family in the eyes of the civil authority, nor by extension, rules governing succession for each member of the family."[54] Official control, according to Altaras's report, must extend over the legal and social bonds that constitute a family. Jewish reformers such as Altaras understood (correctly, as it turned out) that the French model of emancipation required that the state extend its control over the domestic family life of Algerian Jews.

Second, according to Altaras, the "moral interests of civilization" were compromised by the legal fusion of civil and religious spheres. If the French policy favored Algerian Jews' "complete moral and behavioral fusion with the French,"[55] reasoned Altaras, why conserve the difference in civil status? On the contrary, they must "be absorbed into us" legislatively. Altaras saw the apparent failure of Algerian Jews to embrace Europe's particular, historically situated notion of the secular, in which religion occupied a finite sphere of life, as a grave moral deficit.[56] Nevertheless, failing to integrate Jews into the civil (and secular) matrix of authority manifested by the état civil could prove fatal to any future plans to naturalize them. Jews should not be left to "their principles and their law judges" out of fear of provoking a "harmful separation" between them and the population to which they should be assimilated. Polygamy, a practice that "human nature and the purest familial sentiments condemn" presented a particular problem for Altaras.[57]

Divorce was another problem that the Jewish personal status allowed. Fortunately, reflected Altaras, many Algerian Jews already "see [divorce] as shameful, and families distinguished by their social position and morality [can] proudly [note that] there is not a single case of divorce among their members."[58] Only fifteen divorces took place in Algiers in 1840, pointed out Altaras, evidence that this would not be a significant moral hurdle for Algerian Jews to surmount. But no matter how rare the offending practices were morality and reason insisted that since "divorce is proscribed by our laws," there was little room for debate. "We think that our principles on this point," argued Altaras and Cohen, "like the matter of polygamy, should be imposed upon the indigenous Israelites."[59]

Altaras's thinking was colored by ministers' beliefs about colonial assimilation. Even before Altaras issued his report, officials in the civilian ministries made it clear that subjecting Jews to French personal status laws would be necessary to legally assimilate them into the European population. This assimilation, in turn, would help consolidate colonial rule. In an 1839 letter to Governor General Comte de Vallée, Minister of War Soult wrote that the Jewish religion had not yet been effectively subjected to French law. Since 1834, he noted, nothing had been done to bring indigenous Jews further under the jurisdiction of French civil administration, "above all concerning infractions of religious law and contestations related to marriages."[60] Further "organization" was necessary in this domain to "attach" Algerian Jews to France. In another letter, Soult noted that even if the competence of rabbinical tribunals was already reduced to "disciplinary issues of the conjugal union . . . the moment seems to have arrived to remove this exceptional jurisdiction." The remaining power of the rabbis was simply a "leftover juridical competence" from the Regency "that was seldom well-employed."[61]

Relieving rabbis of jurisdiction over marriages and subjecting them to French law was both a moral and a political step. Judaism was "professed by a very considerable portion of the civil population," Soult argued, and their numbers "alone demonstrate that we cannot delay much longer taking care of a religion that was left in a state of abandon by the previous government which the conquest has yet to terminate."[62] In 1841, another official commission noted that legal assimilation would lead to moral improvements, such as the abolition of polygamy and divorce.[63] In 1842, Soult informed the director of the interior at Algiers that he approved of Altaras's "plan to travel to Algeria to study the civil and religious constitution of their co-religionists" and asked him to direct Altaras's attention to the potential obstruction to naturalizing colonized Jews: "the director of the interior should [also] call their particular attention to the question of marriage and divorce, the only points relative to their civil status (état civil) upon which the Israelites differ from us legally."[64] Clearly, by the early 1840s, top officials at the Ministry of War agreed that eliminating Jews' "exceptional jurisdiction" over their families was essential for the interwoven projects of Jewish assimilation and consolidating colonial power.

The 1845 decree establishing the consistories did not require Algerian Jews to marry before an officer of the état civil, a fact that led to much hand wringing among Algeria's civilian administrators.[65] Consequently, prefects and consistorial officers were forced to encourage local Jews to conform voluntarily to French family laws. For example, Rabbi Cahen's 1850 report on the Province of Oran underlined that "since we began operations, we have consistently ensured that the prescriptions of the état civil were obeyed, especially in Oran, relative to marriages."[66] At the same time, "we opposed requests for divorce with everything we had."[67] When, in 1857, a consistorial representative complained that a local functionary was making civil marriages for Jews difficult in the town of Aïn Témouchen, the representative made it clear that "it was a matter of course" to ask marrying couples to undergo civil marriages beforehand.[68] In 1865, the consistory cut off charitable disbursements to an unemployed Algerian rabbi. His crime was having pronounced several divorces despite lacking the authority to do so granted by the consistory. In doing so, the rabbi was guilty of being "a source of discord" in Jewish families. Furthermore, divorce was "frequently the cause of immorality" and that "in the interest of civilization, it will be necessary to put an end to this abuse on the part of the rabbis."[69]

The consistory also made the moralization of Algerian domestic and family life a priority when they chose delegates for outlying communities. In the mid-1850s, for example, Abraham ben Ichou made a tour of peripheral towns in the Province of Oran to report on Jewish communities and bring them under consistorial control. On his voyage, he spoke with military officers in charge of the bureaux arabes and the Muslim legal authorities with whom they worked. In towns such as Tiarat and Frenda on the edge of the Oranais tel (mountainous region before the Sahara), they complained that local Jews were morally dissolute. According to ben Ichou's findings, Jews of these towns tended toward excessive drinking, raucous behavior, and beating their wives. Ben Ichou subsequently warned them that the consistory "will look for ways to severely punish those who continue to engage in such conduct," and laid down rules for the newly organized community. Among a number of enforcement measures, new marital rules were declared: "No one can marry if he is already" and "a foreigner can only marry when and if he certifies that he is not already married." Finally, the new law required that "the rabbi may not issue any act of divorce without sending it to the consistory."[70] Marital and private lives of Algerian Jews immediately factored into the consistorial mandate.

A series of court decisions near the end of the 1850s brought increasing attention to Jews' legal status in Algeria. In 1857, the Imperial Court at Algiers ruled that neither the 1842 law, which effectively ended Jewish legal autonomy, nor any subsequent law regarding the organization of justice in Algeria, required Algerian Jews to conform to the French personal status law. The decision reasoned that even though the 1842 law "removes . . . from members of the Israelite religion any juridical competence over their co-religionists," the law nonetheless held that "contests relative to personal status will be judged according to the religious law of the parties concerned."[71] The 1845 law organizing the Jewish religion in Algeria did not eliminate the right of Algerian Jews to live by their religious law, but it did refer to the 1808 Napoleonic law submitting French-Jewish clergy to the French civil code, thereby obligating Jews to marry in accordance with French law. The judgment explained that Napoleon's law would have to be extended to Algeria if local Jews were to be governed by the French personal status.

The 1858 trial of Simon Courchiya added another layer of confusion. The case involved an Algerian-Jewish woman who sued for divorce in a French court based on the impotence of her husband. The plaintiff claimed to be governed by the Jewish personal status permitting divorce in such a case. The court, however, ruled that since the marriage had been contracted before an officer of the état civil, only Napoleonic family law—not Jewish law—was applicable. The court decided further that Jewish personal status differed from Muslim personal status in this regard. Nevertheless, the 1858 case confirmed that civil marriages between two Jews were entirely separate affairs from Jewish religious marriages. As the 1850s drew to a close, Algerian Jews were still not required to contract civil marriages, and therefore not required to separate the jurisdiction of faith from the domain of the state. This set of affairs would not persist indefinitely.

The prefect understandably saw the Courchiya decision as an obstacle to the naturalization of Algerian Jews and demanded help from higher authorities.[72] In a series of letters, he implored both the governor general and the minister of public instruction and religions to change the law. He warned that the decision to permit Jews to evade the French état civil would thwart the assimilatory mission of the prefecture and the consistory. The Courchiya judgment, he wrote, "puts into question the obligation of a numerous portion of our population to declare their births and deaths, and to precede their religious marriages with the celebration of the marriage before an officer of the état civil." This had negative implications for a range of institutional expressions of the civilizing mission, because "were it to hold, [the decision] would cause a great perturbation in our état civil, in the applications of rules about our schools and in our penal codes. It would effectively result in distancing from our customs a population that our mission is to attach to us, and to bring it into the common laws of civil life, as it is in France."[73] The fact that Algerian Jews neglected (or actively refused) to marry according to the French état civil created a crisis for local officials charged with executing the civilizing mission in Algeria. These local figures responded by asking higher authorities to implement clarifying legislation regarding local Jews' status and obligations. The prefect insisted that "our mission" would fail if laws were not passed allowing him to enforce French marriage laws among the Algerian-Jewish population. It was an opportune time, the prefect suggested to his superiors, for a decree that would submit Algerian Jews, "like their co-religionists in France," to the état civil. The prefect well understood that without official jurisdiction over Jewish families, naturalization remained a distant goal. His response to local circumstances was to ask Paris to alter laws to advance the civilizing mission.

The contradictions faced by local officials also shaped their approach to gathering and processing information about the administered population. To bolster his point, the prefect conferred with Rabbi Cahen about marriage practices of local Jews in Oran. According to Cahen, most Jews in Oran already registered with the état civil. Divorces, in the meantime, were more rare than when he first arrived in Algeria.[74] The prefect interpreted this to mean that most Jews were willing to live by "laws [that] suppress divorce and the ability for sisters- and brothers-in-law to marry without previous authorization . . . the sort of unions established among them and that their rabbis recommend."[75] The prefect argued that if the governor general agreed to make the desired legal reforms, there would be no uproar from the Algerian-Jewish population.[76] The prefect omitted the fact that many Jews were clandestinely contracting marriages (or second marriages) and getting purely religious divorces.[77] An 1863 memo, for example, noted that so many Jews were avoiding civil marriages that official rabbis (required to marry only those already civilly married) could conduct only a small percentage of Jewish weddings in Oran.[78] Algerian Jews continued to avoid the encroachments of French law into the interior of the family.

The emergence of the notion of clandestine or illegal Jewish marriages in Algeria is emblematic of how marriage and family structure had become a battle line in French colonial efforts to civilize Jews. For example, as Cahen's report to the prefect noted: "There have been divorces pronounced by indigenous rabbis, but only between conjoints who were not previously married before the officer of the état civil." In these cases, "the religious marriage is celebrated either in another country, or clandestinely in Algeria."[79] The rabbi testified to the existence of divorces, as well, but again emphasized that they were not only diminishing in number, but were mainly contracted by foreigners or clandestinely in Algeria. He reported that "in 1855, there were only three, of which two were between foreigners and one was between indigenous Jews married illegally. In 1856, I noted two, of which one was between foreigners and the other between indigenous [Jews] whose marriage was illegitimate from a civil perspective. In 1857, there was only one, between Moroccans married in their country."[80] The report coincided with the production of new statistics concerning Jewish demographic trends. With the help of the consistory, charts were forwarded to the prefect showing birth and death rates among Jews, numbers of marriages, and comparisons between Jewish and European growth rates.[81] Like schools, questions relating to families and the état civil were vehicles by which new forms of knowledge and expertise were deployed to understand, categorize, monitor, and govern bodies, populations, and domestic life.

The debate about Jewish marital practices was at least partly rooted in colonial policy debates about the legal assimilation of Algeria into France. The deep rift between civilian colonists and military rulers, in turn, contoured the ongoing tug-of-war about the extent and type of legal assimilation France would pursue. The colonists tended to demand the extension of colonization and civil rule in the colony, while the military hoped to preserve its powers in military territories, limiting civilian colonization. To explain this point, we must review transformations in French colonial rule and thought in Algeria from the late 1850s to mid-1860s, pausing to reflect on what impact these intertwined phenomena had on the project of civilizing Algeria's Jews.

Starting in the late 1850s, Napoleon III began a project of legal assimilation that included the new post of minister of Algeria. The emperor's nephew, Prince Napoleon-Jerome, assumed the post. His assimilatory reforms included expanding civil territory, increasing the prefects' power, and making certain military officers (such as *commandants* of military territory) answerable to the civilian Ministry of Algeria. Officers in command of military territories were, at the same time, saddled with new *conseils des affairs civils,* or civil affair councils, invested with enough authority to curtail effectively military autonomy.[82]

Colonists welcomed these reforms, but they antagonized the military, which often refused to follow orders from the new ministry. Confounding this situation further was Prince Napoleon-Jerome's decision to limit officers' discretionary powers to punish tribes. This ruling was viewed as a blow to both military authority and to the colonists' superior legal status; many colonists reacted in horror to any legal limitation put on Europeans' freedom to punish Arabs. With the army and an important faction of the colonists briefly united against the prince, he resigned in March 1859.[83] Soon after, the Ministry of Algeria itself was eliminated, in 1860. Meanwhile, a freer colonial press and a more vocal population of *colons* (European colonists) continued to press for Algeria's legal assimilation to France.[84] This campaign continued into the 1870s and influenced discussions of Jewish emancipation.[85] In their desire to bolster the civilian population, colonists also lobbied for freer access to citizenship for Italian and Spanish immigrants. The press loudly championed these sentiments, especially between 1858 and 1862.[86]

With the end of the Ministry of Algeria, Napoleon III reinstated the post of governor general and initiated a different colonial policy. In contrast to his nephew, Napoleon III hoped to limit agricultural colonization, end the land expropriations (cantonnements) of natives for the benefit of European settlers, and share civilization with the natives. His Saint-Simonian views favored allowing Arabs to pursue small-scale agriculture, while encouraging the supposedly more dynamic European population to remain in cities and develop commerce and industry.[87] Under the new regime, Arab-European harmony and cooperation was to be accomplished through beneficial and educative day-to-day contact without expropriation. In a famous letter to Governor General Pélissier, Napoleon III declared that Algeria "is not, properly speaking, a colony, but rather an Arab kingdom. The indigenous have, like the colonists, an equal claim to my protection and I am as much the emperor of the Arabs as the emperor of the French." In 1863, Napoleon III extended private property to tribal lands. Two years later, he issued a law that made full French citizenship available to indigenous Muslims and Jews, providing they gave up their personal status and agreed to be bound by French family law. Napoleon III thus posed a radical challenge to the conception of Algeria held by many officers in his military, not to mention the colonists.

The political moment inspired a number of republican-leaning lawyers and magistrates in Algeria to take up the issues of assimilation, citizenship, and personal status laws.[88] What conditions would Muslim or Jewish Algerians have to meet to be considered French? Legists offered different answers, but family customs, divorce, polygamy, and personal status consistently occupied prominent places in their reasoning.[89] Interestingly, these writers often referred to French-Jewish emancipation and to Napoleon's Grand Sanhedrin to develop their legal discussions of Algerian naturalization. For these legal experts, Napoleon was credited with harmonizing Jewish and French law, after which French Jews were required to obey French personal status laws.

Metropolitan Precedents and Colonial Legislation

How and why Napoleon's 1806–1807 Assembly of Jewish Notables and Sanhedrin became a legal precedent for colonial legislation is partly answered by the twelve questions Napoleon's minister Comte de Molé asked the Jewish representatives at the Paris assembly. While the questions spanned a number of issues dealing with morality, usury, and patriotism, the first three dealt with the private domain of marriage and the family.

1. Is it legal for Jews to marry multiple wives?
2. Does the Jewish religion permit divorce? Is divorce valid without it being declared so by the courts, and by virtue of laws that contradict the French code?
3. May a Jewish woman marry a Christian man, or a Christian woman a Jewish man? Or does the law permit Jews to marry only among themselves?[90]

Heading the list were these three questions directly tied to marriage law and family customs, a theme suggesting that Napoleon saw private morality and the relative positions of men and women in the family as a fundamental component of citizenship. Colonial jurists and legal experts found Napoleon's harmonization of Jewish civil law with his legal code a useful guide for regulating colonized Algerians' access to French citizenship.[91]

One of the most notable of the experts who looked back to Napoleon for guidance on the shaping of colonial naturalization laws was the president of the Tribunal of Sétif, Casimir Frégier. He published tens of articles in his series of essays *Études législatives* over the course of the 1860s, frequently dealing with Muslims, Jews, and marriage.[92] For example, in his 1862 pamphlet, *Du marriage français de l'Israélite algérien*, he argued that marrying before an officer of the état civil should not accord citizenship and that the recent court decision was thus ill conceived. Religion, he explained, penetrated all aspects of the "Oriental man," so it was nonsensical to offer him the option of parting with his personal status, even in the interest of being governed by a more perfect law. Furthermore, even if one could disavow one's personal status, marrying before an officer of the état civil did not constitute such a declaration. Frégier argued that a more significant religious and civil transformation was necessary. He suggested that France apply Napoleon's Jewish policy to the colonial situation and convene another Grand Sanhedrin for the Algerian Jews.[93] Frégier's efforts came to the attention of the central consistory in Paris, which subsequently supported him in his next project—a book-length study of the legal history and future of Algerian Jews, which appeared in 1865.[94]

The Parisian legal scholar J. E. Sartor offered a different perspective. Writing after Napoleon III issued the 1865 senatus-consulte he celebrated the emperor's invitation to Algerian Muslims and Jews to embrace civilization. The law deserved additional praise, argued Sartor, for not offending those who sought to retain their current status. Universally imposing French personal status law, he argued, would be foolish, for it "would have required reversing the ideas possessed by peoples of the Orient regarding polygamy, which they see as perfectly natural, but we reject so severely." It would also offend a set of putatively Oriental beliefs regarding "the authority of the father over his children, on the condition of the woman, [and] on repudiation."[95] Changes in women's status and marriage law dominated Sartor's discussion of the requirements for an indigenous Algerian to become French. Echoing earlier writers, such as Altaras, Cohen, and Cahen, women's status and marriage law provided an organizing principle for discussions of citizenship and colonial difference.

Sartor did not believe that Muslims and Jews were incapable of adopting French family morality. Indeed, he believed that when Algerians did opt to cleave to civilization, a dramatic transformation would have occurred: "from the moment when the indigenous decide[s] to ask for naturalization and acquires it . . . a complete transformation operates upon his status and upon his personality. From this moment, he has broken from all that the past might have in contradiction with French law."[96] This would not be a betrayal of one's religion, insisted Sartor, since "it would not be difficult to establish that the great differences that exist between our habits and the customs followed relative to the family do not counter the spirit of either the Qur'an or the Talmud."[97] As this suggests, Sartor saw family law as the most important obstacle to citizenship. Unlike Frégier, he believed that civilizing must be a matter of personal choice to adopt French family law, not a law imposed from above. Conformity to French family law and customs, in other words, was a matter of faith to be willingly embraced by Algerians themselves.

Jules Delsieux, an Algiers-based legist and writer, also suggested that the Sanhedrin offered a legal precedent for modeling colonial indigenous policy.[98] In his *Essai sur la naturalisation collective des Israélites indigènes*, he argued that the Revolution and the Sanhedrin set precedents for the imposition of French nationality upon colonized people without regard to their wishes: "When the [Revolution-era] convention gave the Israelites their rights of men and citizens, it did not consult them. When the Emperor, by his decree of March 17, 1808, confirmed the decree of the convention . . . he did not call upon them to give their advice. They were born on French territory and by that very fact they were French citizens. This was sufficient for them to be given (citizenship), even [if] the title [was] imposed upon them . . . whether they wanted it or not."[99] Delsieux seems to have shared some of Sartor's concerns, noting that in 1808, French Jews raised "ignorant complaints" and "did not understand how this new organization was richly advantageous for them." He drew a parallel between French Jews in 1808 and colonized Jews of 1860, arguing that emancipation sometimes had to be imposed on ignorant beneficiaries. Delsieux was building on an established, post-Enlightenment strain of French thought that held that citizenship could transform men.[100]

Rabbi Mahir Charleville, who in 1864 replaced Lazare Cahen as grand rabbi of the Oran consistory, also considered the Sanhedrin as a useful guide for colonial policy governing family law and related matters. The context in which he expressed his thoughts was the debate leading up to the consistorial reform, eventually enacted September 16, 1867. Reforming the consistory had been discussed since the 1850s, notably when the consistory of Algiers proposed establishing more (French-occupied) rabbinic posts to administer to a surprisingly recalcitrant population.[101] The 1867 law did not establish these additional seats, but it did end Oran and Constantine's nominal subservience to the Algiers consistory. In fact, an 1848 decree had already weakened this relationship by making provincial consistories answerable to the local prefectures. Now, the central consistory in Paris would have authority over the three Algerian consistories. It was an assimilatory reform effectively extending civil government in Algeria. The consistory of Oran had actively pushed for the change, since natural increase and immigration from Morocco over the 1850s and 1860s led Oran's Jewish population to surpass that of Algiers.[102] The reform also ended the consistory's rabbinical posts' limitation to French rabbis.

Charleville himself had opposed this last provision. He argued that Algerian Jews should not be considered for official rabbinical posts in the consistories because they were neither familiar with nor obligated to follow the Sanhedrin's decisions. "Yet the very purpose of these decisions," he stated, "is to destroy the abnormal situation of the indigenous Israelite's status; polygamy, divorce, and marriage without prior civil formalities."[103] Furthermore, Charleville saw in Napoleonic legislation the backbone of his mission in Algeria. He drew attention to the fact that "in order to obtain the rabbinical diploma, it is necessary to know the Sanhedrin's decisions." This law served a particular purpose, "above all so that the rabbi propagates and personifies the enlightened and civilizing spirit."[104] Charleville was not discussing citizenship requirements, but rather France's civilizing mission more generally. He agreed that Napoleon's legislation offered a precedent for articulating the boundaries of France in the colony. Significantly, these boundaries were within the structure of families and domestic life.

Further congealing the importance of Jewish family law and the articulation of citizenship requirements was that some writers were involved in both. As mentioned earlier, Charleville published in 1868 a translation and commentary of the late medieval Jewish text *Eben haEzer* in collaboration with Mr. E. Sautayra, the vice president of the civil tribune of Algiers. This was originally the title of the third section of Rabbi Joseph ben Asher's thirteenth-century halachic code *Arba'ah Turim*, or "four rows" (often referred to as the *Tur*). Charleville's text, however, was based on Rabbi Joseph ben Ephraim Caro's authoritative *Shulchan Aruch*, a sixteenth-century halachic text modeled after the *Tur* that became almost universally authoritative in the Jewish world. The choice of *Eben haEzer* was timely; it dealt significantly with marriage, family law, and sexual relations. Furthermore, the editors explicitly linked their study of Jewish law as a way to advance the colonial administration's authority—notably over Jews. Specifically, the authors noted that Algerian rabbis maintained their jurisdiction over family law, and that French colonial judges were still instructed to seek their advice when issues touching on Jewish family law found their way into their courtrooms. Yet no French translation of the relevant Jewish legal texts existed, giving rabbis a monopoly on this key element of colonial jurisdiction. Therefore "we saw it necessary, in the interest of good administration of justice, of the security of transactions and for the development of credit in the colony, to substitute the simple advice of rabbis with the [actual] law, and therefore fill the lacuna that currently exists in Algerian legislation."[105] To eliminate any ambiguity, the editors subtitled the book "explanations of the Jewish doctors, jurisprudence of the court of Algiers, and comparative notes on the French and Muslim Law."[106]

The translation was well received. The editors of the influential and widely read *Révue Africaine*, for example, saw the publication of Charleville's work as a significant event and in 1869 published a positive review of it. "This code," the reviewer concluded from the book, "does not govern Jews in the same way as, for example, the Napoleonic Code governs the French. Communities may bring modifications and adopt particular customs that time and circumstance may demand. It is by virtue of the practice's adaptive faculty that we have seen rabbinic legislation bend to the exigencies of diverse civilizations, and stay current with the accomplishments of progress."[107] The *Révue* also approved of Charleville and Sautayra's consistent attention to current problems of colonial administration, including their near-constant comparison between Jewish and Muslim law. Indeed, Charleville went so far as to say that Jewish law was ultimately the source of Muslim law, so recent Muslim legal commentaries were actually of less use to colonial administrators.[108] The *Révue* suggested Charleville and Sautayra's work could bring to legal professionals who "devote themselves to the fruitful study of comparative legislations, and to those who wish to know the Orient and realize . . . its influence on our modern civilizations."[109] The book illustrates not only how reformers saw Jewish religious authority as an important field of knowledge for the articulation and advancement of colonial power, but also how they imagined marriage, divorce, polygamy, and related phenomena to be crucibles in the enactment (and legislation) of the civilizing mission.

Public debates about naturalization and personal status by French and Algerian reformers accompanied a broader phenomenon in North Africa. Algerian Jews themselves were creating conditions that forced colonial administrators to introduce new forms of legislation. In response to Algerian Jews' refusal to abandon their local rabbis and conduct civil marriages, Cahen and the prefect multiplied their requests for a law subjecting Algerian Jews to French civil law. The community that the consistory was charged with transforming had managed to put French rabbis such as Cahen in an untenable and contradictory position. He was forbidden to fulfill his mandate of overseeing Jewish marriages in Oran because so few Algerian Jews were married civilly. On April 10, 1862, for example, Rabbi Cahen asked the prefect for help resolving the "irregularity that reigns in the celebration of marriages."[110] He renewed this request on February 27, 1863, noting that the problem of marriages was rooted in the contradictions of Jews' legal status. Currently, "the [state of] incertitude in which we find ourselves regarding the état civil of indigenous Israelites" resulted in legal "anarchy."[111] The rabbi's complicated situation revealed his impotence in successfully controlling families and thereby fulfilling his colonial mandate; the 1845 organizational decree charged him with overseeing indigenous marriages, but at the same time he was forbidden from doing so if the couple in question had not already contracted a civil marriage. This was becoming increasingly problematic; out of 40 or so marriages contracted over the past year (1862–1863), the rabbi had blessed only four.[112]

Cahen's contradictory position signaled a larger obstacle to the French civil authority's civilizing mission. Soon after Cahen's letter, the prefect spelled out the implications of the judicial confusion to higher authorities. He noted that excusing Jews from the requirement to register with the état civil was to "keep this population outside our customs and habits, [despite] our mission to bring it closer to us."[113] In May 1863, the prefect again communicated these thoughts to the governor general, hoping to prompt him to act on the issue, noting that this was not the first time the urgency of the situation had been noted.[114] The prefect then made another call for a decree that would place the Jews of Algeria in the same legal framework as their French co-religionists. Cahen's inability to fulfill his mandate of supervising the marriage of Algerian Jews resulted, as the prefect explained, in their inability to assimilate to the French. Civilization appeared to demand access to and control over the structure of families, and yet access to and control over Algerian Jewry proved more difficult to implement than to imagine.

The prefect of Oran agreed. An internal memo from 1867 noted the French law obligating French rabbis to teach the principles of the Sanhedrin. Furthermore, Jewish law "declares as a religious precept that it is forbidden for any Israelite of any state where polygamy is prohibited by civil laws to marry a second wife while the first is still alive."[115] The prefect communicated his and Charleville's concerns to the governor general. He agreed that "the admission of indigenous Israelites as candidates for . . . grand rabbi appears to me as wise as it is equitable," but "it must be on the condition of a previous renunciation of their personal status, which allows for polygamy, divorce, and [religious] marriage without a prior civil marriage."[116] It would appear that Governor General MacMahon had already taken an interest in the question. In May 1867, he had asked the prefect to consider the possibility of indigenous Jews as candidates for the grand rabbinate and to that end asked the prefect to provide him with statistical and moral information about the Jewish communities of the province.[117]

In 1869, the Imperial Court at Algiers ruled that even Jews who contracted civil marriages before an officer of the état civil remained governed by the Mosaic personal status, bringing the governor general into a prolonged discussion about the normalization of Algerian Jews' status.[118] Following the ruling, officers of the état civil in Algiers began to refuse to contract civil marriages even for those indigenous Jews who presented themselves. As it turned out, functionaries at city hall were simply following orders in the absence of legislation that required them to do otherwise.[119] The governor general requested further advice from the consistory, the prefect, and the director of Arab affairs for the Province of Oran regarding the wisest policy to follow. By the end of the 1860s, the highest-ranking officer in Algeria was involved in resolving the conflict between a religiously defined personal status and the family laws upon which French citizenship depended.

Theorizing Assimilation and Family Law: The 1865 Senatus-Consulte

Napoleon III's senatus-consulte of July 14, 1865, was presented as the second part of the assimilating, and indeed civilizing, reform begun in 1863. "After the constitution of property, the most important point in political legislation or a constitution is the état civil of people," declared *conseilleur d'état*

Louis-Hugues Flandin (the state council is the highest administrative judicial authority in France) when presenting Napoleon's decree to the French Senate. To that effect, the law made the historic if confusing declaration that Algerian Muslims and Jews were French, but since they would both continue to be governed by their respective personal status, they were not to be automatically considered citizens:

> Article 1: The indigenous Muslim is French; nevertheless, he will continue to be governed by Muslim law. He can be admitted to serve in the armies of land or sea. He can be called for civil employment in Algeria. He can, upon his request, be admitted to enjoy the rights of the French citizen; in this case he is governed by the civil and political laws of France.
>
> Article 2: The indigenous Israelite is French; nevertheless . . .
>
> Article 3: The foreigner who can prove three years of residency in Algeria can be admitted to enjoy all the rights of French citizenship.[120]

The law was not what Jewish reformers had wanted. Jews maintained their personal status, and the religiously defined personal statuses of Muslims and Jews rendered the question of their naturalization more complicated than that of the Europeans to whom reformers hoped to see Algerian Jews assimilated. According to Flandin's presentation of the law to the Senate, the key issue remained marriage law. "The full exercise of rights of French citizenship," explained Flandin, "is incompatible with the conservation of the Muslim [personal] status, with its dispositions contrary to our laws and our mores about marriage, on repudiation, divorce, and the état civil of the children."[121] The senatus-consulte allowed both Jews and Muslims to preserve their religious law but, in the spirit of the emperor's Saint-Simonian-influenced notions of association, also gave them the option of civilization. They could, in other words, choose to abandon their religiously defined code and live by French personal status law. This choice, however, was against the spirit of consistorial efforts tending to universally submit Algerian Jews to French civil law.

Flandin's explanations provided the official justification for the law. They also offer us a clear example of how the Sanhedrin's focus on family law structured legislation of colonial inclusion and exclusion. For this reason, it is worth exploring how the highest judicial official in Napoleon III's government explained a law that theoretically offered French citizenship to colonized Jews and Muslims. As we shall see, Flandin's explanation imagined the emancipation of the Jews of France to have pivoted on Napoleon's harmonization of Jewish family law with France's civil code. Now, the logic underpinning France's emancipation of the Jews structured a colonial law also described as an avenue toward enlightenment and emancipation. Yet this colonial emancipation justified the exclusion of almost all colonized Jews and Muslims from the rights guaranteed by French citizenship.

The 1865 law reflected more Saint-Simonian influence than the centralizing but exclusionary liberalism of the prefect and consistory. The law did not, for example, separate Jews and Muslims by giving the former a preferential legal standing. Nor did it impose a new personal status regime on Jews. Rather, the emperor's law looked forward to a "fusion of races," hoping that by opening the path of civilization to Jews and Muslims, they would gradually assimilate willingly. Langlais, a legal scholar whose explanatory essay was included in the official legislative records, expressed this preference for a non-coercive assimilating process geared to the colonized population broadly defined. For example, the provision of the 1865 law permitting Algerians to serve in the military appeared geared toward Muslims, but applied to Jews, as well: "the government thought with reason that of all the proper means to hasten the fusion of races, the most effective would be to allow this essentially warrior population to mix with an army whose valiance has been revealed to it via its own defeats at their hands. . . . In addition, the life of the camps is an experience . . . of [our] habits, tastes, and sacrifices [and] is [therefore] by itself a fecund element of assimilation."[122] The law established something akin to public decency and morality as a central requirement of French citizenship. This would require parting with the statute by which they currently lived. Flandin argued, "if the statute that they have abandoned is the source of the rights and customs that are incompatible with public decency (*pudeur publique*), with morality, with the good order of families," then necessarily, "these rights are abolished." Flandin built on the assumption that Algerian Jews and Muslims currently lived by a statute that provided for families that failed to meet France's basic moral standards. "The acceptance of the quality of French citizen," the law presumed, "constitutes the most formal abdication of [these rights]."[123] The colonial subject was therefore required to explicitly accept the state's sovereignty over the "order of families" before citizenship could be considered.

In a clear indication of how morality, family customs, and domestic practices had become central to the legal construction of colonial difference, Flandin justified colonial rule by Algerians' practice of polygamy and divorce. By abandoning these practices, he suggested, colonized subjects could assume the same rights and responsibilities as Frenchmen: "the Muslim religion authorizes polygamy, repudiation, [and] divorce. The same is true for the Jewish religion. Clearly, the exercise of such rights would be forbidden to the indigenous who become French citizens, and those that practice them after having entered into French life would be subject to laws enacted to repress acts of this nature."[124] Napoleon III's new assimilatory legislation demonstrated how family customs had become a sort of cartographic tool to differentiate the morality and decency demanded by French citizenship from the society of the colonized Algerians. At the same time, the law differed from the reforms demanded by civil officials and the rabbis in that it did not eliminate the Jewish personal status. Rather than implement a collective change of status, it gave Jews and Muslims the choice to accept what was presented as a morally superior law.

The law also demonstrates how lawmakers took Napoleon's early nineteenth-century policies toward French Jews as a blueprint for legislating the colonial hierarchy in Algeria. The resulting social hierarchy was logically coherent within the epistemological structure associated with emergent notion of the "secular." French legists, reflecting a specific intellectual tradition, underlined the Jewish and Muslim failure to distinguish between civil and religious law. Imagining their laws to be divine, French lawmakers reasoned, colonized Muslims and Jews allowed religion to govern all aspects of their lives, for as Flandin wrote: "We know that the Qur'an is at once a religious and a civil law; it is a holy scripture and a code for the Muslim." The 1865 law, therefore, ensured that "no abjuration is to be asked of him, no act that does violence to his conscience; he keeps his religious law, we do not even ask him to renounce—through an express declaration—his civil status." At the same time, if the colonized chose to jettison religion's preeminence, the path was open, since "the senatus-consulte implicitly leads to this renunciation at his own request; since the Muslim status is irreconcilable with French law, his duty is to obey the law, his right is to invoke the law that protects him!" The element of choice distinguished the 1865 senatus-consulte from the Napoleonic Sanhedrin of 1808, which imposed personal status laws upon the Jews of France.

Crucially, for the purposes of this chapter, these two laws—one passed to transform French Jewry, the other meant to promote the assimilation of Algerian Muslims and Jews—were linked in their concern with family law's place in the structure of citizenship. This common principle was not lost on Flandin or his colleagues on the floor of the Senate in 1865: "in 1806, the Israelites wished to become French citizens; at the time, they were governed by the Talmud, which, like the Qur'an, sanctified polygamy, repudiation, et cetera. Napoleon I wanted to separate faith and law. He convoked an assembly of notable Israelites, he constituted a great court of the Jewish nation, and on March 2, 1807, the Great Sanhedrin . . . rendered a doctrinal decision in conformity with the Emperor's thinking. The Israelites then became French citizens."[125] While his history was off (Jews of France had officially been granted civic equality in 1791), Flandin's point was clear. The precedent of the Sanhedrin illustrated that the formal establishment of civil law's preeminence in the family had to be established as a prerequisite for citizenship. The Qur'an, it was implied, was similar to a Muslim Talmud.

According to the 1865 law, civilization and naturalization were intertwined processes.[126] Bearing the imprint of Napoleon III's Saint-Simonianism, Flandin assured the Senate that "Muslim fanaticism has [already] lost quite a bit of its ardor and its intolerance." This was due to "the influence of 35 years of daily interactions, commerce, industry, agricultural development, [and] the needs of an increasingly sedentary existence." As a result, Arabs and Europeans "have moved closer to each other . . . already a ray of civilization has penetrated African society." Flandin also drew on the myth of Kabyle superiority to further illustrate his point. "It would be an error to believe that the law of Muhammad reigns in an absolute manner over the Muslim population," he argued, because "the Kabyles, who descend from Christian refugee families, differ from other Arabs in three ways: morals, laws, and even religious practice." Their ability to be civilized was associated with religion's limited reach. Not surprisingly, family structure and morality played an important role in teasing out this taxonomy of civilization. Flandin assured his listeners that "this million or so men, who do not practice polygamy, whose families are constituted much like our own, who have shown themselves to be sensitive to the advantages of civilization, will want to profit from the new benefits that the senatus-consulte will bring them." According to the explanation of the law of 1865, civilization appeared once again to be located within the family.

The logic of the law depended on grafting the teleology of French-Jewish emancipation to the colonial narrative of civilizing. Flandin's reference to Revolutionary and Napoleonic laws, especially, blurred the historical trajectories of French and Algerian Jews. For example, he noted that "before 1789 in France, the Jews were excluded from all local civic rights, and even after the great Revolution they were admitted neither to the primary assemblies convoked for the nomination of the estates general, nor even to the communal assemblies." It was only Napoleon's 1808 law following the Sanhedrin that "definitively established" Jews' "état civil" in France. Colonialism, in Flandin's explanation had since continued the emancipatory legacy of the French Revolution. "In 1830, the native Israelites of Algeria did not have a better situation than their co-religionists had in France before 1789. The conquest was for them a deliverance, they entered willingly into the ranks of their liberators; they found there an honorable regeneration. By numerous petitions, they requested that the quality of citizen be accorded to them. The senatus-consulte fulfills their wishes."

Flandin was not alone in seeing continuities between Napoleonic and Revolutionary legislation and the 1865 law. Some French lawmakers opposed the bill, arguing that since polygamy was an expression of a larger belief system, granting citizenship upon the sole condition that Jews and Muslims modify one aspect of their behavior was dangerous. Better would be to convene two more Sanhedrins; one each for the Jews and Muslims of Algeria.[127] In other words, both backers and detractors of the 1865 law saw the Sanhedrin as a central point of reference, attesting to the persistence of marriage laws in the conception of citizenship and of the civilizing mission in Algeria.

Naturalization and Its Discontents

It is not difficult to explain why Jewish reformers and civil officials in Algeria were less impressed with Napoleon III's law than was Flandin. First, it treated colonized Muslims and Jews equally, which challenged the colonial mythology that represented the Jews of Algeria as an oppressed but superior minority. Second, it allowed Jews to choose whether to accept the French personal status. Most civil officials knew, however, that Algerian Jews were not eager to give up their personal status in exchange for French citizenship. Indeed, between 1865 and 1870, a mere 142 out of Algeria's 33,000 Jews were naturalized.[128] Muslims did not apply for citizenship in great numbers either. By 1878, only 435 Muslims had accepted citizenship out of more than 3 million. Meanwhile, court decisions affirmed Algerian Jews' independence from French civil law. In 1869, for example, an Algerian court ruled that Algerian Jews who were married before an officer of the état civil were still governable by Jewish personal status. In the mind of Jewish reformers, this attempt at legal assimilation was a total failure.[129]

Debates leading up to the Crémieux Decree of 1870, which made Algerian Jews French citizens, proved marital law to be a defining issue in French reformers' struggle for Algerian Jews' emancipation. This was a fundamental principle upon which both colonial legists and French-Jewish reformers appear to have agreed. As mentioned earlier, Rabbi Charleville used the incompatibility of French-Jewish and Algerian-Jewish family law to demonstrate that Algerian rabbis should not be eligible for consistorial posts in 1867. Three years later, Governor General MacMahon circulated a questionnaire to civil authorities asking if the consistories "consider themselves authorized" to make a declaration "analogue to that of the Grand Sanhedrin of 1808 to absolve their co-religionists from the observations of the Mosaic law that are contrary to the prescriptions of the Napoleonic code and of the ensemble of our civil and political laws."[130] MacMahon's concern about reactions to Jewish naturalization en masse was well founded; the consistory of Oran had refused to participate in a recent petition asking for universal Jewish naturalization.[131] Oran's consistory eventually concluded that naturalization would be welcomed, but the members inquired whether the law would maintain divorce. The letter pointed out that divorce had not been banned by the Sanhedrin, but it "subordinated the religious act to the civil act."[132] Oran's consistory would appear to have taken into account the sensibilities of many local Jews. The conseil général of Algiers called for a new, colonial Sanhedrin, followed by Algerian-Jewish naturalization.[133] Algerian newspapers, meanwhile, published articles questioning whether the mass of Algerian Jews actually desired citizenship.[134]

In the years leading up to 1870, the year in which all Algerian Jews were granted French citizenship, debates about Jews' readiness for naturalization circulated among French and Algerian reformers, colonial officers, and legal experts in France and in Algeria. The outcome of these conversations would crystallize with the passage of the Crémieux Decree, a law that permanently put an end to the question of Algerian Jews' ability to become (legally, at least) French. The decision would also address the issue of which authority would govern the Jewish family.

Former consistory member Adolphe Crémieux became minister of the interior in the wake of the proclamation of the Third Republic in September 1870. Crémieux was a well-known lawyer most recently elected deputy of the third *arrondissement* of Paris. He also had a distinguished liberal record; he served as a minister in the short-lived Second Republic, was a member of both the Paris and central consistories, and was credited with the 1844 decree reorganizing the Jewish religion in France. From its founding in 1860, he had also been a member of the Alliance Israélite Universelle, whose members had tended toward his republican politics.[135]

By the time of his appointment as minister, Crémieux's reformist reputation and support for Algerian-Jewish naturalization had earned him the unofficial title of spokesman for Algerian affairs.[136] The reputation endured despite the brevity of his visits to Algeria and his small base of contacts, generally limited to elite reformist and republican circles. After the rejection of a draft decree that would have given Algerian Jews the option of rejecting citizenship within the first year of its promulgation, the Crémieux Decree, as it would be called, was issued on October 24, 1870. The decree stated simply that Algerian Jews were citizens and that they no longer were governed by their previous personal status: "the indigenous Israelites of the departments of Algeria are declared French citizens. In consequence, their real statute and their personal status will be registered from the promulgation of the present decree, by French law; all rights acquired up to this day shall remain inviolable."[137] The same day, another republican-inspired decree reduced military rule in Algeria and extended civil government in Algeria. Algerian Jews, without the formality of a Sanhedrin, or indeed any choice in the matter, were universally required to abandon their personal status and to conform to the guidelines of the French *statut personel* and the état civil. Apart from some criticism from Jews in the departments of Constantine and Oran, the law went into effect quietly.[138]

Algerian Jews did not, however, rush to conform to the dictates of their new personal status, particularly when it came to their marriage practices. Within the first two years of the decree, the central consistory in Paris, to which Algerian consistories now reported, issued numerous circulars and posters reminding Algerian Jews of their new requirement to contract civil marriages. In September 1872, Rabbi Charleville noted that for 90 percent of the marriages contracted in the Province of Oran since the decree was issued, "the law is eluded or disdained."[139] In December of the same year, the members of the consistory of Oran made a similar complaint, noting that the problem of clandestine marriages was linked to that of private synagogues, where indigenous rabbis continued to celebrate weddings with no regard for French law.[140] The minister of public instruction and religions noted, "the decree of October 24, 1870, according to whose terms the indigenous Israelites of Algeria became French and ceased to be governed by the statute of the law of Moses, has faced a heated opposition in the [now] Department of Oran."[141] The consistories found themselves faced with a population that had accepted citizenship but nonetheless quietly refused to accept French jurisdiction over the legal constitution of the family, which had become not only a primary mark of civilization but also a condition of French nationality. The phenomenon is well illustrated by the Sasportès court case with which this chapter began. Algerian Jews were citizens, but by the standards of family structure and morality as defined in the preceding decades, they remained to be "civilized."

Conclusion

It would be difficult to overemphasize the centrality and consistency of family law, morality, and domestic life to the cultural and legal construction of the French colonial hierarchy in Algeria. Civil administrators and Jewish reformers in Algeria both responded to and helped reproduce this dynamic. The weight of family law in the French notion of citizenship led the consistory to strive to bring Algerian Jews into conformity with French laws and practices. Simultaneously, French rabbis and the prefects made consistent appeals to higher authorities to clarify the legal position of Algerian Jews. Reminiscent of the first fifteen years of the occupation explored in Chapter 1, Algerian-Jewish behaviors and actions once again encouraged French officers, administrators, and lawmakers to tailor the civilizing mission to the needs of colonial rule. The resultant civilizing mission was a product of Algerian-Jewish behaviors and, indirectly, the reformers' understanding and use of the Jewish religion. The legal confusion created by earlier assimilatory laws, institutions, and court decisions eventually created a situation that local administrators sought to resolve through naturalization. The ascent of a republican government in Paris provided the liberal rabbis, prefects, and lawyers of Algeria with a powerful and sympathetic audience.

Meanwhile, Napoleon's Grand Sanhedrin served as a reference point for discussions about naturalization during the Second Empire. Jewish reformers, republicans, military officials, and legal thinkers consistently used the Sanhedrin as an example of how groups possessing different legal/religious codes could be legally absorbed into France. While our discussion concentrated on the continuing importance of this model in the campaign to emancipate Algerian Jews, we also noted that the Sanhedrin's model was raised in discussions concerning Algerian Muslims, as well. In fact, the senatus-consulte of 1865 allowed Muslims to become citizens if they agreed to adopt French laws governing the family, the major requirement imposed on French Jews in 1808.

The laws and discussions leading up to 1870 illustrate how surveillance, control, and access to the domestic sphere of the family were central to the French civilizing mission in Algeria. The 1865 law made citizenship available to Jews and Muslims willing to allow the French état civil to both register and govern the structure of their families. But even before Napoleon III formalized the mutual dependence of French personal status and citizenship local administrators and rabbis spoke of clandestine marriages—family unions hidden from the view of the authorities. Marriages, far from hidden, in actuality were often simply conducted at synagogues and homes rather than in the presence of French civil officers. Not surprisingly, French prefects and rabbis grew concerned that most Algerian Jews were not willing to part with their religiously defined personal status. Evidence suggested, in contrast, that Jews in Algeria resisted French law's intrusion into the intimate domains of their homes and families. Even after the 1870 Crémieux Decree, divorce and polygamy continued to raise the specter that Algerian Jews had rejected France and the French-Jewish community. Algerian-Jewish family customs, French officials worried, were still jealously hidden behind home and synagogue walls.

Conclusion

In late eighteenth-century France, a Portuguese-Jewish merchant from Bordeaux named Samuel Peixotto chose to divorce his wife, Sara Mendes Dacosta. Rather than regulate the affair with a rabbi, he sued for divorce in the Paris royal courts, claiming that he had the right to divorce on the grounds that he was Jewish. Peixotto's odd move—attempting to get a French court to uphold Jewish law and grant him a divorce—triggered an explosion of legal discussion on the question of the status of Jews in France. The discussion centered on what exactly described their status, whether they enjoyed all rights generally accorded to inhabitants of the kingdom (*régnicoles*), were foreigners (*étrangers*) or French (*français*), and what code was to govern their marital practices. Evelyn Oliel-Grausz has noted that the *Répertoire universel et raisonné de jurisprudence civile, criminelle canonique et bénéficiel de Guyot*, perhaps the most important French legal journal of the eighteenth century, had manifested a dramatic new interest in this subject during the 1770s. While the *Répertoire* of 1778 featured only six pages on divorce, the editions of 1784 and 1786 featured more than 60 pages on the subject.[1] The *Collection de décisions nouvelles*, another journal, went from featuring one-half page on divorce in 1778 to 21 pages in the edition of 1787. Almost all of the new text stemmed from the odd case of Peixotto and the wider question of what the code governing Jews' personal status implied for their legal status in France. The case soon grew into a *cause célèbre* and attracted a significant amount of popular attention.

Arabs of the Jewish Faith has emphasized that colonial ideology and policy in Algeria developed in response to local circumstances, actors, and institutions. Yet in interesting ways, Peixiotto's case foreshadows the 1870 trial of Sasportès, the Algerian Jew brought to court by the French authorities for practicing polygamy. In both trials, the question of which authority governed family structure and marriage law served as the locus of a wider debate over the criteria for French nationality. While the Revolution supposedly resolved ambiguities over Jewish status, Napoleon used French Jewish "abuses" as a pretext for reevaluating their citizenship. His approach was to convene representatives of the Jews of France and inquire about their laws and customs, emphasizing those dealing with the family and marriage. For the purposes of French law, the Grand Sanhedrin officially resolved the supposed contradictions between Judaism and the civil code. As we saw earlier, colonial laws used this precedent to locate both the "foreignness" of Jews and their avenue to citizenship in their family practices.

Members of the consistory and civil administration in colonial Algeria worked within this Napoleonic precedent. At the same time, the Algerian consistory system was an effort to export a modified vision of Abbé Henri Grégoire's ideal of Jewish "regeneration." Grégoire's influential essay in favor of Jewish emancipation rested on his faith that the corruption of Jews was due to past persecution, and emancipation would lead to their regeneration as happy and productive citizens. Yet like Napoleon, Grégoire located Jewish vices in the domestic sphere. Certainly, Grégoire criticized Jews' economic behaviors, but he also speculated on their immoral family life, marriage customs, and sexual proclivities.[2] He insisted that the health and morality of the republic depended upon women assuming their proper role in society, avoiding public roles, and helping to preserve monogamous, Christian family life. Foreshadowing colonial critiques of Islamic society, he suggested that non-Christian cultures mistreat their women and regard them as property.

It was no coincidence that Grégoire explained the regenerative power of citizenship in an essay about Jews. Enlightenment and Revolutionary debates used the corrupted Jew as a sort of "anti-citizen," a vehicle for emphasizing the power and meaning of emancipation and citizenship.[3] Seemingly influenced by the moralistic formulations of Grégoire and other eighteenth- and early nineteenth-century writers, consistorial officers in Algeria focused on morality, interior spaces, and family customs of local Jews as crucial loci in which the civilizing project could be worked out. Civil officials and consistorial members thus sought to close private synagogues, certify the morality of teachers, measure and judge the air quality in schools, encourage Jews to conduct civil marriages, and stop prostitution. It would appear that beginning with the writings of Grégoire (if not earlier), regeneration, emancipation, and citizenship were intimate—and often Jewish—affairs in the minds of many French political thinkers.

Debates and laws that concerned Algeria's Jews were conceptually linked not only to earlier French contexts, but also to the French authorities' concurrent treatment of Algeria's Muslim population. Put in dialogue with Second Empire–period legislation, such as the 1865 senatus-consulte, the

Peixiotto case and Napoleon's Jewish policy suggest that early debates over Jewish religious authority, family law, and national belonging colored Muslims' subsequent encounter with French "civilizing" policies. At the same time, Jewish reformers responded to a French colonial discourse that used Muslim family structure and the position of women as a barometer of inferiority and justification for domination. Jacques-Isaac Altaras, Joseph Cohen, Lazare Cahen, and Mahir Charleville spilled considerable ink discussing polygamy, divorce, and the status of women in Algerian-Jewish homes. Jacob Lasry, president of the consistory of Oran, hoped to ban Jewish marriage ceremonies judged to be "Arab" in form. Sometimes, reformers vaunted Jewish superiority over Muslims, but more frequently they lamented Algerian Jews' refusal to conform to the requirements of the French personal status.

Personal status laws applied to French subjects in colonial Algeria in the nineteenth century were logically rooted in these intertwined discourses. They allowed Muslim and Jewish families to be governed by their religious authorities, but also made the family the boundary of French citizenship. When Jews did not willingly submit to be married before an officer of the état civil, the marriage was deemed clandestine by Jewish reformers. The emergence of clandestine marriages suggests the ways in which family law became a battleground in French efforts to secure control of the intimate lives of Jews. These dramatic laws, of course, affected not only Jews. Only five years after the passage of the 1865 law permitting Algerian Jews and Muslims to choose French personal status, the very decree that abolished the Jewish personal status and enfranchised Algeria's Jews left Muslim personal status intact. Put another way, Muslim legal exclusion appears to have rested, in part, on the legal logic that emancipated colonized Jews.

Colonial debates and legislation about personal status and citizenship are but a few examples of how the French civilizing mission was reconstructed and reimagined in Algeria. The economic activities, social status, and demographic weight of Algerian Jews compelled colonial officials to formulate a strategy that effectively dealt with this important urban minority. Governor General Thomas-Robert Bugeaud and the ministers to whom he reported did not agree on a Jewish policy, but all felt it necessary to neutralize this population that seemed both troublesome and potentially useful. Algerian Jews were at once part of the "friendly" urban population, yet strongly intertwined with commercial networks that involved local tribes, trans-Saharan commerce, and France's European rivals. When the Ministry of War sent Jacques-Isaac Altaras to research Algerian Jews in 1842, it helped fuse the historical teleology of French-Jewish emancipation with colonial policy. The answer Altaras generated was that the regime ought to establish an institutional network whose mandate was to more effectively assimilate Algerian Jews into the European population. In the context of

Algeria, then, Enlightenment-influenced Jewish reformers were invited to participate in a colonial project. The French Ministry of War, faced with the realities of the Algerian urban and commercial landscape, chose to adapt and deploy a historically specific notion of emancipation in the service of colonial domination.

Once established, the colonial consistories adopted an ideology of regeneration that privileged corporeal and interior spaces. Reports and correspondence drew attention to Jewish family practices, the organization of their homes, the clothing they wore, and especially to activities conducted within private synagogues. They thus endeavored to penetrate, monitor, and control religious, domestic, educational, and corporeal spaces. Administrators relied upon experts who raised issues of health, hygiene, and morality in their efforts to gain access to such interiors. Religious or private realms became of vital interest to those who hoped to change the relationship of Jews to the colonial state. In official correspondence, Algerian Jews who dodged these efforts were frequently described as averse to civilization. The word took on new meanings as colonial officers charged with regenerating Algerian Jews encountered resistance to their intrusive campaign.

The importation of the regenerating project from France to Algeria had other unintended consequences. Within a year of the installation of consistories in Algeria, members of the Algerian Jewish elite appropriated the civilizing ideology to advance their own political and moral interests, joining municipal councils and the consistory itself. Jacob Lasry and Abraham ben Haim, for example, brought their own economic interests, social perspectives, and religious faith into the very body that metropolitan reformers and the Ministry of War had hoped would transform them. Algerian Jews soon played important roles in determining which local practices, synagogues, or schools would be supported or suppressed. Non-elite Jews, meanwhile, often rejected the French rabbis who were charged with overseeing their communities, refused to get married according to the French personal status, and maintained their own rabbis, schools, and synagogues. Their discontent was articulated in various lexicons that reflected and appropriated French political language, stressing faith, patriotism, civilization, progress, and at times republicanism. Moshe Karsenty, we recall, made his demands based on France's uncontestable authority and civilizing ideal in his petitions to ministers in Paris. In myriad ways, then, the colonial administration's attempt to ameliorate and assimilate Algerian Jews was appropriated and transformed by France's colonial subjects.

Schools were a crucial space of encounters and resistance. In contrast to Jews in other parts of the Mediterranean basin, Algerian Jews often refused to send their children to communal schools, preferring familiar local rabbis and educators. Civil administrators were, as a result, forced to make significant compromises with teachers and rabbis of the midrashim, allowing some to remain in operation, and hiring others to instruct at communal schools. Continuity with preexisting educational and religious forms, rather than the outright elimination of these institutions, distinguished Algerian Jews' confrontation with French colonialism. If regeneration required official organs to penetrate and monitor Algerian-Jewish domestic and religious space, local Algerian Jews in turn shaped the civilizing policies of the consistories.

Before concluding, it is perhaps useful to reflect on how a recent legal case resonates with this historical study. In 2000, a Moroccan Muslim woman known as Faiza M. went to France to rejoin her husband, a French citizen. In the years that followed, the couple had three children and Faiza applied for French citizenship. Her application was denied in 2005 on the grounds of the applicant's "failure to assimilate" (*défaut d'assimilation*). Faiza appealed the ruling, but in June 2008 the conseil d'état upheld the earlier decision, deciding that Faiza M. had "adopted, in the name of a radical practice of her religion, a behavior (*comportement*) in society incompatible with the essential values of the French community, and notably the principle of the equality of the sexes."[4] As it turns out, Faiza M had started wearing a *burqa*, a loose, head-to-toe garment that reveals only the eyes of its wearer. French social service agencies apparently reported that Faiza M. "lived in total submission to male relatives."[5] *Le Monde* described the "innovation" of the decision in a way that recalls central conclusions of our current study: "In the case of Faiza M, it is her clothing and private life that has been put forward in confirming the refusal of French nationality."[6] Several weeks later, the minister of urban affairs, Fadela Amara, expressed her approval of the decision. She predicted that it may "dissuade certain fanatics from imposing the burqa on their wives." In an interview with *Le Parisien*, Amara insisted the burqa is "a prison, it's a straitjacket."[7] The outcome of the decision ensured that Faiza M. could continue to live in France with her family, but without the rights of citizenship. In the name of France's commitment to women's equality, the court denied a woman voting rights and other benefits of citizenship. Her crime was having been supposedly forced by her husband into "total submission," manifested in part by her clothing.

Despite the vast differences of time and circumstance, the case of Faiza M. contains echoes of the debates over civilizing Jews and personal status laws in nineteenth-century Algeria. Early Jewish reformers tried to convince lawmakers that since Algerian-Jewish women did not live in total submission to their husbands, and were used to going out unveiled when they pleased, they should be naturalized. Generals also argued that Jews who wear European clothing could be trusted with firearms. At the same time, French lawmakers and judges denied Algerian Jews citizenship based on their putatively immoral family structure. Observers condemned polygamy, divorce, and other manifestations of Algerian-Jewish women's total submission to their husbands, while striving to submit them to a French (that is, civilized) family structure. Consistorial representatives and civil authorities thereby sought increased access to the private lives of the individuals under their watch. With Napoleon III's 1865 law, both Muslims and Jews were invited to choose the path of civilization by adopting the regime of French family law. Those who did not make the formal abdication of rights threatening the "good order of families," however, would continue to live as imperial subjects until the end of the colonial period. The emancipation of Algeria's Jews was carried out only later, when lawmakers chose to oblige Jewish families to conform to French family law. In nineteenth-century Algeria, as in twenty-first-century France, notions of emancipation, family order, and women's status were mobilized to deny citizenship rights to people living under French authority.

The history of Algerian Jews' confrontation with French colonial power suggests that the notion of emancipation, as it emerged in Revolutionary and Napoleonic debates over Jewish citizenship, was central to France's exclusionary colonial ideology. This Revolutionary and Napoleonic legacy did not predestine France's colonial Jewish policy, but colonial administrators and lawmakers drew on it to understand, structure, and legislate colonial difference. French understandings of citizenship, regeneration, and civilization were subsequently appropriated, translated, and reformed according to colonial strategy, in local forms, and in dialogue with historical contingencies.

What ideological and legal continuities with Napoleonic legislation and the ideology of regeneration were carried forward to the colonial setting had radically different effects in the colonial context than it did in the metropole. In Algeria, Jewish personal status became both a determining marker of colonial inferiority, as well as a source of religious identification and piety. French lawmakers accused Algerians of failing to limit and define a discrete religious domain in conformity with the French secular legislative code, thereby erecting a roadblock to their own naturalization. When French reformers deemed Jews worthy of emancipation, they ensured that the path of this population would diverge radically from that of their Muslim neighbors. And yet, for the many differences in Jewish and Muslim history in late colonial Algeria, Algerian Jews' experience with both colonization and collective naturalization suggests that even recent French discussions that link the family life of Muslim immigrants with their ability to be French have enjoyed a long, colonial history.

NOTES

ABBREVIATIONS FOR ARCHIVAL SOURCES

ACC   Archives du Consistoire Central des Israélites de France

AN   Archives Nationales de France

BNA   British National Archives

CAOM   Centre des Archives d'Outre Mer

SHAT   Service Historique de l'Armée de la Terre

INTRODUCTION

1. Alice Conklin noted the Enlightenment background of the civilizing ideology, but focused her fascinating study on the Republican period. See her *A Mission to Civilize: The Republican Idea of Empire in France and West Africa, 1895–1930* (Stanford: Stanford University Press, 1997). More recently, J. P. Daughton has examined the conflicting ideological strains of French imperialism during this period. J. P. Daughton, *An Empire Divided: Religion, Republicanism, and the Making of French Colonialism, 1880–1914* (Oxford and New York: Oxford University Press, 2006).

2. Jews often represented a sort of anti-citizen in Enlightenment debates over emancipation and citizenship. See Ronald Schechter, *Obstinate Hebrews: Representations of Jews in France, 1715–1815* (Berkeley: University of California Press, 2003), esp. 6–7; idem, "The Jewish Question in Eighteenth-Century France," *Eighteenth-Century Studies* 32:1 (1998): 84–91.

3. The "Kabyle myth" is the best-known example of French colonial mythologies. Charles-Robert Ageron, *Les Algériens musulmans et la France*, vol.1 (1871–1919) (Paris: Presses Universitaires de France, 1968), 267–292; Patricia Lorcin, *Imperial Identities: Stereotyping, Prejudice, and Race in Colonial Algeria* (New York: I. B. Tauris, 1995), 118–166; Marnia Lazreg, "The Reproduction of Colonial Ideology: The Case of the Kablyle Berbers" *Arab Studies Quarterly* 5 (1983): 380–395.

4. See Schechter, *Obstinate Hebrews*, 1–65.

5. Civilizing in the West African context also generally denoted "mastery." See Conklin, *A Mission to Civilize*, 5–6.

6. Pierre Birnbaum, "French Jews and the 'Regeneration' of Algerian Jewry," in *Jews and the State: Dangerous Alliances and the Perils of Privilege*, ed. Ezra Mendelssohn (Oxford: Oxford University Press, 2003), esp. 94–96.

7. R. Estoublon and A. Lefébure, *Code de l'Algérie annoté. Recueil chronologique des lois, ordonnances, décrets arrêtés, circulaires, etc. actuellement en vigueur* (Algiers: A. Jourdan, 1896), 305.

8. Haketia is a form of Ladino (Judeo-Spanish) that was spoken largely in Moroccan cities, such as Tetuan and Tangiers. Like the Ladino spoken in the Ottoman East, it was based on Spanish grammar, written in Hebrew letters, and featured many Hebrew and Arabic loan words.

9. Ranajit Guha suggested transcripts written in the "code" of "committed colonialism" could still provide clues to subaltern consciousness. Like the South Asian peasants that Guha discusses, the colonial "prose of counter-insurgency" often reduced Algerian Jewish resistance to something akin to unconscious "natural history." Here to, the historian can read colonial transcripts "against the grain" to recover the subject. See Ranajit Guha, "The Prose of Counter-Insurgency," in *Selected Subaltern Studies*, ed. Ranajit Guha and Gayatri Chakravorty Spivak (Oxford and New York: Oxford University Press, 1988), 45–88; Rosalind O'Hanlon, "Recovering the Subject: Subaltern Studies and Histories of Resistance in Colonial South Asia," *Modern Asian Studies*, 22:1 (1988): 189–224. Gayatri Chakravorty Spivak excuses efforts to reconstitute subaltern perspectives through official colonialist documents as "a strategic use of positivist essentialism in a scrupulously visible political project" by "Discussion: Subaltern Studies: Deconstructing Historiography," in *Subaltern Studies IV* (Delhi: Oxford University Press, 1985), 342.

10. Gyan Prakash, "Subaltern Studies as Postcolonial Criticism," *American Historical Review* 99, 5 (December 1994): 1475–1490.

11. Ranajit Guha, "The Prose of Counter-Insurgency," 45–88, 74.

12. See *The Antonio Gramsci Reader: Selected Writings, 1919–1938* (New York: New York University Press, 2000), 189–221. I do not deny that colonized Jews carved out real space for themselves in a colonial order, all the while making their claims within a hegemonic discourse.

13. Responsa refers to a genre of literature in which a given rabbi (or his followers) distributes his answers to questions sent to him by fellow Jews who respect his religious authority.

14. Yossef Charvit, *La France, l'élite rabbinique d'Algérie et la Terre Sainte au XIXe siècle: tradition et modernité* (Paris: Honoré Champion Éditeur, 2005), esp. 97–184. See also his *Élite rabbinique d'Algérie et modernization* (Jerusalem: Editions Gaï Yinassé, 1995).

15. This was the case for many rabbis in Oran, including Rabbi Abraham Enkaoua, whose study *Zevachim Shleimim* was at the center of heated debates. See, for example, the volume containing both *Kerem Hemer* and *Taharat haKesef* (Livorno: Dfus Hadash shel Eliahu ben Amuzeg ve-Heverav, 1869). As we shall see, angry responses to the first book became a matter of concern for the consistory of Oran.

16. *Shechita*, or ritual slaughter, was a contentious issue in many Jewish communities. See Robin Judd, *Contested Rituals: Circumcision, Kosher Butchering, and Jewish Political Life in Germany, 1843–1933* (Ithaca, NY: Cornell University Press, 2007). I thank Nathaniel Deutsch for bringing this issue to my attention and introducing me to relevant literature.

17. Examples of recent work exploring the encounter between French Jews and Algerian Jews include Michael Shurkin, "French Nation Building, Liberalism, and the

Jews of Alsace and Algeria, 1815–1870" (Ph.D. diss., Yale, 2000); Pierre Birnbaum, "French Jews."

18. The population of Algeria at the time of the conquest was probably between three and four million. The Jewish population was about 30,000 to 35,000, mainly concentrated in cities and towns. See Simon Schwarzfuchs, *Les Juifs d'Algérie et la France, 1830–1855* (Jerusalem: Institut Ben-Zvi, 1981), 21.

19. Liberal ideas justified exclusive laws in British colonialism as well. Uday Mehta, "Liberal Strategies of Exclusion," in *Tensions of Empire: Colonial Cultures in a Bourgeois World*, ed. Ann Laura Stoler and Frederic Cooper (Berkeley: University of California Press, 1997), 59–86.

20. Some variant of the phrase "Jewish Colonialism" appears in almost every treatment of the topic since the 1970s. See, for example, Simon Schwarzfuchs, "Colonialisme français et colonialisme juif," in *Judaisme d'Afrique du Nord aux XIXe–Xxe siècles: Histoire, société et culture*, ed. Michel Abitbol (Jerusalem: Institut Ben-Zvi, 1980), 37–48; Elizabeth Deborah Friedman, *Colonialism and After: An Algerian Jewish Community* (South Hadley, MA: Bergin and Garvey Publishers, 1988), 1–14; and Shurkin, *French Nation Building*, 11. Pierre Birnbaum does not challenge the formulation when he cites Henri Chemouilli saying the same thing in "French Jews and the 'Regeneration' of Algerian Jews," in *Jews and the State: Dangerous Alliances and the Perils of Privilege*, 90.

21. The implication of the term is that French Jews set up institutions intended to make Algerian Jews more like them, mirroring the wider French "assimilationist" policy in Algeria The French colonial theory of assimilation, was most influentially laid out by Raymond Betts, *Assimilation and Association in French Colonial Theory, 1890–1914* (New York: Columbia University Press, 1960). Assimilation meant different things to different people, but its proponents generally aspired to assimilate the administration of Algeria into the French government. Some understood the theory as tending to integrate colonized subjects into the larger French national community. Betts was careful to distinguish the ideal of assimilation from the reality; see pages 165–176.

22. Michel Abitbol, "The Encounter between French Jewry and the Jews of North Africa: Analysis of a Discourse," in *The Jews in Modern France*, ed. Frances Malino and Bernard Wasserstein (Hanover, NH: Brandeis University Press, 1985), 31–53. See also Benjamin Stora and Geneviève Dermenjian, "Les Juifs dans le regard des militaries et des Juifs de France à l'époque de la conquète," *Révue Historique* 284(2) (1990): 333–339.

23. On the anti-Semitic movement that emerged in Algeria before, but peaked during, the Dreyfus affair, see Lizabeth Zach, "French and Algerian Identity Formation in 1890s Algeria," *French Colonial History* 2 (2002): 115–143. Geneviève Dermenjian argues that popular resentment against Jews was rooted to the perception that they voted in lockstep with their leaders. *La crise anti-juive*, 33–52.

24. Charles-André Julien has described the "psychosis" of repression, noting that "everywhere, massacres and rapes returned as a leitmotif" in officers' correspondence. Captain Lafaye was shocked by the behavior of his troops in 1848: "We have burned a village of Khremis, of the tribe of Beni Snous. Our soldiers . . . were not beyond the murder of old men, women and children. . . . Most hideous was how they killed the women after raping them." Other officers proudly defended their massacres. Thomas-Robert Bueaud, for example, famously defended Gen-

eral Pélissier's *enfumade*, in which hundreds of men, women, and children of the surrendered Ouled Riah were sealed in caves and asphyxiated by smoke. See his *Histoire de l'Algérie contemporaine: Conquête et colonisation, 1827–1871* (Paris: Presses Universitaires de France, 1964), 320.

25. The Comte de la Pinsonnière famously wrote, "We have subsumed in barbarism the 'barbarians' we had come to civilize, and yet we complain that we have not yet succeeded!" Julien, *Histoire de l'Algérie*, 110. François Guizot, who occupied several ministry positions during the July Monarchy (1830–1848), justified the necessity of "civilized" countries using policies of force against the less civilized. François Guizot, "Discours prononcés par M. Guizot, Ministre des Affaires Etrangères, dans la discussion des crédits extraordinaires pour l'Algérie, séance du 10 Juin 1846," in *Chambre des Pairs, Session de 1845–1846* (Paris, 1846).

26. Fanny Colonna, *Instituteurs algériens, 1883–1939* (Paris and Algiers: Presses de la fondation nationale des sciences politiques and Office nationale des publications universitaires [Algiers], 1975).

27. The term is borrowed from Partha Chatterjee, *The Nation and Its Fragments: Colonial and Postcolonial Histories* (Princeton, NJ: Princeton University Press, 1993). Focusing on British India, Chatterjee has argued that the essentialized difference between the colonizer and the colonized subject justified authoritarian, nondemocratic rule.

28. Nathan Godley, "'Almost Finished Frenchmen': The Jews of Algeria and the Question of French National Identity, 1830–1902" (Ph.D. diss., University of Iowa, 2006), 188.

29. Ibid., 190–191. See also Geneviève Dermenjian, *La crise antijuive Oranaise, 1895–1905: L'antisemitisme dans l'Algérie coloniale* (Paris: l'Harmattan, 1986), 33–52.

30. Ibid. See also Joshua Schreier, "Napoleon's Long Shadow: Morality, Civilization, and Jews in France and Algeria, 1808–1870," *French Historical Studies* 30:1 (Winter 2007): 77–103.

31. Richard Ayoun, "Le Décret Crémieux et l'insurrection de 1871 en Algérie," *Revue d'Histoire Moderne et Contemporaine* 35 (January-March 1988): 11–87.

32. Ibid.

33. Literally, "Arabes de religion juive." Charles du Bouzet, *Les Israélites indigènes de l'Algérie: Pétition à l'Assemblée Nationale contre le décrèt du 24 Octobre, 1870* (Paris, 1871), 4.

34. Frederic Cooper has argued that when scholars assign a "causal weight" to an abstracted post-Enlightenment ideology, and allow it to have a determining factor in colonial history, it not only elides past and current political and epistemological struggles in Europe, it also "gives insufficient weight to the ways in which colonized people sought—not entirely without success—to build lives in the crevices of colonial power, deflecting, appropriating, or reinterpreting the teachings and preachings thrust upon them." This book devotes significant space to these "crevices." See his *Colonialism in Question: Theory, Knowledge, History* (Berkeley: University of California Press, 2005), 16.

35. Jewish reformers sometimes described French Jews as Africans or Asians, and this foreignness led to many European accounts comparing overseas peoples with the European Jews. See Jay Berkovitz, *The Shaping of Jewish Identity in Nineteenth-Century France* (Detroit: Wayne State University Press, 1989), 47–48, 122; Tudor

Parfitt, "The Use of the Jews in Colonial Discourse," in *Orientalism and the Jews,* ed. Ivan Davidson Kalmar and Derek J. Penslar (Lebanon, NH: Brandeis University Press, 2005), 51–67. On the Oriental French Jew, see Pierre Birnbaum, *L'Aigle et la synagogue: Napoléon, les Juifs, et l'Etat* (Paris: Fayard, 2007), 75–98.

36. The idea that modern power was located and deployed in part through the explosion of discourses on sexuality and practices of the body is, of course, Michel Foucault's. See his *History of Sexuality: An Introduction,* vol. 1 (New York: Vintage, 1990): esp. 103–131. Focusing on colonial contexts, Ann Laura Stoler has argued that "control over sexuality and reproduction were at the core of defining colonial privilege and its boundaries." Ann Laura Stoler, "Rethinking Colonial Categories: European Communities and the Boundaries of Rule," *Comparative Studies in Society and History* 31, 1 (January 1989): 134–161 (the quote appears on 154). The article was republished in *Carnal Knowledge and Imperial Power: Race and the Intimate in Colonial Rule* (Berkeley: University of California Press, 2002), 22–40. This latter work represents an elaboration of the principle that "matters of the intimate were absolutely central to imperial rule," upon which my study builds. See also Aron Rodrigue's *Images of Sephardic and Eastern Jewries in Transition* (Seattle: University of Washington Press, 1993), 80–93.

37. Suzanne Desan, *The Family on Trial in Revolutionary France* (Berkeley: University of California Press, 2004), 249–310; Alyssa Goldstein Sepinwall, *Abbé Grégoire and the French Revolution: The Birth of Modern Universalism* (Berkeley: University of California Press, 2005), 72, 215.

38. Lisa Moses Leff, *Sacred Bonds of Solidarity: Jewish Internationalism in Nineteenth-Century France* (Stanford: Stanford University Press, 2006). Furthermore, Leff has also shown how Napoleon's *consistoires israélites* would later serve as the model for colonial institutions in Algeria. See "The Impact of the Napoleonic Sanhedrin on French Colonial Policy in Algeria," *CCAR Journal* (Winter 2007): 35–60.

39. Narratives of Jewish emancipation wove together metropole and colony, so the approach of this study is necessarily trans-local. As such, it builds on recent literature on the nature of writing colonial histories. See Ann Laura Stoler and Frederic Cooper, eds., *Tensions of Empire: Colonial Cultures in a Bourgeois World* (Berkeley: University of California Press, 1997). See especially the editors' introduction, "Between Metropole and Colony: Rethinking a Research Agenda," 1–58.

40. On the danger of ahistorical visions of post-Enlightenment modernity and its colonial incarnations, see Frederic Cooper, *Colonialism in Question,* 12–22. On how colonial personal status laws, which echo Revolutionary and Napoleonic requirements for citizenship, were framed to exclude Muslims from citizenship. See Michael Brett, "Legislating for Inequality in Algeria: The Senatus-Consulte of 14 July 1865," *Bulletin of the School of Oriental and African Studies* 51 (1988): 441–461; Jeanne Bowlan, "Polygamists Need Not Apply: Becoming a French Citizen in Colonial Algeria, 1918–1938," *Proceedings of the Annual Meeting of the Western Society for French History* 24 (1997): 110–119.

41. See Sarah Stein, "Modern Jewries and the Imperial Imagination," *AJS Perspectives* (Fall 2005): 14–16; Ivan Kalmar and Derek J. Penslar, eds., "Empire and the Jews," in *AJS Perspectives* (Fall 2005): 18–19.

42. Kalmar and Penslar, "Empire and the Jews," 19.

43. Stein, "Modern Jewries," 16.

44. Any historical picture must be untangled from the powerful modernization narrative of successful assimilation that was "affirmed" by the Jews' full naturalization and eventual emigration to France. Benjamin Stora speaks of Jews' near "invisibility" in the "social landscape of France since 1962, (since) they melted into the mass of Europeans thrown into the exodus at the moment of Algerian independence." See Stora's *Trois exils: Juifs d'Algérie* (Paris: Editions Stock, 2006), 9–10.

45. Ibid., 13. Joel Beinin, in his study of Egyptian Jewry, has discussed the ways in which politics have prevented Jews in Egypt from assuming a place in contemporary Egyptian society or in its national historical narrative. See *The Dispersion of Egyptian Jewry*, 1–30.

46. Hamilton A. R. Gibb and Harold Bowen's explanation of the term was particularly influential. See *Islamic Society and the West: A Study of the Impact of Western Civilization on Moslem Culture in the Near East*, vol. 1, part 2 (London and New York: Oxford University Press, 1950), 206. See also C. E. Bosworth, "The Concept of *Dhimma* in Early Islam" in *Christians and Jews in the Ottoman Empire: The Functioning of a Plural Society*, vol. 1, ed. Benjamin Braude and Bernard Lewis (New York: Holmes & Meier Publishers, 1982), 37–52. For a discussion of the legal position of Jews in Islamic societies, see Mark Cohen, *Under Crescent and Cross: The Jews in the Middle Ages* (Princeton: Princeton University Press, 1994), 52–76. A negative interpretation of the Jews' status as dhimmis was also expressed in earlier works on Algerian Jews specifically, such as Claude Martin, *Israélites algériens de 1830 à 1902* (Paris: Editions Herakles, 1936); and Richard Ayoun and Bernard Cohn's synthetic discussion in *Les Juifs d'Algérie: deux mille ans d'histoire* (Paris: J. Clattès, 1982), 68–86.

47. See, for example, Jacques Taïb, *Sociétés du Maghreb moderne (1500–1900)* (Paris: Maisonneuve & Larose, 2000), 44–45.

48. Ibid., 44.

49. Ibid., 36–37.

50. Amnon Cohen, "Realities of the Millet System: Jerusalem in the Sixteenth Century," in *Christians and Jews in the Ottoman Empire*, ed. Benjamin Braude and Bernard Lewis, vol. 2, 7–18. See also Schroeter's discussion about the dhimmi in the historiography of Jewish life in Morocco in *The Sultan's Jew: Morocco and the Sephardi World* (Stanford, CA: Stanford University Press, 2002), 4–10. A landmark essay treating the mythologies surrounding Jewish life under Islam and Christianity during the Middle Ages appears in Mark Cohen, *Under Crescent and Cross*, 3–16.

51. Not only were some Jews influential in the court of the precolonial Algerian Regency, but there is also evidence that in some circumstances, nomadic or semi-nomadic North African Jews carried weapons, engaged in agriculture, and lived among other Bedouin. For an overview, see Jacques Taïb, *Etre Juif au Maghreb à la veille de la colonization* (Paris, Albin Michel, 1994), 38–39.

52. Julien, *Histoire de l'Algérie contemporaine*, 7.

53. Julia Clancy-Smith, *Rebel and Saint: Muslim Notables, Populist Protest, Colonial Encounters (Algeria and Tunisia, 1800–1904)* (Berkeley: University of California Press, 1997), 1–32.

54. Ibid., 33–65.

55. *Univers Israélite* I (1845). Cited in Taïb, *Sociétés Juives*, 38.

56. Taïb, *Sociétés Juives*, 38.

57. Jean-Louis Miège, "Les Juifs et le commerce transsaharien," in *Communautés Juives des marges sahariennes du Maghreb*, ed. Michel Abitbol (Jerusalem: Institut Ben Zvi, 1982), 391–404.

58. Ibid., 39.

59. Some scholars have suggested that despite customs requiring that the community approve the choice of moqaddem, communal input may have become less frequent by the late eighteenth century. The customary laws set down by Rabbi Yitzhak bar Sheshet (often known by the acronym formed by his Hebrew initials "RiBaSH") and Rabbi Shimon bar Tsemach Duran ("RaSHBaTZ") in earlier centuries had expressly decreed that this was to be an elected post. See Yossef Charvit, *Elite rabbinique d'Algérie et modernisation* (Jerusalem: Editions Gaï Yinassé, 1994), 44.

60. Isaac Bloch, *Les Israélites d'Oran de 1792 à 1815* (Paris: A. Durlacher, 1886), cited in Richard Ayoun, "Les Juifs d'Oran Avant la Conquête Française," *Revue Historique* 267, 2 (1982): 375–390.

61. To encourage trade with ports such as Algiers and Oran, the government of Spain relaxed its ban on Jewish settlement. See Ayoun, "Les Juifs d'Oran," 389. See also Tito Benadi, "The Jewish Community of Gibraltar," in *The Sephardi Heritage: Essays on the History and Cultural Contribution of the Jews of Spain and Portugal*, vol. II, ed. R. D. Barnett and W. M. Schwab (Grendon, Northamptonshire: Gibraltar Books, 1989), 144–179.

62. Morton Rosenstock, "Economic and Social Conditions of the Jews of Algeria: 1790–1848," *Historia Judaica* 18 (1956): 3–26.

63. Essaouira (Mogador), Algiers, Tripoli, Benghazi (in modern Libya), Alexandria, and Cairo were the most significant ports for the export for this commodity. Jews dominated the trade in numerous locations throughout the nineteenth century, bringing the feathers to Livorno, Marseilles, Paris, and London, among other ports. The boom occurred after 1880, but women were wearing feathers as early as the eighteenth century. See Sarah Abrevaya Stein, "Mediterranean Jewries and Global Commerce in the Modern Period: On the Trail of the Jewish Feather Trade," in *Jewish Social Studies: History, Culture, Society* 13, 2 (Winter 2007): 5–6.

64. Ayoun, Ibid.

65. Miege, "Le commerce transsaharien," 394; Stein, "Mediterranean Jewries," 9–13.

66. Jean-Pierre Filippini, "Les Juifs d'Afrique du Nord et la Communauté de Livourne au XVIIIe siècle," in *Les relations intercommunautaires juives en méditerranée occidentale aux XIIIe–XXe siècles* (Paris: Editions du CNRS, 1984), 60–69.

67. Ibid. See also Matthias Lehmann, "A Livornese 'Port Jew' and the Sephardim of the Ottoman Empire," *Jewish Social Studies* 11, 2 (2005): 51–76; Lionel Lévy, *La Nation Juive Portugaise: Livourne, Amsterdam, Tunis, 1591–1951* (Paris: Harmattan, 1999).

68. Max Kortepeter, "Jew and Turk in Algiers in 1800," in *The Jews of the Ottoman Empire*, ed. Avigdor Levy (Princeton, NJ: Darwin Press, 1994), 335.

69. Jacob Coen Bacri, for example, who held considerable French debts and whose desire to have them repaid contributed to the disintegration of ties between the Regency of Algiers and France in the 1820s, was given special privileges to trade in Marseilles in 1795 as the representative of Dey Hassan Pasha. Kortepeter, "Jew and Turk in Algiers in 1800," 335–336.

70. A fascinating example of French concern about Jewish relations with Arab merchants comes from SHAT, Series 1 H 62, dos. 2, Lt. Colonel to Lieutenant General, Superior Commander of the Province of Oran, 5 June 1839.

71. Rosenstock, "Economic and Social Conditions," 3–26.

72. William Shaler, *Sketches of Algiers, political, historical, and civil; containing an account of the geography, population, government, revenues, commerce, agriculture, arts, civil institutions, tribes, manners, languages, and recent political history of that country* (Boston: Cummings, Hilliard and Co., 1826), 29.

73. M. Rozet, *Voyage dans la régence d'Alger*, vol. 3 (Paris: Arthus Bertrand Librarie, 1833), 227. Also William Shaler, *Sketches of Algiers*, 65.

74. For example, CAOM, Series 1 E Liasse 150 18 MIOM 45, Minister of War Correspondence: Bugeaud, 25 September 1839. See also Anthony Thrall Sullivan, *Thomas-Robert Bugeaud, France and Algeria, 1784–1849: Politics, Power, and the Good Society* (Hamden, CT: Archon Books, 1983), 107–113.

75. Rosenstock, "Economic and Social Conditions," 3–26; Isaac Bloch, *Les Israélites d'Oran de 1792 à 1815* (Paris: A. Durlacher, 1886).

76. The ownership of private synagogues was a means of bolstering the prestige and probably the income of their owners. CAOM, fol. 3U/2, dos. "Synagogues Particulieres," Consistoire Israelite de la Province d'Oran to Director of Civil Affairs, Province of Oran, 30 November 1847.

77. See, especially, CAOM, fol. 3U/1 and 3U/2.

78. Susan Slyomovics, "Geographies of Jewish Tlemcen," in *The Walled City in Literature, Architecture, and History: The Living Medina in the Maghreb*, ed. Susan Slyomovics (Portland, OR and London: Frank Cass & Co., 2001), 81–96.

79. For the significant Jewish role in various components of this commerce, see Stein, "Mediterranean Jewries and Global Commerce"; as well as Jonathan I. Israel, *Diasporas Within a Diaspora: Jews, Crypto-Jews, and the World of Maritime Empires (1540–1740)* (Lieden: Brill, 2002), 5; Daniel Schroeter, *Merchants of Essaouira: Urban Society and Imperialism in Southwestern Morocco, 1844–1886* (Cambridge: Cambridge University Press, 1988); and his *The Sultan's Jew*, esp. 1–35; For the trans-Saharan leg of Mediterranean commerce, see Jean-Louis Miege, "Les Juifs et le commerce transsaharien au dix-neuvieme siècle," in *Communautés juives des marges sahariennes du Maghreb*, ed. Michel Abitbol (Jerusalem: Institute Ben-Zvi, 1982), 391–404.

80. Salo Baron coined the expression "lachrymose conception of Jewish history." He argued that Jewish history was mistakenly seen as a long chronicle of suffering and oppression. See his *A Social and Religious History of the Jews* (New York: Columbia University Press, 1928). For how this conception influenced studies of Jews in Islamic societies, see the chapter cited above by Mark Cohen in *Under Crescent and Cross*, 3–16. In recent years, politics have fueled neo-lachrymose portrayals of Middle Eastern or North African Jewish history. See Sarah Abrevaya Stein, "Sephardi and Middle Eastern Jewries Since 1492," in *The Oxford Handbook of Jewish Studies*, ed. Martin Goodman, Jeremy Cohen, and David Sorkin (London and New York: Oxford University Press, 2002), 327–362; Joel Beinin, *The Dispersion of Egyptian Jewry*, 14–19. Regarding the Jews of Algeria, an example of scholarship echoing the colonial model of the conquest as an "emancipation" from an Oriental "state of abasement," see Richard Ayoun, "Les efforts d'assimilation intellectuellle et

l'émancipation législative des Juifs d'Algérie," in *Cultures juives méditerranéennes et orientales*, ed. Centre Georges Pompidou (Paris: Syros, 1982), 171–188.

81. H. Z. Hirschberg, *A History of the Jews in North Africa*, vol. 2, *From the Ottoman Conquests to the Present Time* (Leiden: E. J. Brill, 1981), 56–79.

82. Richard Ayoun, *Typologie d'une carriere rabbinique: l'example de Mahir Charleville*, vol. 1 (Nancy: Presses Universitaires de Nancy, 1993), 231–232.

83. AN, fol. F19 11143, Central Consistory to Minister of Justice and Religions, 12 December 1836.

84. AN, fol. F19 11143, Minister of War to Minister of Justice and Religions, 9 November 1839.

85. Jacques-Isaac Altaras, member of the Marseille consistory, wrote the most influential early report on the Jews of Algeria after being commissioned by the Ministry of War. In it he describes the variety of Jewish occupations while still describing Jewish life under Muslim rule as a "state of abasement." See "Rapport sur l'état moral et politique des Israélites de l'Algérie et des moyens de l'améliorer," reproduced in Schwarzfuchs, *Les Juifs d'Algérie*, 67–201. Hereafter Altaras, "Report."

86. Phillip Nord, *The Republican Moment: Struggles for Democracy in Nineteenth-Century France* (Cambridge, MA: Harvard University Press, 1998).

87. See Leff, *Sacred Bonds*, 127–137.

88. On the deployment of authoritative knowledge to construct colonial or postcolonial subjects in the Middle East, see Omnia El Shakry, *The Great Social Laboratory: Subjects of Knowledge in Colonial and Postcolonial Egypt* (Stanford: Stanford University Press, 2007), and Michael Gasper, *The Power of Representation: Publics, Peasants, and Islam in Egypt* (Stanford: Stanford University Press, 2008).

CHAPTER 1 JEWS, COMMERCE, AND COMMUNITY IN EARLY COLONIAL ALGERIA

1. Charles-André Julien, *Histoire de l'Algérie contemporaine: Conquète et colonisation, 1827–1871* (Paris: Presses Universitaires de France, 1964), 83.

2. SHAT, series 1 H 12, fol. 3 *Rapport sur la Province d'Oran*, General Boyer to Governor General of Algeria, 1 March 1832.

3. Ibid.

4. Indeed, the wording of the decree even instructs rabbis to encourage Jews to take up "agricultural work." See R. Estoublon and A. Lefébure, *Code de l'Algérie annoté. Recueil chronologique des lois, ordonnances, décrets arrêtés, circulaires, etc. actuellement en vigueur* (Algiers: A. Jourdan, 1896), 83.

5. For motto, see Michael Shurkin, "French Nation Building, Liberalism, and the Jews of Alsace and Algeria, 1815–1870" (Ph.D. diss., Yale, 2000), 195.

6. Shurkin, *French Nation Building*, 146, 186–189; Richard Ayoun, "Les efforts d'assimilation intellectuelle et l'émancipation législative des Juifs d'Algérie," in *Cultures juives méditerranéennes et orientales*, ed. Centre Georges Pompidou (Paris: Syros, 1982), 171–188; Simon Schwarzfuchs, "Colonialisme français et colonialisme juif" in *Judaïsme en Afrique du Nord aux XIXe–XXe siècles: Histoire, société, et culture*, ed. Michel Abitbol (Jerusalem: Institut Ben Zvi, 1981), 37–48; Zosa Szajkowski, "The Establishment of the Consistorial System in Algeria" *Jewish Social Studies* 18, 1 (1956): 41–54, and "The Struggle for Jewish Emancipation in Algeria After the

French Occupation," *Historia Judaica* 18(1) (1956): 27–40; Lisa Moses Leff, *Sacred Bonds of Solidarity*, 127–137.

7. In this I differ slightly from Lisa Moses Leff's reading of the liberal Jewish influence on colonialism. See her fine *Sacred Bonds of Solidarity: Jewish Internationalism in Nineteenth-Century France* (Stanford: Stanford University Press, 2006), 117–156.

8. According to Charles-André Julien, by 1840, almost 90 percent of the 25,000 Europeans living in Algeria were urban, and of them, 44 percent were French. The others included Spanish, Italians, Maltese, and some Swiss and Germans. By the end of the 1840s, the European population had grown steadily and reached more than 125,000. See Julien, *Histoire de l'Algérie Contemporaine*, 158.

9. CAOM, fol. F80 1670/B, *Rapport sur la province d'Oran et sur l'etat de l'occupation dans cette partie de la Regence*, 25 April 1853.

10. Julien, *Histoire de l'Algérie Contemporaine*, 158.

11. CAOM, fol. F80 1670/B. Chief of Algiers Bureau to Minister of War, 3 July 1832; SHAT, Series 1 H 11, dos. 2, *Rapport Particulier*, Algiers, 20 February 1832.

12. CAOM, fol. F80 1670/B, *Rapport sur la province d'Oran et sur l'etat de l'occupation dans cette partie de la Regence*, 25 April 1853.

13. On poor Europeans of precolonial Tunis, see Julia Clancy-Smith, "'Making It' in Pre-Colonial Tunis: Migration, Work and Poverty in a Mediterranean Port-City, c.1815–1870," in *Subalterns and Social Protest: History from Below in the Middle East and North Africa*, ed. Stephanie Cronin (London and New York: Routledge, 2008), 213–236.

14. Communities from the M'zab Valley, centered around the city of Ghardaia in the northern Sahara, were established in a number of Algerian cities. See Julien, *Histoire de l'Algérie contemporaine*, 13. On their presence in Oran specifically, see SHAT 1 H 20, dos. 2, *Rapport sur la Province d'Oran et sur l'état de l'occupation dans cette partie de la Regence*, 23 April 1833.

15. SHAT, series 1 H 11, dos. 2, *Rapport Particulier*, Algiers, 20 February 1832.

16. Thomas Robert Bugeaud, duc d'Isly, *Mémoire sur notre établissement dans la province d'Oran: Par suite de la paix*, reproduced in Maurice Henri Weil, *Oeuvres militaries du maréchal Bugeaud, duc d'Isly, réunis et mises en ordre* (Paris: L. Baudouin, 1883), 219. The original brochure was published in 1838.

17. SHAT, series 1 H 93, dos. 2, Bugeaud to Minister of War, 10 November 1843.

18. CAOM, 18 Mi 2EE 5, Bugeaud to Minister of War, 19 November 1843. The historian Michel Ansky went so far as to suggest that by the seventeenth century, and until the arrival of the French, Jews essentially dominated commerce in Algerian cities. See Michel Ansky, *Les Juifs d'Algérie: Du décret Crémieux à la liberation* (Paris: Editions du Centre, 1950), 23–24.

19. Louis de Baudicour, *Des indigènes de l'Algérie* (Paris: Charles Douniol, 1852), 4. Cited in Nathan Godley, "'Almost Finished Frenchmen': The Jews of Algeria and the Question of French National Identity, 1830–1902" (Ph.D. diss., University of Iowa, 2006), 54. Translation is Godley's.

20. De Genvray and Lapointe, "Les juifs à Alger," in *Le Journal de Rouen*, 13 February 1852, cited in Nathan Godley, *Almost Finished Frenchmen*, 53.

21. Baron Baude, *L'Algérie* (Paris: A. Bertrand, 1841): 287, cited in Godley, *Almost Finished Frenchmen*, 55–56.

22. Daniel Holsinger, "Trade Routes in the Algerian Sahara in the Nineteenth Century," *Revue de l'Occident Musulman et de la Méditerranée* 30, 1 (1980): 57–70.

23. Ibid., 62.

24. In a letter to the Ministry of War, Bugeaud noted that he had managed to revive Bedouin trade in French markets, but that the results were not entirely encouraging: "I have succeeded reasonably well [to re-establish trade] with all the submitted groups, and our markets are abundant. The Arabs are coming back, loaded with merchandise—mostly English, unfortunately." Bugeaud to Minister of War, 20 September 1842. CAOM, fol. 2 EE 3, microfilm 18 MIOM 2; Holsinger, "Trade routes," 63.

25. Most of this traffic went from Tripoli. See Marion Johnson, "Calico Caravans: The Tripoli-Kano Trade after 1880," *Journal of African History* 17, 1 (1976): 95–117; Daniel Holsinger, "Trade Routes," 60; A. Adu Boahen, *Britain, the Sahara, and the Western Sudan, 1788–1861* (Oxford: Oxford University Press, 1964), cited in Sarah Abrevaya Stein, "Mediterranean Jewries and Global Commerce in the Modern Period: On the Trail of the Jewish Feather Trade," in *Jewish Social Studies: History, Culture, Society* 13, 2 (Winter 2007): 8.

26. SHAT, Series 1 H 62, dos. 2, Lt. Colonel to Lieutenant General, Superior Commander of the Province of Oran, 5 June 1839. For Algeria at the time of the treaty of Tafna, see Julien, *Histoire de l'Algérie Contemporaine*, 131–151.

27. SHAT, Series 1 H 62, dos. 2, Lt. Colonel to Lieutenant General, Superior Commander of the Province of Oran, 5 June 1839.

28. It is, however, worthy of note that the treaty was negotiated with the help of ben Duran, a member of one of the more powerful Spanish Jewish families in Algeria. See Julien, *Histoire de l'Algérie Contemporaine*, 136.

29. Francesca Trivellato, "The Sephardic Diaspora and Cross-Cultural Trade in the Early Modern Period," paper presented to the Economic History Seminar at Harvard University, February 8, 2008. See also her *The Familiarity of Strangers: The Sephardic Diaspora, Livorno, and Cross-Cultural Trade in the Early Modern Period* (New Haven: Yale University Press, 2008).

30. CAOM, fol. 3U/1, Colonel Commander of the Subdivision of Oran to General Pelissier, 5 April 1853.

31. CAOM, fol. 3U/1, Extract of Register of Deliberations of the Consistory of Oran, 11 February 1855.

32. CAOM, 1 E, Liasse 150, 18MIOM 45, Minister of War to Governor General of Algeria, 6 November 1839.

33. SHAT, 1 H 11, dos. 2, Muhammad abd al-Kadi to General Boyer, undated, but likely February 1832.

34. The family had since become connected to the Bujnah (Busnach) family, one of the two leading mercantile families of Algiers (alongside the Bacri family). By the early nineteenth century, the family also had marital ties with the Macnins, one of the leading Moroccan Jewish trading families based in Essaouira, and the subject of a fascinating study by Daniel Schroeter. See *The Sultan's Jew*, 43.

35. CAOM, fol. F80 1670/B, *Rapport sur la province d'Oran et sur l'etat de l'occupation dans cette partie de la Régence*, 25 April 1853.

36. Ibid. Also, SHAT 1 H 11, dos. 1, General Boyer to Governor General of Algeria, 21 January 1832.

37. CAOM, fol. F80 1670/B, Minister of War to Director of the Department of War, Algiers Bureau, 28 May 1832.

38. CAOM, fol. F80 1670/B, *Rapport sur la province d'Oran et sur l'etat de l'occupation dans cette partie de la Regence*, 25 April 1853.

39. Marcel Emerit, "Les tribus privilegées en Algérie dans la prémiere motié du XIXe siècle," *Annales* 21, 1 (1966): 44–58.

40. Marcel Emerit, "Les tribus privileges," 49; see also Julien, *Histoire de l'Algérie contemporaine*, 96. For location of the Doua'ir, see Plate V.

41. By 1835, the Doua'ir had a formal treaty with France. See Emerit, "Les tribus privilegés," 50.

42. SHAT, 1 H 11, dos. 2, Muhammad al-Qadi to General Boyer, undated, but likely February 1832.

43. Ibid.

44. SHAT, 1 H 11, dos. 2, Commandant of the Station, Mers el-Kabir, 13 February 1832.

45. SHAT, 1 H 11, dos. 2, Boyer to Muhammad al-Qadi, 13 February 1832.

46. Ibid.

47. SHAT, fol. 1 H 12, dos. 3, Boyer to Minister of War, 1 March 1832.

48. SHAT, fol. 1 H 20, dos. 2., *Rapport sur la Province d'Oran et Sur l'état de l'occupation dans cette partie de la Regence*, 23 April 1833.

49. CAOM, fol. F80 1631, Civil Intendant in Algiers to Governor General, 2 December 1835.

50. SHAT, fol. 1 H 12, dos. 3, Boyer to Minister of War, 1 March 1832.

51. SHAT, fol. 1 H 11, dos. 1, Boyer to Governor General, 21 January 1832.

52. BNA, F.O. 335/57/13, James Welsford to Colonel Sir Thomas Reed, Tunis, 18 January 1832.

53. BNA, F.O. 335/57/2, British Consul in Algiers to Lord Viscount Goderich, 5 October 1831.

54. BNA, F.O. 335/57/2, British Consul in Algiers to Lord Viscount Goderich, 5 October 1831.

55. BNA, F.O. 335/57/2, French Army of Africa, General Behaghel by invitation of General Landois, copy of section of minutes, 22 August 1831.

56. BNA, F.O. 335/57/2, British Vice Consul Welsford, certified copy of note by Civil Intendant Banachin of Oran, 27 October 1831.

57. Ibid.

58. See Daniel Schroeter, *The Sultan's Jew: Morocco and the Sephardi World* (Stanford, CA: Stanford University Press, 2002), as well as Stein's "Feather Trade." See also Stein's essay on the historiography on Jews and modern European empires, "Modern Jewries and the Imperial Imagination," *AJS Perspectives* (Fall 2005): 14–16.

59. BNA, F.O. 335/57/13, James Welsford to Sir Thomas Reade, 18 January 1832.

60. Ibid.

61. BNA, F.O. 335/57/2, Pierre Boyer to British Vice Consul, 11 October 1831.

62. A fanega is a Spanish unit of measure apparently in common use in the region. It is similar in quantity to an English bushel.

63. BNA, F.O. 335/57/13, James Welsford to Sir Thomas Reade, 30 January 1832.

64. BNA, F.O. 335/58/12, Consul for the King of Two Sicilies in Tunis to Hussein Basha Bey, 24 August 1832.

65. CAOM, fol. 3U/1, Proposal of Consistory of Oran for Notables of the Circumscription, 5 May 1853.

66. CAOM, fol. F80 1631, Twenty Jews of Oran to "Géneral," 7 June 1835.

67. Ibid.

68. CAOM, fol. F80/1631, Bureau of Civil Intendant to Governor General, 25 July 1835.

69. Clancy-Smith, "'Making It' in Pre-Colonial Tunis," 214.

70. CAOM, fol. 3U/1, Royal Commissioner to Civil Intendant, 2 November 1837.

71. SHAT, Series 1 H 62, dos. 2, Lt. Colonel to Lieutenant General, Superior Commander of the Province of Oran, 5 June 1839.

72. This affair is also summarized in Shurkin, *French Nation Building*, 164–165.

73. While of the same extended clan, this Duran is in all likelihood *not* the same as the moqaddem of early nineteenth-century Oran, mentioned in the introduction. CAOM, fol. F80/1631, Bureau of Civil Intendant to Governor General, 2 December 1835.

74. Ibid.; Julien, *Histoire de l'Algérie coloniale*, II. For another reference to Duran in his role as cattle merchant and confidante of the French command in Algiers, see SHAT, fol. 1 H 62, dos. 2, General Valée to Emir Abd al-Qader, 11 June 1839.

75. Claude Martin, *Israélites algériens de 1830 à 1902* (Paris: Editions Herakles, 1936), 53–58. For a resumé of Jews reported double dealing between the French and Abd al-Qader, see also Godley, *Almost Finished Frenchmen*, 57–58.

76. CAOM, fol. F80/1631, Duran to Civil Intendant, 24 November 1835; Civil Intendant to Governor General, 2 December 1835.

77. CAOM, fol. F80/1631, Duran to Civil Intendant, 24 November 1835.

78. CAOM fol. F80/1631, ben Shimon to Governor General, 3 November 1835.

79. Ibid.

80. CAOM fol. F80/1631, Governor General to Civil Intendant, 3 November 1835.

81. Ibid.

82. CAOM, F 80 1631, Civil Intendant to Governor General, 2 December 1835.

83. SHAT, fol. 1 H 62 dos. 2, Governor General Valée to Abd al-Qader, 11 June 1839.

84. Once again, the phrase is borrowed from Gyan Prakash, "Subaltern Studies as Postcolonial Criticism," 1475–1490.

85. CAOM, fol. F80/1631, Duran to Civil Intendant, 24 November 1835.

86. Ibid.

87. Ibid.

88. I thank Hartley Lachter for bringing this possibility to my attention and suggesting the kabbalistic and hallachic implications.

89. Fez emerged as a center for the production of Kabbalistic scholarship in the wake of the expulsion from Spain. From there, many rabbis made their way to centers in Italy and Palestine. See Moshe Idel, "Jewish Mysticism Among the Jews of Arab/ Moslem Lands," *Journal for the Study of Sephardic and Mizrachi Jewry* I, 1 (February 2007): 14–39. At least one well-known fifteenth-century kabbalist, R. Ephraim ben Israel al-Naqawah (Enkaoua), was buried in Tlemcen in western Algeria, and his

tomb became a center for pilgrimage. See Susan Slyomovics, "Geographies of Jewish Tlemcen," 81–96.

90. David Nadjari, *Juifs en terre coloniale: Le culte israélite à Oran au début du XXe siècle* (Nice: Editions Jacques Gandini, 2000), 79. Nadjari also draws on Haïm Zafrani's observations of Moroccan Judaism in Tetuan and Tangiers, from which increasing numbers of Oran's Jews were migrating. See his *Mille ans de vie juive au Maroc* (Paris: Maisonneuve & Larose, 1983), 223.

91. The Jewish principle of *mar'at ayin* is possibly invoked here—the prohibition on conducting technically permissible behavior that would appear to be forbidden or to sanction the forbidden. In the case at hand, the rabbis may have warned Ben Shimon that whether or not his wife was adulterous (an accusation that may have been difficult to prove), it was his obligation to prevent members of his family from appearing adulterous.

92. CAOM, fol. F80/1631, Duran to Civil Intendant, 24 November 1835.

93. An important caveat: Most references to Jewish prostitution do not appear until the 1840s, when the presence of French occupying forces was more than ten years old. By then, circumstances may have favored the inception or growth of a previously insignificant local sex trade. See Altaras, "Report," in Simon Schwarzfuchs, *Les Juifs d'Algérie et la France, 1830–1855* (Jerusalem: Institut Ben-Zvi, 1981), 101; CAOM 3U/1, Minutes of Meeting of Consistory, 7 September 1847; CAOM, fol. 3U/1, Rector to Prefect of the Province of Oran, 2 August 1853.

94. Julien, 322.

95. *Le Courier d'Afrique*, 12 July 1845.

96. See, for example, Schwarzfuchs, *Napoleon, the Jews, and the Sanhedrin* (Boston and London: Routledge and Kegan Paul, 1979), and Ronald Schechter, *Obstinate Hebrews: Representations of Jews in France, 1715–1815* (Berkeley: University of California Press, 2003).

97. Anthony Thrall Sullivan, *Thomas-Robert Bugeaud: France and Algeria, 1784–1849 Politics, Power, and the Good Society* (North Haven, CT: Archon Books, 1983), 129.

98. Ibid., 110.

99. CAOM, Series 1 E Liasse 150 18 MIOM 45, Minister of War Correspondence: Bugeaud, 25 September 1839.

100. Moritz Wagner, *The Tricolor on the Atlas: Algeria and the French Conquest*, trans. Francis Pulzky (New York: T. Nelson and Sons, 1855).

101. Captain Daumas to Auvray. Mascara, 28 January 1838. From Captain Daumas and Georges Yver, *Correspondance du Capitaine Daumas, consul à Mascara (1837–1839)*, part of series: Gouvernement Général de L'Algérie, Collection de Documents Inédits sur l'Histoire de l'Algérie après 1830. IIe Série; *Documents Divers* (Algiers: Jordan, 1912), 88–89; CAOM, series E 16, 18 MIOM 37, Daumas to General Guelhec, 8 January 1839.

102. Anonymous, *Guide du voyageur en Algérie: Itinéraire du Savant de l'Artiste, de l'Hômme du monde, et du Colon* (Paris, 1848), 15–16.

103. Sullivan, *Thomas-Robert Bugeaud*, 110.

104. Ibid.

105. CAOM, series 2 EE 5, microfilm 18 MIOM, Bugeaud to Minister of War, 19 November 1843. See also Sullivan, *Thomas-Robert Bugeaud*, 110.

106. ACC, Register of Deliberations, 24 November 1833. Also cited in Martin, *Les Israélites Algériens*, 68.

107. AN, fol. F19 11143, Central Consistory to the Minister of Justice and Religions, 12 December 1836.

108. AN, fol. F19 11143, Central Consistory to the Secretary of State of the Department of War, 4 September 1839.

109. AN, fol. F19 11143, Central Consistory to the Minister of Justice and Cults, 12 December 1836.

110. By 1839, Algeria had attained what Charles-André Julien described as its *état civil* and its "administrative personality." On October 14, the minister of war officially baptized "*le pays occupé par les Français dans le Nord de l'Afrique*" as *Algérie*. Algeria was declared a colony by the ordinance organizing government finances, issued in 1839. See Julien, *Histoire*, 157.

111. Ministère de la Guerre, *Tableau de la Situation des Etablissements Françaises dans l'Algérie* (Paris: Imprimerie Royale, 1838–1845).

112. Valée was Bugeaud's predecessor and nemesis. He served as governor general from December 1, 1837 to January 29, 1841.

113. As a reminder, Jewish autonomy was already on the way to being dismantled by 1839. The ordinance of August 1834 mentioned here marked a significant reduction of Jewish autonomy (and the first major difference in colonial policy toward Jews and Muslims). Rabbis were divested of any jurisdiction save over marriages, divorces, and matters judged purely religious. The *arrêtés* of 28 February 1841 and 26 September 1842, which organized the system of justice throughout Algeria, essentially confirmed the loss of Jewish autonomy.

114. AN, fol. F19 11143, Minister of War to General Valée, 2 April 1839.

115. AN, fol. F19 11143, Minister of War to General Valée, 3 April 1839.

116. The commission included another member of the important Livornese Algerian family discussed above, Mordecai Amar, who was also the current moqaddem in Algiers. It also included Mayor Clément of Algiers. See Szajkowski, "The Struggle for Jewish Emancipation in Algeria after the French Occupation," *Historia Judaica* 18(1) (1956): 29.

117. Gustave de Beaumont, *Etat de la question d'Afrique: Réponse à la brochure de M. le Général Bugeaud intitulée: L'Algérie* (Paris: Paulin, 1843), 7. Bound in *Chambre de Députés: Impressions diverses et feuilletons* (Paris: Imprimerie Royale, 1843).

118. Gustave de Beaumont, *Ministère de la Guerre, Commission de Colonisation de l'Algerie: Rapport fait au nom de la Seconde Sous-Commission* (Paris: Imprimerie du Gouvernement, 1843), 1.

119. Gustave de Beaumont, *Etat de la question d'Afrique: Réponse à la brochure de M. le Général Bugeaud intitulée: L'Algérie* (Paris: Paulin, 1843), 17. Bound in *Chambre de Députés: Impressions diverses et feuilletons* (Paris: Imprimerie Royale, 1843).

120. Beaumont, *Commission de Colonisation*, 5.

121. For the generals' conviction that Jews were an obstruction to French economic control, see Sullivan, *Thomas-Robert Bugeaud*, 110. For Bugeaud's rejection of civil colonization, see CAOM, fol. 18, MIOM EE 3, Bugeaud to Martin du Nord, Minister of Justice, Algiers, 17 October 1843. For his hope to resist further civil penetration into Algeria, see CAOM, series 2 EE 5, 18 MIOM 3, Bugaud to Minister of War, 19 November 1843.

122. Julien, *Histoire*, 144–145.

123. CAOM, fol. F80 1675, Minister of War to General Valée, 6 November 1839.

124. Ibid.

125. General Thomas-Robert Bugeaud, *Mémoire sur notre établissement dans la Province d'Oran par suite de la Paix*. Reproduced in Weil, *Oeuvres militaries du maréchal Bugeaud*, 212.

126. CAOM, series 2 EE 5, fol. 18 MIOM 3. Bugeaud to Minister of War, 19 November 1843.

127. AN, fol. F80 11143, Minister of War to Minister of Justice and Religions, 6 November 1839.

128. Rosenstock, "The Establishment of the Consistorial System in Algeria," 49.

129. The French title was *Rapport sur l'état moral et politique des Israélites de l'Algérie et des moyens de l'améliorer*. In all likelihood, the report's echo of Abbé Henri Grégoire's 1788 *Essai sur la régénération physique, morale, et politique des Juifs*, was conscious. The original work represents one of the Revolutionary era's most influential arguments in favor of Jewish emancipation. See Pierre Birnbaum, "French Jews and the 'Regeneration' of Algerian Jewry," in *Jews and the State: Dangerous Alliances and the Perils of Privilege*, ed. Ezra Mendelsohn (Oxford: Oxford University Press, 2003), 88.

130. Altaras, "Report," in Schwarzfuchs, *Les Juifs de l'Algérie*, 67–68.

131. *Archives Israélites* IV (1843): 188.

132. Morton Rosenstock, "Economic and Social Conditions of the Jews of Algeria: 1790–1848," *Historia Judaica* 18 (1956): 49.

133. AN, fol. F19 11143, Minister of Justice and Religions to Minister of War, 16 August 1843.

134. CAOM, series E, fol. 170, 18 MIOM 49, Minister of War to General Bugeaud, 12 December 1843.

135. *Archives Israélites*, VI (1845): 919.

136. CAOM, fol. F80 1675, Minister of War memo, 8 November 1845.

137. Ibid.

138. CAOM, fol. F80 1675, Minister of War to King Louis-Philippe, 8 November 1845.

139. Ibid.

140. In this sense, it differed markedly from Napoleon's Infamous Decree of March 17, 1808, promulgated in response to Jewish usury in Alsace. The decree both prevented Jews from engaging in money lending and suspended debt payments for loans made by Jewish lenders for a period of ten years. It annulled debts made at interest rates higher than 5 percent, which thereafter were declared usurious. Napoleon's law also imposed new residency restrictions on Jews.

141. R. Estoublon and A. Lefébure, *Code de l'Algérie annoté*, 83.

142. The terms *juifs indigènes* and *israélites indigènes*, which the French used quite frequently, are misleading and imprecise. They were used to describe Moroccan immigrants, local Algerians, and even those with Livornese family connections. One of the first "indigenous" members of the consistory was Amran Senanès, who was actually of Moroccan descent.

143. CAOM, fol. 3U/1, Direction of the Interior and of Colonization (Algiers) to Sub-director of the Interior and of Colonization (Oran), 4 January 1847. The letter is based on orders from the Ministry of War in Paris, dated 25 November 1846.

144. CAOM, fol. 3U/1, Sub-director of the Interior and of Colonization to Director of the Interior, 9 January 1847.

145. CAOM, fol. F80 1631, Rabbi Cahen to Minister of War, 25 February 1847.

CHAPTER 2   REVOLUTION, REPUBLICANISM, AND RELIGION

1. CAOM, fol. 3U/1, Minutes of Meeting of the Consistory of Oran, 7 September 1847.

2. Ibid. See also the fascinating discussion about the origins and development of the term mission civilisatrice on the H-France archive from June 2005 (http://lists. uakron.edu/archives/h-france.html).

3. CAOM, fol. 3U/1, *Etat nominatif des Israélites ramenés de Mascara en Decembre 1835, présentement fixés à Oran*, Civil Intendant of Oran, 18 November 1836; *Etat nominatif des Israélites ramenés de Mascara en Decembre 1835, présentement fixés à Mostaganem*, Civil Intendant of Oran, 26 October 1836.

4. Most recently, Pierre Birnbaum, "French Jews and the 'Regeneration' of Algerian Jewry," in *Jews and the State: Dangerous Alliances and the Perils of Privilege*, ed. Ezra Mendelssohn (Oxford: Oxford University Press, 2003); Michael Shurkin, "French Nation Building, Liberalism, and the Jews of Alsace and Algeria, 1815–1870" (Ph.D. diss., Yale, 2000); Leff, "Jews, Liberals, and the Civilizing Mission in Nineteenth-Century France," in *Historical Reflections/Réflexions Historiques* 32, 1 (2006): 105–128.

5. Birnbaum, "French Jews and the 'Regeneration' of Algerian Jewry," 88.

6. Most notably, Claude Martin, *Israélites algériens de 1830 à 1902* (Paris: Editions Herakles, 1936).

7. Michael Gasper, *The Power of Representation: Publics, Peasants, and Islam in Egypt* (Palo Alto, CA: Stanford University Press, 2009), 17.

8. Frederic Cooper has clearly laid out the pitfalls of granting either post-Enlightenment thought, or the supposedly monolithic colonial modernity upon which it was based, an uncontested or all-powerful quality. See his *Colonialism in Question: Theory, Knowledge, History* (Berkeley: University of California Press, 2005), 3–32. Alice Conklin rightly argues that earlier critiques of the civilizing mission wrongly dismissed it as "window dressing." See *A Mission to Civilize: The Republican Idea of Empire in France and West Africa, 1895–1930* (Stanford: Stanford University Press, 1997), 2.

9. *L'Univers Israélite*, I (1844).

10. R. Estoublon and A. Lefébure, *Code de l'Algérie annoté. Recueil chronologique des lois, ordonnances, décrets arrêtés, circulaires, etc. actuellement en vigueur* (Algiers: A. Jourdan, 1896), 82.

11. Text of the 1806 *Règlement* is reproduced in Phyllis Cohen Albert, *The Modernization of French Jewry: Consistory and Community in the Nineteenth Century* (Hanover, NH: Brandeis University Press, 1977), 345–347.

12. The anti-Jewish bishop of Langres thought it indicative of the death of the Jewish religion that the Jews would accept such reforms. As he put it: "The source of all the temporal and even spiritual powers (now) is the state, the government, the minister of religions!" See *Le Spectateur*, Dijon, 24 and 27 May 1845, reprinted in *l'Univers Israélite* I (1844–1845); 174–180. The first issue of *l'Univers Israélite* (a more conservative French-Jewish journal founded in the wake of the reformist *Archives*

Israélites de France) lambasted the 1844 decree for not appreciating the progress the Jews of France had made since Napoleon instituted the consistories. Notably, the editor of the *l'Univers* complained that secular notables (as opposed to rabbis) dominated Judaism in France, and that the ordinance was inappropriate "for the nineteenth century" because the state usurped the right to approve low-level rabbis, who did not even receive governmental compensation. *L'Univers Israélite* I (1844–1845): 168–173.

13. Lisa Moses Leff, "The Impact of the Napoleonic Sanhedrin on French Colonial Policy," *CCAR Journal* (Winter 2007): 35–60. See esp. 47–49.

14. This authority should not be confused with the day-to-day direction of the consistories. The directors of civil affairs and prefectures were more directly involved.

15. Estoublon and Lefébure, *Code de l'Algérie annoté*, 82.

16. Nahon's subsequent career remained deeply enmeshed in the French colonial service. After being pushed out of the consistory, he was interpreter at the local prefecture; a year and a half later, he became the French consul in Tetuan, Morocco. *Akhbar*, 12 September 1850.

17. Ibid. In a sense, the hiring of Cahan represents a clear intersection between schools, prisons, and the expansion of state power. Michel Foucault's insistence on the centrality of these institutions in the development of modern forms of power over the eighteenth and nineteenth centuries focused on the Western European experience. It is of note that the same sorts of institutions are here seen as the obvious training ground for colonial consolidation. See Michel Foucault, *Discipline and Punish: The Birth of the Modern Prison* (New York: Vintage, 1995), esp. 170–308.

18. CAOM, fol. F80 1631, Memo, Second Bureau (of Ministry of War), 17 March 1847.

19. CAOM, fol. GGA, dos. 10/3/32, *Etat du mouvement de la prison civile d'Oran pendant l'anné 1847*. Given the Jewish proportion of Oran's population, such figures are not particularly surprising, especially given the social disruption and poverty characterizing the colonial cities at this point.

20. CAOM, fol. F80 1631, Lazare Cahen to Minister of War, 25 February 1847.

21. CAOM, fol. 3U/1, Petition from Jews of Oran to Governor General, 1 April 1848. Not only was Amran Sénanès related by marriage to Nahon, he shared his last name with another Moroccan Jew in Sidi-Bel-Abbes on whose part the Oran consistory attempted to intervene when he was arrested. See CAOM, fol. 3U/1, Consistory of Oran to General Commander of the Province of Oran, 28 March 1853.

22. *Akhbar*, 8 January 1850.

23. CAOM, fol. F80 1631, Memo, General Direction of Civil Affairs, 17 March 1847.

24. Regarding French instructors, CAOM, fol. F80 1631, Memo, General Director of Civil Affairs, 17 March 1847; regarding translation of oath, CAOM, fol. 3U/1, Sub-director of the Interior and of Colonization, Oran Office, 22 June 1847.

25. CAOM, fol. 3U/1, Minutes of Meeting of Consistory, 7 September 1847 and 9 September 1847.

26. CAOM, fol. 3U/1, various correspondences between Director of the Interior and General Administration of Algeria, 1842.

27. This moralizing posture would also characterize efforts of the Alliance Israélite Universelle in the Mediterranean basin in later decades. See Aron Rodrigue,

Images of Sephardic and Eastern Jewries in Transition (Seattle: University of Washington Press, 1993) 80–93.

28. CAOM, fol. 3U/1, Minutes of Meeting of Consistory, 7 September 1847.

29. E. A. Duchesne, *De la prostitution dans la ville d'Alger depuis la conquète* (Paris: J. B. Bailliere, 1853), 58.

30. See, for example, Julia Clancy-Smith, "Islam, Gender and Identities in the Making of French Algeria," in *Domesticating the Empire: Race, Gender and Family Life in French and Dutch Colonialism*, ed. Julia Clancy-Smith and Frances Gouda (Charlottesville and London: University Press of Virginia, 1998), 154–174; and "The Colonial Gaze: Sex and Gender in the Discourses of French North Africa," in *Franco-Arab Encounters: Studies in Memory of David C. Gordon*, ed. L. Carl Brown and Matthew S. Gordon (Beirut: American University of Beirut Press, 1996), 201–228. For the importance of family morality in the debates over Algerian Jewish citizenship, see Joshua Schreier, "Napoleon's Long Shadow: Morality, Civilization, and Jews in France and Algeria, 1808–1870," *French Historical Studies* 30, 1 (Winter 2007): 77–104.

31. Scholars of other areas have examined the efforts of colonial and post-colonial states to discipline their subjects to obey regular rhythms of work or study. Also relevant here is how the use and organization of space both represented and reinforced colonialists' notions of what constituted "modern" activities or sensibilities. See Timothy Mitchell, *Colonising Egypt* (Berkeley: University of California Press, 1991).

32. CAOM, fol. 3U/1, Minutes of Meeting of Consistory, 7 September 1847.

33. Ibid.

34. Ibid.

35. CAOM, fol. 3U/1, Note from Police to Consistory of Oran, 9 September 1847.

36. CAOM, fol. 3U/1, Minutes of Meeting of Consistory, 27 October 1847.

37. CAOM, fol. 3U/1, Consistorial Correspondence, 1847–1855.

38. CAOM, fol. 3U/1, President of Consistory to Director of Civil Affairs, 4 November 1847.

39. Ibid.

40. CAOM, fol. 3U/1, Minutes of the Meeting of the Consistory, 7 September 1847.

41. CAOM, fol. 3U/1, Minutes of the Meeting of the Consistory, 26 December 1847.

42. BNA, F.O. 335/58, Items 10–12.

43. CAOM, fol. F80 1631, translation by Nahon for the Minister of War, 28 February 1846.

44. Tefillin, or phylacteries, are two small leather boxes in which scrolls of scripture are kept, attached to leather straps. Jewish men put them on their arms and foreheads during *Shachrit* (morning prayers) on weekdays.

45. CAOM, fol. F80 1631, Lasry to the Minister of War, transcribed and attached to letter from Ministry of War, Direction of Algerian Affairs, to Governor General, 24 February 1846.

46. Ibid.

47. Ibid.

48. Ibid.

49. Charles-André Julien, *Histoire de l'Algérie contemporaine: Conquète et colonisation, 1827–1871* (Paris: Presses Universitaires de France, 1964), 255.

50. "Left" must be understood contextually. Many supported the Republic and were hostile to established religion. Later in the century, active socialist parties emerged in Algeria. At the same time, European immigrants later in the century were frequently violently racist against indigenous Arabs. See Emanuel Sivan, "Colonialism and Popular Culture in Algeria," *Journal of Contemporary History* 14, 1 (January 1979): 21–53. See also Maurice Agulhon, *The Republican Experiment: 1848– 1852* (Cambridge/Paris: Cambridge University Press and Editions de la Maison des Sciences de l'Homme, 1983), 38–40.

51. See Peter Amman, "The Paris Club Movement in 1848," in *Revolution and Reaction: 1848 and the Second French Republic*, ed. Roger Price (New York: Barnes and Noble, 1975), 115–132; and Amman's book, *Revolution and Mass Democracy: The Paris Club Movement of 1848* (Princeton, NJ: Princeton University Press, 1975). See also Maurice Agulhon, *The Republican Experiment*, 38–40.

52. Ibid.

53. Marcel Emerit, "L'Esprit de 1848 en Algérie," in *La Révolution de 1848 en Algérie: Mélanges d'histoire*, ed. Marcel Emerit (Paris: Editions Larose, 1949), 16–19.

54. Julien, *Histoire de l'Algérie Contemporaine*, 346.

55. One should note that the political effervescence in Algeria differed from that in the metropole, shaped as it was by particularities of the colonial situation. Notably, despite the stratification of white colonial society and their differences in political perspective, racism against indigenous Muslims had a unifying effect upon the various social classes of white Algeria. Few European colonists actually wanted to overthrow the French administration in Algeria for fear of losing their dominant position vis-à-vis the colonized population.

56. CAOM, fol. 3U/1, Civil Commissioner of Mostaganem to Director of Civil Affairs of Oran, 26 January 1848.

57. Ibid.

58. CAOM fol. F80/1631, Petition from Jews of Mostaganem to Duc d'Aumale, Governor General of Algeria. February 1848.

59. Lazare Cahen, *Rapport sur la situation des Israélites de la Province d'Oran*, 6 October 1850. Cited in Schwarzfuchs, *Les Juifs d'Algérie et la France, 1830–1855* (Jerusalem: Institut Ben-Zvi, 1981), 232–233.

60. CAOM, fol. 3U/1 Nahon to Director of Civil Affairs, 4 February 1848.

61. Henri-Eugène-Philippe-Louis d'Orléans, duc d'Aumale, was soon to be replaced by Cavaignac, whom the provisional government did not fear might aid a House of Orleans–inspired royalist coup. By March 3, the prince was on his way to a self-imposed exile in England.

62. CAOM, fol. 3U/1, Governor General of Algeria to General Director of Civil Affairs in Oran, February 1848.

63. CAOM, fol. F80/1631, Governor General to Director General of Civil Affairs, 6 April 1848.

64. Cavaignac was a republican, though quite conservative, and like his predecessor, related to the Orléans. He was to become infamous among the left for his slaughter of Parisian workers during the uprising of June 1848.

65. CAOM, fol. 3U/1, Jews of Oran to General Cavaignac, Governor General of Algeria, copy dated 1 April 1848.

66. CAOM, fol. 3/U1, Director of Civil Affairs to President Nahon, 7 April 1848.

67. *Archives Israélites*, IX (1848): 338.

68. Martin, *Les Israélties algériens*, 85.

69. Michael Shurkin, "French Nation Building, Liberalism, and the Jews of Alsace and Algeria: 1815–1870" (Ph.D. diss., Yale University, 2000), 270–271.

70. BNA, F.O. 3/53, leaf 20, British Consulate in Algiers to Viscount Palmerston, 23 April 1848.

71. Martin, *Les Israélites algériens*, 86.

72. CAOM, fol. 3U/1, Çahen to Director of Civil Affairs for the Province of Oran, 13 July 1848.

73. CAOM, fol. 3/U1, Nahon to Director of Civil Affairs, 29 March 1848.

74. CAOM, fol. 3U/1, Sénanès to Director of Civil Affairs, 29 March 1848.

75. CAOM, fol. 3/U1, Director of Civil Affairs to Nahon, 7 April 1848.

76. CAOM, fol. 3/U1, Nahon to Director of Civil Affairs, 22 May 1848.

77. CAOM, fol. F80 1631, Director of Civil Affairs to Governor General, 27 May 1848.

78. Cavaignac had been called to Paris to serve as minister of war in mid-May.

79. CAOM, fol. 3/U1, Governor General to Director of Civil Affairs in Oran, 16 August 1848.

80. CAOM, fol. 3/U1, Decision of Central Consistory of Algiers, issued 11 November 1848.

81. The consistories of Algiers and Constantine, however, were *not* remade in 1848.

82. CAOM, fol. 3/U1, Civil Commissariat of Mostaganem to Director of Civil Affairs of Oran, 26 January 1848.

83. CAOM, fol. 3U/1, Ben Oliel and Salomon Sarfati to Consistory of Oran, 1 February 1848.

84. Ibid.

85. On the importance of visiting tombs of departed rabbis, see Susan Slyomovics, "Geographies of Jewish Tlemcen," in *The Walled City in Literature, Architecture, and History: The Living Medina in the Maghreb*, ed. Susan Slyomovics (Portland, OR and London: Frank Cass & Co., 2001), 81–96.

86. CAOM, fol. 3U/1, Jews of Mostaganem to General Director of Civil Affairs in Algiers, February 1848.

87. CAOM, fol. 3U/1, Jews of Oran to General Cavaignac, copy dated 1 April 1848.

88. Ibid.

89. Ibid.

90. Emerit, "l'Esprit de 1848 en Algérie," 16–19.

91. CAOM, fol. 3U/1, Jews of Oran to General Cavaignac, copy dated 1 April 1848.

91. CAOM, fol. 3U/1, Consistory to Director of Civil Affairs of Oran, 11 April 1848.

92. Ibid.

93. Ibid.

94. CAOM, fol. 3/U1, Nahon to Director of Civil Affairs, 22 May 1848.

95. CAOM, fol. F80/1631, Petition from Jews of Mostaganem to Governor General, February 1848.

96. As stated earlier, Ranajit Guha has explained that British colonial correspondence often described rebels in colonial India as incapable of grasping relevant issues. Their rebellions were subsequently described as akin to "natural phenomena." See his "The Prose of Counter-Insurgency," in *Selected Subaltern Studies*, ed. Ranajit Guha and Gayatri Chakravorty Spivak (Oxford and New York: Oxford University Press, 1988), 45–88.

97. CAOM, fol. 3U/1, Consistory of Oran to Director of Civil Affairs, 11 April 1848.

98. Ibid.

99. Shurkin, *French Nation Building*, 271.

100. CAOM, fol. 3U/1, Nahon to Director of Civil Affairs, 4 February 1848.

101. CAOM, fol. 3U/1, Cahen to Director of Civil Affairs, 13 July 1848.

102. CAOM, fol. 3U/1, Nahon to Director of Civil Affairs, 11 April 1848.

103. CAOM, fol. 3U/1, Nahon to Director of Civil Affairs, 29 March 1848.

104. Ibid.

105. *Archives Israélites* IX (1848): 434.

106. *Archives Israélites* IX (1848): 435.

107. CAOM 3U/1 Director of Civil Affairs to Civil Commissioner in Mostaganem, 5 February 1848 (draft).

108. Agulhon, *The Republican Experiment*, 49–80.

109. Shurkin, *French Nation Building*.

110. Ibid.

111. See, for example, Albert, *The Modernization of French Jewry*, 232–233.

112. AN, fol. F19 11015, Central Consistory to Minister of Public Instruction and Religions, 17 April 1848.

113. The club also blended religious themes with discussions of class politics. For example, in one of Créhange's publications, he argued about God's concern for labor relations: "The fourth commandment of God (observe the Sabbath and keep it holy) is a proof of the benevolent concern of the Supreme Being for the workers." See Abraham Ben Baruch Créhange, *Des droits et des devoirs du citoyen instruction tirée de l'histoire sainte, ou entretiens d'un maître d'ecole avec ses elèves* (1848).

114. *La Vérité*, 17 April 1848.

115. Ibid.

116. AN, fol. F19 11015, Petition from Jews of Paris to Members of the Provisional Government of France.

117. *Archives Israélites*, IX (1848): 338.

118. Conklin, *A Mission to Civilize*.

119. As Ronald Schechter has argued, Jews became an important conceptual vehicle for discussing the meaning of citizenship and regeneration in the eighteenth century. See *Obstinate Hebrews: Representations of Jews in France, 1715–1815* (Berkeley: University of California Press, 2003), esp. 6–7; idem, "The Jewish Question in Eighteenth-Century France," *Eighteenth-Century Studies* 32, 1 (1998).

120. For the role of preformed "expectations" in forming French experiences of Muslims, see Timothy Mitchell, *Colonizing Egypt*. On how the Orientalist tradition influenced how Frenchmen viewed actual Muslims once significant numbers arrived in France, see Tyler Stovall, "Love, Labor, and Race: Colonial Men and

White Women during the Great War," in *French Civilization and Its Discontents: Nationalism, Colonialism, Race*, ed. Tyler Stoval and Van Den Abbeele (Ithaca, NY: Cornell University Press, 2004), 297–321.

121. See, for example, Martin, *Les Israélites algériens*; H. Z. Hirschberg, *A History of the Jews in North Africa*, vol. 2, *From the Ottoman Conquests to the Present Time* (Leiden: E. J. Brill, 1981), 56–79; and Richard Ayoun, "Les Juifs d'Oran Avant la Conquête Française," *Révue Historique* 267, 2 (1982): 375–390.

CHAPTER 3 SYNAGOGUES, SURVEILLANCE, AND CIVILIZATION

1. CAOM, fol. 3U/1, Nahon to Director of Civil Affairs for the Province of Oran, 19 March 1848.

2. CAOM, fol. 3U/1, Director of Civil Affairs to Governor General, September 1848.

3. Andrew Aisenberg, *Contagion: Disease, Government and the Social Question in Nineteenth-Century France* (Stanford: Stanford University Press, 1999). See also David Arnold, *Colonizing the Body: State Medicine and Epidemic Disease in Nineteenth Century India* (Berkeley: University of California Press, 1993). On the use of medicine to control colonial subjects in France, see Clifford Rosenberg, "The Colonial Politics of Health Care Provision in Interwar Paris," *French Historical Studies* 27, 3 (2004): 637–658. For an example of the focus on hygiene in Jewish schools of Eastern Europe, see Stephen Zipperstein, *Imagining Russian Jewry* (Seattle: University of Washington Press, 1999), esp. 41–62. For cleanliness and hygiene in nineteenth-century France, see Julia Csergo, *Liberté, Égalité, Propreté: La morale de l'hygiène au XIXe siècle* (Paris: Albin Michel, 1988); Jean-Pierre Goubert, *The Conquest of Water*, trans. Andrew Wilson (Oxford: Polity Press, 1986); Georges Vigarello, *Concepts of Cleanliness: Changing Attitudes in France Since the Middle Ages* (Cambridge: Cambridge University Press, 1988).

4. Patricia Lorcin, "Imperialism, Colonial Identity, and Race in Algeria, 1830–1870: The Role of the French Medical Corps," *ISIS* 90, 4 (1999): 653–659; Olivier Le Cour Grandmaison, *Coloniser. Exterminer: Sur la guerre et l'état colonial* (Paris: Fayard, 2005).

5. Anne Marcovich, "French Colonial Medicine and Colonial Rule: Algeria and Indochina," in *Medicine and Empire: Perspectives on Western Medicine and the Experience of European Expansion*, ed. R. MacLeod and M. Lewis (London: Routledge, 1989), 103–117.

6. Yvonne Turin, *Affrontements culturels dans l'Algérie coloniale: écoles, médecines, religion, 1830–1880* (Paris: F. Maspero, 1971), 80. See also William Gallois, *The Administration of Sickness: French Medical Imperialism in Nineteenth-Century Algeria* (London: Palgrave, 2007), as well as his "Local Responses to French Medical Imperialism in Late Nineteenth-Century Algeria," *Social History of Medicine* 20, 2 (2007): 315–331.

7. "The bourgeoisie [first] underlined the high political price for its body, sensations, and pleasures." Michel Foucault, *The History of Sexuality*, vol. 1, *An Introduction* (New York: Vintage, 1990), 123.

8. Julia Clancy-Smith, "Islam, Gender and Identities in the Making of French Algeria," in *Domesticating the Empire: Race, Gender and Family Life in French and Dutch Colonialism*, ed. Julia Clancy-Smith and Frances Gouda (Charlottesville and London: University Press of Virginia, 1998), 154–174; and "The Colonial Gaze: Sex and Gender in the Discourses of French North Africa," in *Franco-Arab Encounters: Studies*

in Memory of David C. Gordon, ed. L. Carl Brown and Matthew S. Gordon (Beirut: American University of Beirut Press, 1996), 201–228.

9. Altaras, "Report," in Simon Schwarzfuchs, *Les Juifs d'Algérie et la France, 1830–1855* (Jerusalem: Institut Ben-Zvi, 1981), 85.

10. Joseph Cohen, "Apercu Général sur les Moeurs des Israélites Algériens," in *Archives Israélites* IV (1843): 26.

11. For a discussion of Daumas, see Clancy-Smith, "Islam, Gender and Identities in the Making of French Algeria," 164.

12. Cohen, "Apercu Général," 32.

13. Ibid., 217.

14. Gustave de Beaumont, *Ministère de la Guerre, Commission de Colonisation de l'Algerie: Rapport fait au nom de la Seconde Sous-Commission* (Paris: Imprimerie du Gouvernement, 1843), 5.

15. *Archives Israélites*, I, (1840): 478. See also Michael Shurkin, "French Nation Building, Liberalism, and the Jews of Alsace and Algeria, 1815–1870" (Ph.D. diss., Yale, 2000), 175; Benjamin Stora and Geneviève Dermenjian, "Les Juifs dans le regard des militaries et des Juifs de France à l'époque de la conquète," *Révue Historique* 284(2) (1990): 333–339.

16. *Archives Israélites*, I (1840): 136, cited in Shurkin, *French Nation Building*, 177.

17. Most religious authorities would probably agree that when it comes to physical structures, a *mikva*, or ritual bath, is more important to the observance of Jewish law.

18. I borrow here from Jürgen Habermas, *The Structural Transformation of the Public Sphere: An Inquiry into a Category of Bourgeois Society* (Cambridge, MA: MIT Press, 1996).

19. Rabbi Lazare Cahen, 1850 "Report to Prefect," reproduced in Schwarzfuchs, *Les Juifs de l'Algérie et la France*, 233.

20. CAOM, fol. 3U/1, Petition of Jews of Mostaganem to the Director of Civil Affairs in Algiers, 18 February 1848.

21. CAOM, fol. 3U/1, Command of the Subdivision of Sidi-Bel-Abbes to General Pélissier, 5 April 1853.

22. CAOM, fol. 3U/1, Consistory of Oran to General Commander of Province of Oran, 28 March 1853.

23. CAOM, fol. 3U/1, General of the Subdivision of Oran to President of Consistory of Oran, 13 April 1853.

24. CAOM, fol. 3U/1, Report to Prefect, 7 June 1853.

25. Ibid.

26. Ibid.

27. CAOM, fol. 3U/1, Cahen to Prefecture, 4 October 1852.

28. CAOM, fol. 3U/1, Prefecture to Consistory of Oran, 22 October 1852.

29. CAOM, fol. 3U/1, Civil Commissioner of Tlemcen to Prefect of Oran, 26 January 1853.

30. CAOM, fol. 3U/1, Police of Oran to Mayor of Oran, 5 November 1852.

31. CAOM, fol. 3U/1 includes numerous lists of local notables sent from consistory of Oran to Prefecture of the Province of Oran.

32. Information on the uses of the consistorial budget at the beginning of the 1850s is noted in a memo originating in the Prefecture of the Province of Oran. See CAOM, fol. 3U/1, Prefecture of the Province of Oran, Extract of Meeting Minutes, 9 April 1853.

33. CAOM, fol. 3U/1, Minutes of Meeting of Prefecture of Province of Oran sent to Prefect of Algiers, 23 May 1853. How many of the non-Jewish inhabitants went with him is unclear from the correspondence.

34. CAOM, fol. 3U/1, Domain Registration Service/Oran Department to Prefect of Oran, 7 April 1853.

35. CAOM, fol. 3U/1, Shemtov Bliah to Prince Louis Napoleon, 23 April 1852.

36. Ibid.

37. CAOM, fol. 3U/1, Cahen to Prefect of Oran, 17 June 1852.

38. CAOM, fol. 3U/1, Prefecture of Oran to Civil Commissioner of Tlemcen, 24 June 1852.

39. CAOM, fol. 3U/1, Domain Registration Service/Oran Department to Prefect of Oran, 7 April 1853.

40. CAOM, fol. 3U/1, Minutes of Meeting of Prefecture of Oran, sent to Prefecture of Algiers, 23 May 1853.

41. CAOM, fol. 3U/1, ben Ichou to Minister of Public Instruction and Religions, 24 September 1855.

42. CAOM, fol. 3U/1, Report to Minister of Public Instruction and Religions, 8 August 1855.

43. CAOM, fol. 3U/1, Cahen to Prefect, 4 June 1855.

44. CAOM, fol. 3U/1, Minutes of Consistory Meeting, 23 November 1855.

45. CAOM, fol. 3U/1, Minutes of Consistory Meeting, 3 December 1854.

46. CAOM, fol. 3U/1, Minutes of Consistory Meeting, 10 December 1854.

47. CAOM, fol. 3U/1, Cahen to Prefect, 4 June 1855.

48. Ibid.

49. CAOM, fol. 3U/1, Minutes of Consistory Meeting, 4 November 1855.

50. CAOM, fol. 3U/2, Governor General to Prefect of Oran, 28 January 1869.

51. CAOM, fol. 3U/1, Cahen to Prefect, 4 June 1855.

52. CAOM, fol. 3U/1, ben Ichou to Prefect, 5 April 1855.

53. CAOM, fol. 3U/1, Report of prefect's commission investigating complaints made by Rabbi Cahen against Mr. ben Ichou and Mr. ben Haim, Prefecture of Oran, July 1855.

54. Ibid.

55. Ibid.

56. Ibid.

57. CAOM, fol. 3U/1, Report to Minister of Public Instruction and Religions, 8 August 1855.

58. Ibid.

59. CAOM, fol. 3U/1, ben Ichou to Prefect, 24 September 1855.

60. CAOM, fol. 3U/1 Civil Commissioner of Mascara to Prefect of Oran, 25 November 1856.

61. Ibid.

62. CAOM, fol. 3U/1, Letters from Civil Commissioners to Prefect of Oran, 1853–1856.

63. As the prefect put it, Lasry was a "man independent of the two parties that divide the indigenous Jewish population" and yet "sufficiently strong in his [social] position that the partisans of El Kanoui and ben Ichou will agree to entrust their goals [to him]." While civil administrators probably exaggerated his aloofness from local quarrels, he was targeted as capable of bringing dignity back to the consistory. See CAOM, fol. 3U/1, Report to Minister of Public Instruction and Religions, 8 August 1855.

64. CAOM, fol. 3U/1, Extract of Minutes of Consistory Meeting, 25 November 1856.

65. CAOM, fol. 3U/1, Extract of Minutes of Consistory Meeting, 25 November 1856; Extract of Minutes of Consistorial Meeting, 4 November 1855.

66. CAOM, fol. 3U/1, Extract of Minutes of Consistory Meeting, 30 November 1856; CAOM, fol. 3U/1, Copy of Decree of Ministry of Public Instruction and Religions, 25 October 1856.

67. CAOM, fol. 3U/1, Copy of Decree of Ministry of Public Instruction and Religions, 25 October 1856.

68. CAOM, fol. 3U/1, Sub-prefecture of Mostaganem to Prefect of Oran, 15 April 1858.

69. Ibid.

70. CAOM, fol. 3U/1, Prefect of Oran to Minister of Public Instruction and Religions, 29 August 1856.

71. Ibid.

72. CAOM, fol. 3U/1, Extract of Minutes of Consistory Meeting, 30 October 1856.

73. Aron Rodrigue's *Images of Sephardic and Eastern Jewries in Transition* (Seattle: University of Washington Press, 1993) makes a similar point with regard to the teachers of the Alliance Israélite Universelle in the Mediterranean basin.

74. Various communications attest to this fact. See CAOM, fol. 3U/1 and fol. 3U/2.

75. CAOM, fol. 3U/1, Civil Commissioner of Mascara to Prefect of Oran, 25 November 1856.

76. Rabbi Avraham Enkaoua, *Zevachim Shleimim veKesef Aher* (Livorno: Dfus Hadash shel Eliahu ben Amuzeg ve-Heverav, 1858)

77. CAOM, fol. 3U/2, Lasry to the Prefect of the Province of Oran, 10 January 1859.

78. Ibid.

79. CAOM, fol. 3U/2, Prefect of Oran to President of the Consistory, 14 January 1859.

80. CAOM, fol. 3U/2, Prefect of Oran to Chief of Police, 14 January 1859.

81. CAOM, fol. 3U/2, letter from rabbis of Jerusalem, November 1858.

82. The second edition of Enkaoua's work includes a letter from a group of Algerian rabbis describing Enkaoua as a "perfect wise man, the excellent judge" whose "hand (produced) a book written in two parts . . . a collection of laws on *shechita* and *trefut* (that which is not kosher)." According to the (possibly apocryphal) haskama, the evildoers "wrapped meat and tripe with them . . . and they made the pages into the fuel for fire. And they waved it around and used it as a fan (*marah-wah*) for fanning themselves." See Abraham Enkaoua, *Taharat HaKesef* (Livorno: Dfus Hadash shel Eliahu ben Amuzeg ve-Heverav, 1858). The Hebrew text uses an Arabic term for "fan."

83. Ibid.

84. This in keeping with the approach of Matt Goldish in his recent *Jewish Questions: Responsa on Sephardic Life in the Early Modern Period* (Princeton, NJ: Princeton University Press, 2008).

85. CAOM 3U/2, Moshe Karcenty to the Prefect of Oran, 21 January 1859.

86. "This work . . . has such a passionate character that one should be suspicious. It flatters the vanity of the author of a book entitled *Kesef Aher* and *Zevahim Shleimim* and it has no other goal but to cloak his own interests as religion." Ibid.

87. Ibid.

88. CAOM, fol. 3U/2, August Pierre Médard (*huissier*), to Lasry, 22 January 1859.

89. CAOM, fol. 3U/2, Minister of Algeria and the Colonies to Prefect of Oran, 8 April 1859.

90. *Archives Israélites* VII (1846), 613.

91. In contrast, for example, to Arabs and Kabyles. See Charles-Robert Agéron, *Les Algériens Musulmans et la France*, vol.1 (1871–1919) (Paris: Presses Universitaires de France, 1968), 267–292; Patricia Lorcin, *Imperial Identities: Stereotyping, Prejudice, and Race in Colonial Algeria* (New York: I. B. Tauris, 1995), 118–166; Marnia Lazreg, "The Reproduction of Colonial Ideology: The Case of the Kablyle Berbers," *Arab Studies Quarterly* 5 (1983): 380–395.

92. As a reminder, the *état civil* is a French institution that legally records the civil status of individuals, including age and marital status.

93. CAOM, fol. 3U/1, Cahen to Prefect, 21 May 1856.

94. CAOM, fol. 3U/1, Minutes of Consistory Meeting, 11 March 1855.

95. CAOM, fol. 3U/1, Sub-inspector Youssouf to Prefect, 6 February 1855.

96. CAOM, fol. 3U/1, Mrs. Jacob Djouno to Prefect, 12 June 1855.

97. CAOM, fol. 3U/1, Cahen to Prefect, 21 May 1856.

98. CAOM, fol. 3U/1, Cahen to Prefect, 8 June 1856; Lasry to Prefect, 24 June 1856.

99. CAOM, fol. 3U/1, Prefect to Rector Delacroix, 2 May 1855.

100. CAOM, fol. 3U/1, Chief Architect to Prefect, 25 April 1855.

101. Csergo, *Liberté, Égalité, Propreté*.

102. CAOM, fol. 3U/1, Chief Architect to Prefect, 25 April 1855.

103. CAOM, fol. 3U/1, Prefect to Cahen, 2 April 1855.

104. CAOM, fol. 3U/1, Cahen to Prefect, 5 June 1856.

CHAPTER 4   TEACHING CIVILIZATION

1. CAOM, fol. 3U/2, Sub-prefect of Oran to Prefect, 18 January 1859.

2. Alice Conklin, *A Mission to Civilize: The Republican Idea of Empire in France and West Africa, 1895–1930* (Stanford: Stanford University Press, 1997).

3. Aron Rodrigue, *Images of Sephardic and Eastern Jewries in Transition* (Seattle: University of Washington Press, 1993). The Alliance was a French organization (though with an international membership base) founded in 1860, which operated primarily in North Africa, the Ottoman Empire, and Iran.

4. Aron Rodrigue, *French Jews, Turkish Jews; The Alliance Israélite Universelle and the Politics of Jewish Schooling in Turkey, 1860–1925* (Bloomington: Indiana University

Press, 1990); Esther Benbassa, "Education for Jewish Girls in the East: A Portrait of the Galata School in Istanbul," *Studies in Contemporary Jewry* 9 (1993): 163–173; Yaron Tsur, "Haskalah in a Sectional Society, Mahdia (Tunisia), 1884," in *Sephardi and Middle Eastern Jewries, History and Culture in the Modern Era*, ed. Harvey E. Goldberg (Bloomington: Indiana University Press, 1996): 146–167. See also Norman Stillman, *Sephardic Religious Responses to Modernity* (Luxembourg: Harwood Academic Publishers, 1995).

5. Some communities in Morocco rejected Alliance schools. See Michael Laskier, *The Alliance Israelite Universelle and the Jewish Communities of Morocco: 1862–1962* (Albany: State University of New York Press, 1983), 89.

6. The first director of the Ecole Normale d'Alger commented in 1865, "Schools are the workshops which manufacture the most reliable arms for the conquest and pacification of the colony." See Antoine Léon, *Colonisation, enseignement et éducation* (Paris: l'Harmattan, 1991), 19.

7. See, for example, Marie-Paule Ha, " From 'Nos Ancêtres, Les Gaulois' to 'Leur Culture Ancestrale': Symbolic Violence and the Politics of Colonial Schooling in Indochina," *French Colonial History* 3 (2003): 101–118; Vickie Langohr, "Colonial Education Systems and the Spread of Local Religious Movements: The Case of British Egypt and Punjab," *Comparative Studies of Society and History* (2005): 161–189; Gregory Starrett, *Putting Islam to Work: Education, Politics, and Religious Transformation in Egypt* (Berkeley: University of California Press, 1998).

8. Assad argues that secularism was at first a European perspective; it emerged out of a specific set historical, political, and intellectual circumstances permitting religion to be reinterpreted as a limited and definable sphere of life. Talal Assad, *Genealogies of Religion: Discipline and Reasons of Power in Christianity and Islam* (Baltimore: Johns Hopkins University Press, 1993), 207.

9. Raymond Grew and Patrick Harrigan, *School, State, and Society: The Growth of Elementary Schooling in Nineteenth-Century France* (Ann Arbor: University of Michigan Press, 1991); Edwy Plenel, *La République inachevée: l'état et l'école en France* (Paris: Payot, 1985); Mona Ozouf, *L'école, l'église, et la République, 1871–1914* (Paris: Armand Colin, 1963); Eugene Weber, *Peasants into Frenchmen: The Modernization of Rural France, 1870–1914* (Berkeley: University of California Press, 1977). For other parallels between colonial education and developments in metropolitan France, see Harry Gamble, "The Regionalist Movement in French West Africa: Colonial Schooling from the Great Depression to Vichy," *Proceedings of the Western Society for French History* 29 (2001): 133–141. Education as a means of discipline in the colonies is also treated in Timothy Mitchell, *Colonizing Egypt* (Berkeley: University of California Press, 1989).

10. John Ruedy, *Land Policy in Colonial Algeria: The Origins of the Rural Public Domain* (Berkeley: University of California Press, 1967); David Powers, "Orientalism, Colonialism, and Legal History: The Attack on Muslim Family Endowments in Algeria and India,' *Comparative Studies in Society and History* 31, 3 (1989): 535–571; Julien, *Histoire de l'Algérie contemporaine*.

11. Yvonne Turin, *Affrontements culturels dans l'Algérie coloniale: Ecoles, medicines, religions, 1830–1880* (Paris: Maspero, 1971); E. G. Guedj, *L'enseignement indigène en Algérie au cours de la colonisation, 1832–1962* (Paris, 2000); Alf Andrew Heggoy, "Arab Education in Colonial Algeria," *Journal of African Studies* 2 (1975): 149–160.

12. Alf Andrew Heggoy and Paul J. Zingg, "French Education in Revolutionary North Africa," *International Journal of Middle East Studies* 7, 4 (October 1976): 571–578; Fanny Colonna, *Instituteurs algériens, 1883–1939* (Paris: Presses de la Fondation nationale des sciences politiques, 1975).

13. Heggoy and Zingg, "French Education," 573.

14. Altaras, "Report," reproduced in Schwarzfuchs, *Les Juifs de l'Algérie et la France,* 128.

15. The archives only mention a "French instructor," or "instructors" for the larger schools. In one 1856 note, the prefect mentioned the value of "history and geography," but made no mention of schools that were teaching them. Besides the French language, no other information is available about the curriculum. See CAOM, fol. 3U/1, Prefect of Oran to Sub-inspector of Schools, June 1855.

16. For more on the schools associated with the regeneration movement in France, see Jay Berkovitz, *The Shaping of Jewish Identity in Nineteenth-Century France* (Detroit: Wayne State University Press, 1989); Phyllis Cohen Albert, *The Modernization of French Jewry: Consistory and Community in the Nineteenth Century* (Hanover, NH: Brandeis University Press, 1977); and Jeffrey Haus, "Liberté, Egalité, Utlité: Education and the State in Nineteenth-Century France," *Modern Judaism* 22 (2002): 1–27.

17. Léon, *Colonisation, enseignement et éducation,* 96.

18. From 1832 to 1848, Inspector Lepescheux served in the Algerian Service de l'Instruction publique. The service fell under the authority of the civil intendant, the director of the interior, and the director general of civil affairs successively. In 1848, the service was replaced by the *rectorat*. See Léon, *Colonisation, enseignement et éducation,* 103.

19. AN, fol. F17 7677, "Tableau statistique de l'instruction publique en Algérie, année 1840," cited also in Léon, *Colonisation, enseignement et éducation,* 98.

20. Altaras, "Report," in Schwarzfuchs, *Les Juifs de l'Algérie et la France,* 122–125.

21. AN, fol. F19 11144, Cahen, "Report on the Situation of Jews of the Province of Oran," in Schwarzfuchs, *Les Juifs de l'Algérie,* 225.

22. Léon, *Colonisation, enseignement et éducation,* 99. See also Rodrigue, *French Jews, Turkish Jews.*

23. Ibid., 105.

24. As Martin Deming Lewis pointed out, *assimilation* in French colonial policy meant many things to many people. The assimilatory program of the Second Republic generally involved integrating the colony legally and administratively with France, so that "colonies are considered as a simple prolongation of the soil of the mother country." See Martin Deming Lewis, "One Hundred Million Frenchmen: The 'Assimilation' Theory in French Colonial Policy," *Comparative Studies in Society and History* 4, 2 (1962): 129–153; also Raymond Betts, *Assimilation and Association in French Colonial Theory* (New York: Columbia University Press, 1961).

25. Julien, *Histoire de l'Algérie contemporaine,* 411.

26. Léon, *Colonisation, enseignement et éducation,* 120.

27. These were to be supervised versions of the traditional religious school, known locally as a *kuttab* or *msid*.

28. R. Estoublon and A. Lefébure, *Code de l'Algérie annoté. Recueil chronologique des lois, ordonnances, décrets arrêtés, circulaires, etc. actuellement en vigueur* (Algiers: A. Jourdan, 1896), 83.

29. CAOM, fol. F80 1632, dos. 404, "Project of Law for the Indigenous Jewish Schools."

30. Ibid.

31. Léon, *Colonisation, enseignement et éducation*, 115.

32. This should not be taken to mean that the military ceased to be an influence—they continued to play a role despite the decree (unpopular among the ranks) removing matters of religion from their competence. See Schwarzfuchs, *Les Juifs de l'Algérie et la France*, 53.

33. Altaras, "Report," in Schwarzfuchs, *Les Juifs de l'Algérie et la France*, 122.

34. Léon, *Colonisation, enseignement et éducation*, 111.

35. Ibid., 112.

36. Ibid.

37. Ibid., 113.

38. Ibid., 89–90.

39. *Les Archives Israélites* I (1840): 542.

40. Ibid.

41. Altaras, "Report," in Schwarzfuchs, *Les Juifs de l'Algérie et la France*, 170.

42. *Les Archives Israélites* IV (1843): 343.

43. Altaras, "Report," in Schwarzfuchs, *Les Juifs de l'Algérie et la France*, 70–177.

44. Ibid., 172.

45. *Les Archives Israélites* I (1840): 542.

46. Altaras, "Report," in Schwarzfuchs, *Les Juifs de l'Algérie et la France*, 128.

47. *Archives Israélites* VII (1846): 478–487.

48. Cahen, "Report on the Situation of Jews in the Province of Oran, 1850," in Schwarzfuchs, *Les Juifs de l'Algérie et la France*, 214.

49. CAOM, fol. 3U/1, Sub-inspector Youssouf to Prefect, 9 November 1854. *Communal* in this context refers to the municipality, not to a pedagogical or administrative philosophy.

50. CAOM, fol. 3/U1, Cahen to Prefect, 13 February 1855.

51. CAOM, fol. 3U/2, Extract of the Register of Deliberations of the Municipal Council of Mascara, 28 February 1856; and Prefect to Rector Delacroix, 2 June 1855.

52. CAOM, fol. 3U/1, Delacroix to Prefect, 2 August 1853.

53. CAOM, fol. 3U/1, Sub-inspector Youssouf to Prefect, 9 November 1854.

54. CAOM, fol. 3U/1, Prefect to Minister of Public Instruction and Religions, 8 August 1855.

55. Ibid.

56. CAOM, fol. 3U/1, Prefect to Consistory of Oran, 2 December 1854.

57. CAOM, fol. 3U/1, Delacroix to Prefect, 2 August 1853.

58. Ibid.

59. CAOM, fol. 3U/1, Sub-inspector Youssouf to Prefect, "Report on the Jewish School of Oran," 9 November 1854.

60. CAOM, fol. 3U/1, Sub-inspector Youssouf to Prefect, 9 November 1854.

61. CAOM, fol. 3U/1, Prefect to Minister of Public Instruction and Religions, 8 August 1855.

62. CAOM, fol. 3U/1, Prefect to Consistory of Oran, 2 December 1854

63. Ibid.

64. CAOM, fol. 3U/1, ben Ayoun and Zarca to Prefect, 16 November 1854.

65. CAOM, fol. 3U/1, Minutes of Meeting of Consistory, 13 and 23 November 1854. Both from extracts of deliberations produced in 1856.

66. CAOM, fol. 3U/1, Minutes of Meeting of Consistory, 19 December 1854.

67. Ibid.

68. CAOM, fol. 3U/1, Minutes of Meeting of Consistory, 30 November 1854.

69. CAOM, fol. 3U/1, Minutes of Meeting of Consistory, 11 February 1855.

70. CAOM, fol. 3U/1, Minutes of Meeting of Consistory, 10 December 1855.

71. CAOM, fol. 3U/2, Minutes of Meeting of Consistory, 4 May 1859.

72. CAOM, fol. 3U/1, Minutes of Meeting of Consistory, 25 December 1854.

73. CAOM, fol. 3U/1, Minutes of Meeting of Consistory, 11 February 1855.

74. CAOM, fol. 3U/1, Delacroix to Prefect, 28 February 1855.

75. CAOM, fol. 3U/1, Prefect to Delacroix, 22 May 1855.

76. We remember that in 1850, a decree submitted Muslim tolbas to government authorization.

77. CAOM, fol. 3U/1, Letters between Consistory and Prefecture, 1856.

78. CAOM, fol. 3U/1, Prefect to Mayor of Oran and Civil Commissioners of Tlemcen and Mascara, 5 February 1855.

79. CAOM, fol. 3U/1, Delacroix to Prefect, 26 April 1855; and Minutes of Meeting of Prefecture of Oran, 2 July 1855.

80. CAOM, fol. 3U/1, ben Ichou to Prefect, 11 August 1855; and Civil Commissioner of Mascara to Prefect, 27 August 1855.

81. CAOM, fol. 3U/1, Cahen to Prefect, 16 August 1855.

82. CAOM, fol. 3U/1, Delacroix to Prefect, 17 August 1855; and Prefect to Delacroix, 31 August 1855.

83. CAOM, fol. 3U/1, Extract of Deliberations of Municipal Council of Mascara, 28 February 1856.

84. CAOM, fol. 3U/1, Civil Commissioner of Mascara to Prefect, 11 March 1856.

85. CAOM, fol. 3U/1, Consistory to Prefect, 5 April 1857.

86. CAOM, fol. 3U/2, Delacroix to Prefect, 17 August 1855.

87. CAOM, fol. 3U/2, Civil Commissioner of Tlemcen to Prefect, 31 October 1855.

88. CAOM, fol. 3/U1, Prefect to Civil Commissioner of Mascara, 7 May 1855.

89. The issue of native schools' putative fanaticism, as well as the competition posed to official schools, also concerned observers of French Muslim schools. Teachers in the msids (estimated to teach about 27,000 students in 2,000 schools by 1865) were accused of inculcating a fanatic version of Islam and drawing students away from the French Muslim schools. Official responses to these problems varied. In Constantine, the prefect ordered 24 Muslim schools closed in 1857, while the prefect of Algiers resolved to pay 1.5 francs per student to any teacher who sent one of

his charges to the French Muslim school of Blida. French Muslim schools retained 1,350 students in 1880. See Léon, *Colonisation, enseignement et éducation*, 117–122.

90. CAOM, fol. 3U/1, Prefect to Delacroix, 2 May 1855.

91. CAOM, fol. 3U/1, Minutes of Prefecture of Oran, 2 and 24 July 1855.

92. CAOM, fol. 3U/1, Minutes of Prefecture of Oran, 24 July 1855.

93. CAOM, fol. 3U/1, Delacroix to Prefect, 17 August 1855.

94. CAOM, fol. 3U/1, Sub-inspector Youssouf to Prefect, 21 October 1855.

95. CAOM, fol. 3U/2, Prefect to Delacroix, 18 May 1858.

96. CAOM, fol. 3U/2, Delacroix to Prefect, 4 May 1858.

97. CAOM, fol. 3U/2, Prefect to Sub-inspector Youssouf, 3 May 1858.

98. CAOM, fol. 3U/2, Inspector of Public Instruction to Prefect, 13 July 1859. I thank Sarah Stein for pointing out the probability of this family relationship.

99. CAOM, fol. 3U/1, Delacroix to Prefect, 23 March 1857.

100. CAOM, fol. 3U/1, Cahen to Prefect, 27 October 1856.

101. CAOM, fol. 3U/1, Delacroix to Prefect, 14 November 1856.

102. CAOM, fol. 3U/1, Prefect to Delacroix, 26 November 1856.

103. CAOM, fol. 3U/1, Prefect to Delacroix, 12 March 1856.

104. CAOM, fol. 3U/1, Delacroix to Prefect, 18 August 1856.

105. CAOM, fol. 3U/1, Mayor of Oran to Prefect, 1 September 1856.

106. CAOM, fol. 3U/1, Consistory to Prefect, 4 June 1856.

107. CAOM, fol. 3U/1, Lasry and Cahen to Prefect, 8 September 1856.

108. Ibid.

109. CAOM, fol. 3U/1, Delacroix to Prefect, 13 November 1856. The relationship between the two Ben Ayouns remains unclear.

110. CAOM, fol. 3U/1, Prefect to Delacroix, 22 May 1855.

111. CAOM, fol. 3U/1, Lasry to Prefect, 14 December 1857.

112. CAOM, fol. 3U/2, Minutes of Meeting of Consistory, 4 May 1859.

113. CAOM, fol. 3U/1, Prefect to Delacroix, 18 May 1858.

114. CAOM, fol. 3U/1, Prefect to Lasry, 18 November 1856.

115. CAOM, fol. 3U/1, *Compte-rendu des travaux du Consistoire israélite d'Oran: du 1ᵉʳ janvier 1856 au 31 décembre, 1858* (printed brochure).

116. Richard Ayoun, *Les Tétuanais à Oran* (n.d., located at Bibliothèque de l'Alliance Israélite Universelle), 202–204.

117. Ibid., 205.

118. CAOM, fol. 3U/2, Nahon to Prefect, 22 May 1860.

119. CAOM, fol. 3U/2, Mayor of Oran to Prefect, 24 May 1860; and Lasry to Prefect, 26 June 1860.

120. CAOM, fol. 3U/2, Prefect to Mayor of Oran, 5 June 1860.

121. *Univers Israélite* XVII (September 1860): 17–19.

122. CAOM, fol. 3U/2, Lasry to Prefect, 26 June 1860.

123. CAOM, fol. 3U/2, Lévy to Prefect, December 1863.

124. CAOM, fol. 3U/2, Charleville to Prefect, 24 June 1867.

125. Ibid.

126. CAOM, fol. 3U/2, Prefect to Governor General of Algeria, 29 June 1867.

127. CAOM, fol. 3U/1, Prefect to Lasry, 5 June 1856.

128. CAOM, fol. 3U/1, Prefect to Lasry, 9 March 1856. In another example, an unnamed rabbi was outside walking with his students when an observer saw him hit several of his students with a baton. The observer informed the prefect who then told Lasry how important it was "that the notables of the Israelite nation make it clear to all of their rabbinic teachers that corporal punishments that were once in common use among them is banned by the French Law." Such punishments were contrary to the mission of "moraliz[ing] the youth that are entrusted to them." Such events demonstrated "just how the system of corporal punishment rejects our ideas, our civilization." The prefect charged the president of the consistory with explaining the importance of obeying the decree of January 1, 1855, and with ensuring that "[his] co-religionists know to conform to the conventions of the more advanced civilization that France offers."

129. *Archives Israélites*, V (1844): 693.

130. *Archives Israélites*, I (1840): 543.

131. *Archives Israélites*, VII (1846): 479.

132. CAOM, fol. 3U/1, Sub-inspector to Prefect, 9 November 1854.

133. CAOM, fol. 3U/1, Delacroix to Prefect, 29 May 1855.

CHAPTER 5   FROM NAPOLEON'S SANHEDRIN
TO THE CRÉMIEUX DECREE

1. *l'Univers Israélite* XXXI (September 1875): 48–51; also AN, fol. F19 11146, copy of transcript of trial.

2. Ibid.

3. This was not actually the case.

4. AN, fol. F19 11146, Correspondence between Central Consistory and Ministry of Justice, 1875.

5. As a reminder, the statut personel determined which laws governed a French subject's family status and inheritance rights.

6. Susan Desan, *The Family on Trial in Revolutionary France* (Berkeley and Los Angeles: University of California Press, 2004), esp. 249–310.

7. Jennifer Ngaire Heurer, *The Family and the Nation: Gender and Citizenship in Revolutionary France, 1789–1830* (Ithaca, NY: Cornell University Press, 2005), 130.

8. Ibid., esp. 140–141.

9. Pierre Birnbaum, *L'Aigle et la Synagogue: Napoléon, les Juifs, et l'Etat* (Paris: Fayard, 2007).

10. Talal Assad, *Genealogies of Religion: Discipline and Reasons of Power in Christianity and Islam* (Baltimore: Johns Hopkins University Press, 1993).

11. Lisa Moses Leff, The Impact of the Napoleonic Sanhedrin on French Colonial Policy in Algeria," *CCAR Journal* (Winter 2007): 35–60; Joshua Schreier, "Napoleon's Long Shadow: Morality, Civilization, and Jews in France and Algeria, 1808–1870," *French Historical Studies* 30, 1 (Winter 2007): 77–103.

12. Julia Clancy-Smith, "Islam, Gender and Identities in the Making of French Algeria," in *Domesticating the Empire: Race, Gender and Family Life in French and*

Dutch Colonialism, ed. Julia Clancy-Smith and Frances Gouda (Charlottesville and London: University Press of Virginia, 1998), 154–174; Malek Alloula, *The Colonial Harem*, trans. Myrna Godzich and Wlad Godzich (Minneapolis: University of Minnesota Press, 1981). Such representations of women and families represented one privileged subject in a larger field of colonial mythologies, including well-studied examples such as that pertaining to the Kabyles. See Ageron, *Histoire de l'Algérie Contemporaine*, vol. 2, *De l'insurrection de 1871 à la guerre de liberation de 1954* (Paris: Presses Universitaires de France, 1979), 130–151; Patricia Lorcin, *Imperial Identities: Stereotyping, Prejudice, and Race in Colonial Algeria* (New York: I. B. Tauris, 1995), 149.

13. Ibid. Also, Emanuel Sivan, *Interpretations of Islam* (Princeton, NJ: Darwin Press, 1979), 157–188.

14. Michael Brett, "Legislating for Inequality in Algeria: The *Sénatus-Consulte* of 14 July 1865," *Bulletin of the School of Oriental and African Studies* 51 (1988): 441–461; Jeanne Bowlan, "Polygamists Need Not Apply: Becoming a French Citizen in Colonial Algeria, 1918–1938," *Proceedings of the Annual Meeting of the Western Society for French History* 24 (1997): 110–119; Ellen McLarney, "The Algerian Personal Statute: A French Legacy," *The Islamic Quarterly* 41, 3 (1997): 187–217.

15. See Clancy-Smith "Islam, Gender and Identities," 154–174.

16. Altaras, "Report," in Schwarzfuchs, *Les Juifs d'Algérie et la France*, 84–85.

17. As discussed in the previous chapter, only one Jewish girls' school had been opened at the time of the report. Although at one point, it had counted 80 to 100 students, attendance trailed off.

18. *Akhbar* (Algiers), 22 October 1850.

19. Joseph Cohen, "Apercu Général sur les Moeurs des Israélites Algériens," published in *Archives Israélites* IV (1843): 26.

20. For a discussion of Daumas and the need to expose what was covered to reveal the sickness of indigenous society, see Clancy-Smith, "Islam, Gender and Identities in the Making of French Algeria," 164.

21. As cited earlier: "Furthermore, the interior of the Israelite family is more expansive and open than the domestic interior of the Muslim. Nothing, besides the laws of modesty and the demands of virtue, prevent Jewish women from developing more or less intimate relations (*connaissances*) with the French." From Cohen, "Apercu Général," 32.

22. Ibid.

23. Ibid., 217.

24. Ibid.

25. See Clancy-Smith, "Islam, Gender and Identities in the Making of French Algeria, 155. See also Timothy Mitchell, *Colonising Egypt* (Berkeley: University of California Press, 1991), 19–26.

26. For sexual stereotyping later in the century, see Emanuel Sivan, "Colonialism and Popular Culture in Algeria," *Journal of Contemporary History* 14, 1 (January 1979): 21–53.

27. Cahen, "Report," in Schwarzfuchs, *Juifs de l'Algérie et la France*, 214.

28. Altaras, "Report," in Schwarzfuchs, *Juifs de l'Algérie et la France*, 101.

29. Ibid.

30. E. A. Duchesne, *De la prostitution dans la ville d'Alger depuis la conquète* (Paris: J. B. Bailliere, 1853), 58.

31. Ibid., 59.

32. Ibid., 87.

33. The campaign for paternity suits was a moral concern in different colonies in the nineteenth century. The issue united a spectrum of groups, from conservative moral reformers to feminists seeking to secure basic rights for women. In addition to fears about "cunning women," the debate evoked class and race anxieties in France and the colonies. See Jean Elisabeth Pedersen, "'Special Customs: Paternity Suits and Citizenship in France and the Colonies, 1870–1912," in *Domesticating the Empire: Race, Gender and Family Life in French and Dutch Colonialism*, ed. Clancy-Smith and Gouda, 43–64.

34. Zosa Szajkowski, "The Struggle for Jewish Emancipation in Algeria After the French Occupation," *Historia Judaica* 18(1) (1956): 27–40.

35. Cahen, "Report," in Schwarzfuchs, *Les Juifs de l'Algérie et la France*, 217.

36. Michel Aron Weill, "Situation des Israélites en Algérie: Rapport Général," reproduced in Schwarzfuchs, *Les Juifs de l'Algérie et la France*, 287.

37. Weill, "Report," in Schwarzfuchs, *Juifs de l'Algérie et la France*, 289.

38. *Le Courrier d'Afrique*, 24 December 1845.

39. *Le Courrier d'Afrique*, 31 December 1845.

40. *Archives Israélites de France* IV (1843): 336–337.

41. Cahen,"Report," in Schwarzfuchs, *Les Juifs de l'Algérie et la France*, 203–241.

42. CAOM, fol. 3U/1, Rector to Prefect, 2 August 1853.

43. CAOM, fol. 3U/1, Minutes of Meeting of Consistory, 3 February 1856.

44. CAOM, fol. 3U/1, Lasry to Prefect, 17 March 1856.

45. CAOM, fol. 3U/2, Consistory to Prefect, 1860 (not dated).

46. CAOM, fol. 3U/2, Mymoun to Prefect, 28 February 1859; Extract of Minutes of Meeting of Consistory, 8 March 1859.

47. Ibid.

48. See Brett, "Legislating for Inequality in Algeria: The *Sénatus-Consulte* of 14 July 1865." For more on the bureaux arabes, see Charles-André Julien, *Histoire de l'Algérie contemporaine: Conquète et colonisation, 1827–1871* (Paris: Presses Universitaires de France, 1964), 333–341. Alan Christelow, looking at court records of the region of Mascara, provides a picture of Muslim justice under the bureaux. He shows the influence of saintly lineage on divorce cases in the 1850s and 1860s, among other issues. See Allan Christelow, "Saintly Descent and Worldly Affairs in Nineteenth-Century Mascara, Algeria," *International Journal of Middle East Studies* 12, 2 (September 1980): 139–155.

49. Notably on February 28, 1841, and September 28, 1842.

50. R. Estoublon and A. Lefébure, *Code de l'Algérie annoté. Recueil chronologique des lois, ordonnances, décrets arrêtés, circulaires, etc. actuellement en vigueur* (Algiers: A. Jourdan, 1896), 27.

51. Even at this early date, some Jewish reformers predicted that family law would eventually present an obstacle to the assimilation of Algeria's Jews into France. The journal *Archives Israelites*, for example, noted that the commission charged

with drafting the 1845 decree split over the issue of divorce. Banning the practice was important, although the editor admitted, "the Jews of Algeria, while demanding a better status, wish to maintain this custom." See *Archives Israélites de France* V (1844): 354.

52. For a brief overview of the process of Algerian Jewish legal assimilation, see Miriam Hoexter, "Les Juifs français et l'assimilation politique et institutionelle de la communauté juive en Algérie (1830–1870)," in *Les Relations intercommunautaires juives en mediterranée occidentale XIIe–Xxes siècles: Actes du colloque international de l'histoire des pays d'outre mer, Aix-en-Provence* (Paris: Editions du CNRS, 1984), 154–161.

53. Altaras, "Report," in Schwarzfuchs, *Les Juifs de l'Algérie et la France*, 113.

54. Ibid.

55. Ibid., 114.

56. Assad, *Genealogies of Religion.*

57. Altaras, "Report," in Schwarzfuchs, *Les Juifs de l'Algérie et la France*, 162.

58. Ibid.

59. Ibid, 162–163.

60. AN, fol. F19 11143, Minister of War to Governor General, 3 April 1839.

61. AN, fol. F19 11143, Minister of War to Minister of Justice and Religions, 6 November 1839.

62. Ibid.

63. Szajkowski, "The Struggle for Jewish Emancipation," 27–40.

64. CAOM, fol. E 152, 18 MI 50, Minister of War to Director of the Interior in Algiers, 1842.

65. Estoublon and Lefébure, *Code de l'Algérie annoté*, 27.

66. Altaras, "Report," in Schwarzfuchs, *Juifs de l'Algérie et la France*, 217–218.

67. Ibid.

68. CAOM, fol. 3U/2, Delegate of Aïn Témouchen to Lasry, 23 March 1857.

69. CAOM, fol. 3U/2, Minutes of Meeting of Notables, Consistory of Oran, 10 December 1865.

70. CAOM, fol. 3U/1, Ben Ichou to Consistory, 1 August 1854.

71. CAOM, fol. 3U/2, "arreté du cour imperial," 27 January 1857.

72. CAOM, fol. 3U/2, Prefect to Governor General, 27 February 1858.

73. CAOM, fol. 3U/2, Prefect to Governor General, 18 August 1857.

74. CAOM, fol. 3U/2, Cahen to Prefect, 27 July 1857.

75. CAOM, fol. 3U/2, Prefect to Governor General, 18 August 1857.

76. Actually, this was the case only in the city of Oran. In provincial cities, such as Tlemcen, Jews were not listed at all in the état civil by the late 1850s. See, for example, CAOM 3U/2, Civil Commissary of Tlemcen, "Etat des naissances, mariages et décès de la population Israëlite de Tlemcen, pendant les annés 1852, '53, '54, et '55," 23 July 1857.

77. CAOM, fol. 3U/2, Cahen to Prefect, 27 July 1857; and Martin, *Les Israélites algériens*, 112.

78. CAOM, fol. 3U/2, Prefect to Governor General, 20 May 1863.

79. CAOM, fol. 3U/2, Cahen to Prefect, 27 July 1857.

80. Ibid.

81. CAOM, fol. 3U/2, Prefecture Correspondence, 1857.

82. Julien, *Histoire de l'Algérie contemporaine*, 412–414.

83. Ibid., 415.

84. Ibid.

85. Martin, *Les Israélites algériens*, 113.

86. Ibid., 116.

87. Saint Simonianism was a utopian-socialist movement whose members hoped for a harmonious (if non-egalitarian) "fusion" of East and West in Algeria. The movement had a number of very high-placed adherents in nineteenth-century France.

88. Interestingly, brochures specifically discussing Jews in Algeria began to appear some years before the general spike in interest in naturalization in the late 1880s and 1890s. Examples of this later literature would include Albert Hugues, *De la nationalité française chez les Musulmans d'Algérie* (Paris: A. Chevalier-Maresq & cie., 1899); Georges Klein, *De la condition juridique des indigènes d'Algérie sous la domination française* (Paris: V. Giard et E. Brière, 1906); J. Bouillié, "De l'application du droit civil aux Musulmans d'Algérie" (Ph.D. diss., Paris University, 1896). On Europeans, there was Alfred Dain, *Naturalisation des étrangers en Algérie* (Algiers: A. Jourdan, 1885); E. Rouard de Card, *Etude sur la naturalisation en Algérie* (Paris: Berger-Levrault 1881); Fabre de Parrel, *Observations sur les lois de naturalisation des étrangers en Algérie* (Algiers: A. Jourdan 1901).

89. Despite the importance of divorce to republican thinking leading up to and after the 1884 *loi Naquet*, which legalized it, few of these writers expressed an explicit interest in changing the law as a way of clearing the way to Algerian Jewish citizenship.

90. Anonymous, *Harmonie des Cultes: Catholique, Protestant et Mosaique, avec Nos Constitutions* (Paris: Dufriche-Foulaines, 1809), 174–175.

91. Napoleonic discussions tended to associate many "foreign" attributes to France's Jews. See Birnbaum, *L'Aigle et la Synagogue*, 7–46. For the focus on Jewish autonomy, or the danger of Jews living as "a nation within a nation" in Napoleonic debates, see Simon Schwarzfuchs, *Napoleon, the Jews, and the Sanhedrin* (Boston and London: Routledge and Kegan Paul, 1979), 22–114.

92. Casimir Fregier, *Esquisses sur la justice musulmane* (Algiers: Imprimérie et Librairie de Vincent, 1862), *Du mariage français de l'Israelite algérien* (Algiers: M. Lévy, Frères, 1862), and *La question juive* (Algiers: Imprimérie et Librairie de Vincent, 1862).

93. Casimir Frégier, *Du mariage français de l'Israélite algérien*.

94. Casimir Frégier, *Les Juifs algeriens: Leur passe, leur present et leur avenir juridique* (Paris: M. Lévy, Frères, 1865).

95. J. E. Sartor, *De la naturalisation en Algérie (senatus-consulte du 5 juillet 1865) Musulmans, Israélites, Europeans* (Paris: Retaux, frères, 1865).

96. Sartor, *De la naturalisation*, 11.

97. Ibid., 26.

98. Jules Delsieux, *Essai sur la naturalisation collective des Israélites indigenes* (Algiers: Duclaux, 1860).

99. Delsieux, *Essai sur la naturalisation*, 22.

100. Ronald Schechter, "The Jewish Question in Eighteenth-Century France;" idem, *Obstinate Hebrews*.

101. CAOM, fol. F80 1748, M. Bequet, *Organization du culte israélite en Algérie: rapport au conseil de gouvernment* (Algiers: Imprimerie du Gouvernement, 1858).

102. ACC, fol. ICC 40, Messaoud Karoubi (Consistory of Oran) to President of Central Consistory in Paris, 16 January 1866; ben Ichou to Munk, 22 May, 1866; Members of Consistory of Oran to Central Consistory of Paris, 4 October 1867.

103. CAOM, fol. 3U/2, Charleville to Prefect, 27 May 1867.

104. Ibid.

105. E. Sautayra, M. Charleville, *Code rabinique: Eben Haezer* (Paris: Challamel, 1868), 10.

106. Ibid.

107. Anonymous, "Code rabbinique," in *La Revue Africaine* 13 (1869): 179–180.

108. E. Sautayra, M. Charleville, *Code rabbinique*, 10–11.

109. Ibid.

110. CAOM, fol. 3U/2, Cahen to Prefect, 27 February 1863.

111. Ibid.

112. Ibid.

113. CAOM, fol. 3U/2, Memo of Prefect, 16 March 1863.

114. CAOM, fol. 3U/2, Prefect to Governor General, 20 May 1863.

115. CAOM, fol. 3U/2, Memo of Prefect, (undated) 1867.

116. CAOM, fol. 3U/2, Prefect to Governor General, 14 June 1867.

117. CAOM, fol. 3U/2, Governor General to Prefect, 14 May 1867.

118. CAOM, fol. 3U/2, Governor General to Prefect, 13 October 1869.

119. CAOM, fol. 3U/2, Director of Arab Affairs to Governor General, 3 November 1869.

120. Estoublon and Lefébure, *Code de l'Algérie annoté*, 302–309.

121. Ibid., 303.

122. Ibid., 305.

123. Ibid.

124. Ibid.

125. Ibid.

126. The endurance of this symbolic power suggests that Ronald Schechter's observation about eighteenth-century debates is also valid for political discussions of a considerably later period. For more on the senatus-consulte, see Brett, "Legislating for Inequality in Algeria," 441–461; McLarney, "The Algerian Personal Statute: A French Legacy," 187–217.

127. Martin, *Les Israélites algériens*, 122.

128. Ibid., 123.

129. Ibid., 125.

130. ACC, fol. ICC40, Prefect to Consistory of Oran, 7 April 1870.

131. Ibid.

132. ACC, fol. ICC40, Minutes of Meeting of Consistory of Oran, 10 April 1870.

133. Martin, *Les Israélites algériens*, 135.

134. Ibid.

135. For more on the part played by the Alliance in the emerging republican culture in 1860s France, see Peter Nord, *The Republican Moment: Struggles for Democracy in Nineteenth Century France* (Cambridge, MA: Harvard University Press, 1995), 64–89.

136. Martin, *Les Israélites algériens*, 141.

137. Estoublon and Lefébure, *Code de l'Algérie annoté*, 302–309.

138. AN, fol. F19 11146, Minister of Public Instruction and Religions to Consistory of Oran, 25 October 1875.

139. ACC, fol. ICC 40, Charleville to Central Consistory, 4 September 1873.

140. ACC fol. ICC 40, Consistory of Oran to Central Consistory, 15 December 1872.

141. AN, fol. F19 11146, Minister of Public Instruction and Religions to Consistory of Oran, 25 October 1875.

CONCLUSION

1. Evelyne Oliel-Grausz, "Divorce Mosaique et la Législation Révolutionaire," *in Les Juifs et la Révolution française: Histoire et mentalités*, ed. Mireille Hadas-Lebel (Louvain, France: C. Peeters, 1992).

2. Alyssa Goldstein Sepinwall, *Abbé Grégoire and the French Revolution: The Birth of Modern Universalism* (Berkeley, University of California Press, 2005), esp. 72, 190–193.

3. Ronald Schechter, *Obstinate Hebrews: Representations of Jews in France, 1715–1815* (Berkeley: University of California Press, 2003).

4. *Le Monde*, 15 July 2008, http://lemonde.fr/societe/article/2008/07/11/une-maro-caine-en-burqa-se-voit-refuser-la-nationalite-francaise_1072401_3224.html.

5. BBC News, 16 July 2008, http://news.bbc.co.uk/2/hi/europe/7509339.stm.

6. *Le Monde*, 15 July 2008.

7. Ibid.

INDEX

Abd al-Qader: as administrator of Mascara, 39, 43, 121; Jewish relations with, 38, 39, 97, 98; as resisting French colonialism, 10, 28, 30

Abou, Moshe ben Jacob, 70, 74–75, 91

Abu al-Madayn, Shu'ayb, 16

Academy of Algiers, 109, 114, 120, 125, 131–132, 141

Addi, Judah, 130

adultery, 40–41

'Afandiya (Egypt), 58

Agha, Mustapha, 30

agricultural work, 54, 123, 162

Ahmed (bey of Tunis), 33, 34

Aïli, Shlomo ben, 101–102

Aïn Témouchent (Algeria), 138, 139, 158

AIU. *See* Alliance Israélite Universelle schools

Algeria: colonial administration's centralizing efforts in, 15–16, 47, 56, 58–59, 62, 65, 86, 93, 104, 113; currency trading in, 4, 15, 43–44; efforts to effect legal assimilation of, to France, 36–37, 153–176, 188n44, 211n24; French commercial interest in, 23, 26–35, 43–44, 54, 162; French liberals as supporting colonization of, 47–48, 50–52, 54, 57, 78; French military administration of, 1, 2, 4, 23–49, 112; interior of, 27–32, 35, 44, 179; Jewish trading networks as not limited by borders of, 12, 13–16, 20, 24, 27–28, 32, 38, 39, 43–44, 66, 179; multiethnic composition of, 24, 25–26; population of, 185n18, 192n8; sources for this study of, 5–6. *See also* Algerian Jews; colonialism; communal autonomy; Europeans; France; Muslims; personal status laws; resistance; *specific places and people in*

Algerian Jews: as "Arabs of the Jewish faith," 8, 9, 12; behavior of children of, 63–65, 89; demographic significance of, in Algeria's cities, 1, 2, 12–13, 15, 25–26, 31, 32, 45, 46, 50–51, 54, 154, 158, 179, 185n18; diversity and divisions among, 4,

6, 12, 15, 19, 29–33, 36–42, 44, 54, 60, 62, 65–67, 69, 74, 91–92, 94–108, 112, 113, 127–129, 134–135, 138; economic significance of, 1, 2, 4, 5, 14–16, 19, 23, 24, 26–38, 43–46, 54, 55, 179; fanaticism attributed to, 5, 6, 9, 58, 79, 84, 93, 119, 120, 122–124, 126, 129, 137, 213n89; France's abolition of communal autonomy of, 13, 32, 36–37, 42, 46, 50–51, 154–155, 159, 197n113; French as privileging, over Muslims, 2, 4, 10, 11, 20, 78–79, 87–89, 98–99, 145, 147–153, 155, 166–167, 173, 179; French citizenship extended to, in 1870, 1, 7, 8–9, 45, 54, 83, 142–144, 146, 156, 173–176, 182; French reformers as concerned to regenerate, 7, 25, 29, 44, 47–50, 52–53, 57–59, 61, 72, 79, 83, 86, 88, 108, 112, 157–158, 173, 174–175, 179–181; French view of, as isolated and miserable, 10–12, 15, 17, 19, 20, 24, 51, 58, 84, 88; ignorance attributed to resistance of, 5, 54, 77–81, 83, 84–85, 93, 123, 124, 126, 135, 140, 165; internal communal issues among, and French administration, 29–33, 36–42, 44, 54, 91–92, 94–96; international networks of rabbis among, 6, 105–108; as interwoven with Muslim society, 4, 8–15, 27–39, 41, 64, 92, 97, 153, 179; Muslim law on, 11; mysticism among, 41, 195n89; as "Oriental," 8, 24, 61, 63, 151, 163, 164, 171; overview of history of, 10–19; preconquest communal autonomy of, 13–14, 30–31; proposals to remove from Algeria, 49–50, 52; resistance of, to France's assimilation efforts, 1, 2–3, 5, 8–10, 20, 21, 42–43, 69–81, 84–85, 91–92, 113, 175–176, 180–181; as security risks for the French, 32–33; seen as corrupt and immoral, 2, 4, 84, 89, 90, 145, 159, 178, 182 (*see also* family customs); seen as European, 32, 37, 39, 42, 46, 47, 49, 52, 63, 98; seen as French allies in Algeria's conquest, 2, 4, 20, 32, 33, 39, 40, 53, 68; similarities of religious practices of, to

186n25; in French metaphors about unveiling Muslim women, 148–149; ignorance to be overcome through, 79–81; by Muslims against Algerian Jews, 11; of resistance to consistories, 70–71, 83, 86; in schools, 114, 115, 117, 124, 126–129, 131, 135, 137, 140; spousal, 159; in synagogues, 38–41, 93, 104, 105–106
vocational training, 117, 122, 123

Wagner, Morritz, 43
wakil, 28–29, 32, 37
Weill, Michel Aron (grand rabbi of Algiers), 42, 108, 140–141, 148, 151

Welsford, James, 33, 34–35
women: morality of, as marker of "colonial difference," 63, 147–152, 179; rights of French, 9, 146, 178; veiling vs. unveiling of, 88–89, 148–151, 153, 181–182

yeshivas, 66–67

Zarca, Salomon, 110, 111, 129, 136
Zermaty, Joseph, 34
Zevachim Shleimim (Enkaoua), 104, 106, 184n15
Zevachim Shleimim veKesef Aher (Enkaoua), 104, 106

ABOUT THE AUTHOR

JOSHUA SCHREIER is an assistant professor of history, as well as a member of the Jewish Studies and International Studies programs, at Vassar College. His previous work has focused on French colonial uses of religious family law to deny or confer citizenship to Muslim and Jewish subjects. He lives with his family in New York City.